The
Fathers' Book

Shared Experiences

© *Carol Palmer*

The Fathers' Book

Shared Experiences

Edited by
Carol Kort *and*
Ronnie Friedland

G.K.HALL & CO.

70 LINCOLN STREET, BOSTON, MASS.

G. K. Hall & Co., 70 Lincoln Street, Boston, MA 02111.
Copyright 1986 by Carol Kort and Ronnie Friedland

86 87 88 89 / 1 2 3 4
Manufactured in the United States of America.
Library of Congress Cataloging-in-Publication Data
Main entry under title:

The Fathers' book.

1. Fathers—United States—Addresses, essays,
lectures. 2. Father and child—United States—
Addresses, essays, lectures. 3. Fathers—United
States—Psychology—Addresses, essays, lectures.
I. Kort, Carol. II. Friedland, Ronnie.
HQ756.F384 1986   306.8'742   85-30552
ISBN 0-8161-9051-8
ISBN 0-8161-9052-6 (pbk.)

Copyedited under the direction of Michael Sims.
Designed and produced by Fred Welden.

Grateful acknowledgment is made to the following for permission to use material copyrighted or controlled by them:

"Pregnancy and Sexuality" by Michael Rossman. © 1985 by Michael Rossman.

"Barrage" and "The Meaning of Life" by Douglas Worth. From Douglas Worth, *From Dream, From Circumstance: New and Selected Poems, 1963–1983* (Cambridge, Mass.: Apple-Wood, 1984). © 1984 by Douglas Worth. Reprinted courtesy of Apple-Wood Press.

Portions of Gordon Baxter's "A Very Old Daddy" first appeared in his *Jenny 'n' Dad* (New York: Summit Books, 1985).

"Bedtime with Sarah" by Jerry Howard. © 1985 by Jerry Howard.

"On Common Ground" by Michael Goodwin. © 1984 by *The New York Times Magazine*. Reprinted by permission.

"Conflicting Interests" by Donald H. Bell. © 1985 by *The New York Times Magazine*. Reprinted by permission.

"Uncle Dad" by C. W. Smith. First printed in *Esquire*, March 1985. © 1985 by C. W. Smith. Reprinted courtesy of *Esquire*.

"Stepping In" by Jacques Leslie. © 1985 by *The New York Times Magazine*. Reprinted by permission.

"Life Miscarried" by Tim Page. © 1985 by *The New York Times Magazine*. Reprinted by permission.

"Peace of Mind" by Richard Moore. © 1985 by *The New York Times Magazine*. Reprinted by permission.

"Fatherhood Postponed" by Carey Winfrey. © 1985 by *The New York Times Magazine*. Reprinted by permission.

We dedicate our second book to our second children,
Tamara Kort and Rebecca Friedland-Little
and to our fathers,
Jack Chvat and in memory of Abner Friedland

Contents

Foreword

Since the early 1970s, approximately three dozen new books about parenting have been published each year. As a part of my professional work, I do my best to evaluate most of them. They vary quite a bit as to focus and quality. The most popular, Dr. Spock's, is a common sense book on baby and child care that principally addresses physical health and care issues, but does extend to a degree into psychological areas such as discipline. Dr. Brazelton's books focus mostly on the emotional needs of parents, and my own deal with learning. Many were written by lay people, some on topical issues such as child care. For whatever reasons, after over twenty-eight years in the field of early human development, I don't believe I have given rave reviews to more than two dozen books out of the more than five hundred or so published over the last fifteen years. One book I have recommended with enthusiasm is *The Mothers' Book* by Friedland and Kort.

The main reason for my enthusiasm for that book is that *The Mothers' Book* fills a gap. The authors collected high-quality, passionate essays from a broad variety of perspectives about mothering. The collection had unusual power, probably because each writer was not only talented but had intense and geniune feelings about her subject at hand. It was the emotional power of the collection along with its uniqueness that set *The Mothers' Book* apart. Furthermore it was published at a time when long-standing ideas about motherhood were undergoing heartfelt reevaluation by women, as feminist ideas took root.

I've always been impressed by clearly articulated, genuinely passionate, and humane ideas about basic issues having to do with babies. *The Mothers' Book* struck me as an important addition to the core collection of books I suggest for new parents. That collection includes one book on the physical well-being of babies, for example, Dr. Spock or *The Children's Hospital Encyclopedia* by Feinbloom; one book on the emotional needs of parents, for example, perhaps by T. Berry Brazelton; and one on behavior and learning, my own. *The Mothers' Book* is a fine example of a fourth core selection on the emotional and personal significance of becoming a mother, and as such it seems to me to belong in that select group.

Now these authors have come up with the logical sequel, *The Fathers'
Book*—once again, a book unlike any other, a book that will be of considerable
value to many new fathers. The editors again have done a masterful job of
selecting authors and topics. The writing is first-rate. The broad range of subject
matter is fascinating. The editing and composition is excellent. The book
contains over fifty essays written by fathers on just about any conceivable facet
of fatherhood. Topics range from the expectations of fathers-to-be through such
profound topics as the meaning of life to such modern issues as paternity leaves
and on and on. Altogether, these short presentations are remarkably diverse;
yet they show one special quality—they each mean a lot to the writer.

Not many people would deny the profound impact that motherhood
makes on women. No one can say whether that power is as great in respect to
men. Nevertheless, my experiences with young families have convinced me
that the feelings of new fathers are very often equally overpowering. For such
men this collection will hold the same kind of appeal *The Mothers' Book* held
for women. It will enable them to expand and enrich the extraordinary feelings
that have been visited on them by the birth of their child. Any document that
has the potential to provide that kind of special gift is worthy of high praise
indeed.

Burton L. White, Ph.D.
Director
Center for Parent Education

Acknowledgments

We would like to thank Ron Levant, director of the Boston University Fatherhood Project, and Margaret Lieber for their networking help. And special thanks, also, to our husbands, Michael Kort and Daniel Little, for their contributions and support.

Introduction

Six years ago we began coediting *The Mothers' Book*. We had recently become mothers ourselves, and we realized that no book existed that reflected the diverse feelings and reactions to motherhood we saw in ourselves and in our friends. And so we decided to put together *The Mothers' Book*, a collection that illuminates and supports the many ways in which mothers actually experience motherhood, as opposed to what books or theorists claim we should feel.

But we sensed that there was a missing link. Didn't men also need support for their reactions to fatherhood? Were they, in fact, experiencing the same mixture of pride, ambivalence, guilt, fear, and joy as the many women we had heard from? Or were fathers experiencing something very different—perhaps more focused on the conflict between career and family, or on the fact that men had role models in their own fathers who, for the most part, were relatively uninvolved with family matters? We were curious; we wanted to know the answers. Although we searched the bookstores for a counterpart to our *Mothers' Book*, it did not seem to exist. We therefore created our own forum for fathers of all kinds to air diverse feelings about fatherhood. It was a natural evolution to offer first mothers, and now fathers, a resource in which they could find support for the realities of parenting. Ours is not yet another "how to father" manual, but rather a "how fatherhood felt for me and very well might feel for you" book.

We wrote to myriad publications that we knew fathers or fathers-to-be were reading, from *Esquire* to *Nurturing News*, to invite men to contribute to our book. And we asked every father we knew to participate. Although we were extremely pleased with the response, we must admit that we were surprised by the number of men who sincerely wanted to respond, but said, simply, that they could not. Perhaps that is why the majority of our contributors are "new style" fathers, who are more accustomed to sharing feelings, as opposed to "traditional" fathers, who have a much more difficult time mapping out their emotional reactions. Many fathers told us that they definitely planned to write, and then sat down and could not do it. Or they found that they had a few sentences to say and nothing more. On the other hand, those who did respond—and they did so from all over the country—were eager to share their strongly felt experiences.

We heard from many academics, perhaps because they are used to writing—more so than, for example, the lawyers or doctors who wrote for the book—and because they tend to have larger chunks of free time.

We included as broad a range as possible of opinions and responses to fatherhood. We chose essays that spoke honestly and forthrightly. We avoided preachy or sarcastic pieces in favor of those that were sincere and reflective. Often the personal account we selected exemplified the feelings of many other respondents; we chose the essay that best expressed a particular feeling or point of view.

Our collection includes personal accounts by all kinds of fathers in various personal and professional situations and relationships. We have writings of older fathers and teenage fathers, fathers who are house husbands by choice and fathers who are committed to high-powered careers. We heard from fathers who always wanted a child and fathers who only had a child to please their partners. We reached fathers of adolescents, and adolescents who were fathers. We found gay fathers, stepfathers, and a large number of single fathers. We cried with fathers in great pain—whose children had experienced freak accidents, diseases, or death—and we sympathized with fathers coping with special-needs children. Men in this book have shared their intimate feelings about infertility, sadness over the loss of prechild freewheeling sexuality, rage at their own fathers, noninvolvement during pregnancy, exhaustion, tenderness, and pride. We have included the voices of fathers who are ecstatic, and others who are at times despondent. Always they spoke of the enormous changes brought about by becoming a parent.

While we are not trained sociologists or psychologists, we could not help but observe the differences expressed by women and men in the two books. Our observations are informal, but several themes did seem to emerge. For example, mothers appeared to receive much more support from their peers, while fathers received more warnings, from "This will ruin your life," to "You'll never be free again." The expectation for women, according to our contributors, is to enjoy parenting; men are supposed not to enjoy it.

Men also usually have a noninvolved father of their own as a role model. The female contributors, for better or worse, had mothers who were usually active participants as role models. Many fathers wrote about wanting to be much more active in the parenting process than their own fathers had been.

On the whole, fathers seemed to experience less guilt in relation to their parenting than did the women who wrote for *The Mothers' Book*. This is perhaps due to the higher expectations society and the women have placed on themselves as mothers, or possibly is because women's role as mother is often more central to their sense of self. For the most part, possibly because of the ways in which they are conditioned in this society, fathers were more cautious in sharing their deepest feelings, and certainly less open than the women contributors. The fathers seemed to be more expressive and open when they were writing poetry than when they were writing prose; perhaps poetry is a safer format, where emotions are more permissible.

More men had to cope with being separated from their children after divorce, more women with having custody and supporting their children both emotionally and financially. Both situations seemed terribly difficult for all involved.

Although many of our male contributors obviously were profoundly touched by the parenting experience, it does seem that more of the women who wrote were transformed by it, perhaps because of having carried the child, or because their lives were more fundamentally altered. It still is usually the women who spend more time caring for the child, although—as this book reflects—this is beginning to change.

Several of our contributors were seeking ways to spend more time with their families than their own fathers had spent with them, even if it necessitated changing their work patterns. In varying ways, the desire to be a "new-style father"—more directly involved with child caring and decision making—seems definitely here to stay. But as many fathers attested in our book, it does not come easily, and an internal struggle usually ensues between traditional and new-style values.

In their actual enjoyment of or disappointments with parenting, the men and women we heard from were similar in many ways. Both sexes agreed that parenting had altered their lives drastically, and largely for the better. There was also a significant group of women and men that felt very ambivalent about parenting, usually because of the loss of personal free time or alone time with their spouse. Both male and female new parents felt the weight of sheer exhaustion. Like the women, men told us about their feelings of pride and elation at being at the birth, watching the first step, helping a child master a task, and participating in decision making. Fathers who missed out on these firsts (as did full-time working mothers) often deeply regretted it. But many felt they had no choice given their career commitments.

Working on both of these books has made us feel that we are part of a powerful, ongoing movement of parents everywhere who have similar struggles, joys, heartaches, and pleasures. We feel close to all of them, and hope that *The Fathers' Book* will reach out to them, and to anyone considering fatherhood, to let them know that whatever they are experiencing, they are not alone. There are many ways to be a father, no one ideal or right way. We hope our book will encourage readers to do the best they can, in their own fashion, and let them know that there is support for them and a deep understanding of what they are feeling at this important point in their lives.

Perhaps this book is even more important than *The Mothers' Book* in that men have fewer support systems, and fewer avenues for expression of their real feelings. They need something that takes them beyond a friendly "hello" to other dads in the park, or a trip to the supermarket where they see other men, but where they are still unlikely to approach one another, looking haggard, and ask for advice about colic. Women are more used to getting what they need: practical advice and emotional encouragement. Men have less access to this; we hope this book becomes an important tool in honing their ability to find out what other fathers are feeling.

In parenthood,
Ronnie Friedland
Newton, Massachusetts
Carol Kort
Brookline, Massachusetts

POSITIVE IMAGES, © *Jerry Howard*

Chapter One
Pregnancy: Planned

The Expectant Father

Daniel J. Wise

At last, after I had tried for months (maybe years) to expand my solitary rumi-
nations on childbirth into a dialogue, my wife had agreed to discuss the topic.
For the occasion we'd chosen a restaurant that, although not elegant, was a
cut above our usual fare. We'd barely settled into our seats when my wife,
Jane, zeroed in on the point. "Okay, I'm ready. Let's have a child. But we
have to do it right now because if I think about it for too long I might change
my mind." She then added, "Remember, it has to be fifty-fifty. You promised
that."

Jane and I are both lawyers. She's the practical one, and I'm the romantic. Jane's reticence was rooted in her uncertainty as to how much of her
present life would be left intact by the demands of parenthood. What would
happen to her body, her career, her time, and to casual evenings spent, like
the present one, dining in neighborhood restaurants? I was untouched by such
concerns, as my picture of the future was filled with nostalgia-ripened memories
of my childhood. Looking back on those pre–parent times, I can honestly say
that I had absolutely no idea of how a child was supposed to fit into my life.
Yes, I knew life would be different, but as to how my emotions would change,
what daddy-love would feel like, and how the contours of my relationship with
Jane would be transformed—the thought of a baby was too far away, the reality
unimaginable.

Distanced from life after birth, I was content to let Jane take over the pregnancy.
And that she did as she gobbled up books on mothering, breast-feeding, child
care, and the medical aspects of pregnancy, including its most exotic complications. Through her network of women friends, she drafted lists of the equipment, clothing, and other infant paraphernalia we would need. She arranged
for the obstetrician, Lamaze classes, a pediatrician—everything. She had re-

searched and resolved issues before I even thought about them. Basically, when Jane got on the case, I got off.

Partly because of my biological distance from the pregnancy, and partly because of my unwillingness to confront my feelings, I floated through the early months—indeed the entire pregnancy—as a spectator. I watched admiringly as Jane's lines became curves, her long face round, and her porous skin soft and translucent. I was not worried when Jane's early tests came back with ambiguous results indicating that all sorts of things I'd never heard of (but Jane had thoroughly researched) might become problems. The possibility that something might seriously go wrong never registered because the idea that there was life—much less my own child—growing inside Jane remained foreign to me.

Even as Jane's stomach ballooned and I could see and hear evidence of the child growing inside of her, I remained unconnected to it. There were certain moments—such as the chugging sound of the baby's amplified heartbeat—when a current of recognition flickered. Later in the pregnancy I was amazed to see some knobby part of the baby traverse Jane's stomach. But despite the thrill of these moments, the baby remained an unvisualized abstraction.

I received daily reports from Jane on the baby's habits. It was prone to hiccups and very active at just those moments when Jane was most inclined to rest. While intriguing, the reports did not stir an emotional response in me. I did not feel the hiccups or the movement. Everything was derivative, filtered through Jane. I did not experience the pregnancy; I only experienced Jane as she experienced the pregnancy. When Jane lost sleep as she struggled to find a comfortable position, I lost sleep. When Jane needed reassurance because her figure was lost in the expanding lines of her pregnant body, I became the comforter. When the pregnancy unleashed Jane's appetite and she could no longer play the role of mealtime cop, we feasted together as never before.

These were all secondhand experiences, which never brought me to the base of my emotions about the pregnancy. Despite my efforts to give the baby a human form, it remained an "it"—an aloof abstraction beyond the plane of my emotions.

The distance was also in part self-inflicted. On some level, despite my efforts to will the baby into my conscious sphere, powerful feelings of denial were at work. As a liberated man, I certainly wanted to go with her on all her visits to the obstetrician. But once I got there I was more than content to let Jane take the lead. I wanted the lowest possible level of respectable visibility. Similarly, in Lamaze class, I didn't want to get involved with the other couples and what they were (or, as in my case, were not) feeling. This was obviously dangerous territory—too great an involvement and surely the barrier protecting me from my emotions would crumble.

My greatest involvement during the pregnancy was a protracted negotiation with Jane over the baby's last name. (We had picked out first names long before the issue of whether we would have children was resolved.) Perhaps this was my way of safely giving some substance to that abstraction growing in Jane's belly. Eventually, we agreed that a boy baby would have my last name and a girl would have Jane's.

The closer we came to the birth, the more intense my emotional defection became. That last night, as Jane's cramps grew into contractions, it was clear that something was happening. Worried that Jane would need strength in her ordeal, I cooked her dinner. It was a fiasco. Jane took one look at the baked potato and refused to eat it because she was afraid she would vomit and choke on it during the labor. I felt that my sole contribution to the labor had been rejected. I sat back with my bruised ego and waited for Jane and the doctor to make the next move.

My blocking efforts intensified at the hospital. I couldn't sit still in the labor room for more than fifteen minutes at a time and continually bounced out of the room to phone in reports to friends and relatives. Jane seemed perfectly in control as the contractions rose and then subsided. Nevertheless, she asked me to stay with her and not make the calls. Good as that made me feel, I couldn't understand why she felt that way, since I couldn't see that I was making any tangible contribution.

As the hours stretched toward dinner time and Jane struggled to maintain her control, I was consumed with the desire to devour a pastrami sandwich (on rye with mustard). It became an obsession. I was saved when one of the residents came by and asked if I wanted anything ordered in. As I waited for my sandwich, Jane entered the most intense stage of labor. I could feel her belly knotted as hard as a cannonball. She was too absorbed to ask for help, and I was too distracted with my pastrami sandwich to volunteer it. The labor nurse moved in to fill the void, and watching her, I learned what I needed to do. Belatedly I took up my station and began pacing Jane through her rhythms.

My pastrami sandwich (I was furious they forgot the mustard) and a television program preserved my emotional distance during this critical period. At every lull in the labor I tore huge bites out of my sandwich. And intermittently throughout the long hours I zeroed in on the TV as I counted out Jane's rhythms, though to my credit I have no memory of the program.

The final pushing and delivery stages required a different stratagem to preserve my distance. I looked on in wonderment as Jane strained, her face contorted beyond recognition, to release the baby. To avoid being overwhelmed, I concentrated on capturing the power of her effort on film. Right down to the instant of birth the camera shutter framed the event and held back the flood tide of my feelings.

Before I knew what had happened, a newborn baby was lying on Jane's stomach struggling to suckle at her breast. While Jane was busy counting fingers, I was frantically trying to determine the baby's sex. Mistaking the umbilical cord for the male organ, I shrieked, "It's a boy!" only to be quickly corrected by the doctor.

Moments later, when I was over at a side table where a nurse was sponging birthing fluids off Johanna, the wall finally broke. The abstraction had been transformed into flesh and blood—jet black hair, rich olive skin, and huge brown eyes. The miracle of Johanna and the fact that she would be just that—Johanna—no longer an invisible "it," overwhelmed me. At long last, I was lost in something larger than myself.

I am a man who can't sing. Whenever I've been so rash as to try to sing in public, I've been the subject of intense ridicule. Even those who love me cringe when they hear me. But that night, no longer in control, I burst into song to tell "Johanna, don't you cry." Nobody will ever be able to convince me those weren't the most perfectly pitched notes and verses ever sung.

Daniel J. Wise lives in New York City where he is a reporter for the *New York Law Journal*. His wife, Jane, is also an attorney. They have two children, Johanna and Benna.

Love Letters to My Unborn Child

Tom Zink

December 20

I think that I should be called a father now and Beth a mother and our parents be officially declared "grand," because the process of our child's growth has already begun.

To the warning, "Ah, but you should not get your hopes up until the child's actually born because something may go wrong" which echoes in my mind, I reply, "Does the fact that a born child will die someday keep us from calling her parents father and mother on her day of birth? Of course not. And I don't see what makes it different for an unborn child."

We surely will celebrate your birthday, little one, in the Chinese tradition, which is on the anniversary of your conception. For it is then that your life truly began.

January 30

I must say that the mystery of the miracle that is you overwhelms me. There you are, inside your amniotic fluid inside your placenta inside your mother's uterus, as still and motionless (apparently) as can be, and yet so busy every second with the business of growing. The miracle of human life, told and retold billions upon billions of times, might just as well never have been told before because to me it is happening for the very first time, and I am awed. May I always regard you, little one, as the miracle you are.

Who can explain the mysteries of life? Doctors and scientists may describe them in great detail so that I can know how large my unborn child is right now, but who can say why it is so and why it works or fails to work? Tonight I am thankful for my Christian faith and my ability to accept and to celebrate what I cannot understand. Good night, my dear one-who-is-yet-to-be-born-but-who-already-is.

February 14

Valentine's Day. I woke up before Beth, and an hour or so later, I came upstairs to see if she'd awakened yet, and she said, "Do you want to feel my uterus *now*? Let me go to the bathroom first." So she went and returned and I felt, and low on her abdomen, about four or five inches below her navel, there's this hard place. It's a definite solid lump. Why's, it's you! There's something going on in there!

It's scary to feel that lump inside of Beth. Before this, her pregnancy was barely noticeable. But not any more. It's clear now there's no turning back. You, our developing fetus, are growing rapidly and are making your presence known. And, oh, how that growing presence will enter our lives with insistence and demands in a very short while! I guess that's why I'm afraid. You will need so much from us; will we be able to give what you need and still have some left for ourselves?

April 6

At one time I thought, at a gut level, that I really hoped you would be a girl. I want to raise a child who is comfortable being affectionate, sensitive, and nurturing, and it seemed to me that you'd have a better chance of holding onto those qualities as a female than as a male in this North American society.

I now think differently. I also want to nurture a person who trusts her or his own thinking, who is confident of her or his own abilities, and who is physically active. The current social system is set up to make those things easier for males. My choice of gender for you really boils down to the fact that it doesn't matter. I love you as you are, whichever you are.

April 10

Tonight a new idea came to my mind. What if I were the person who was pregnant? It's not biologically possible, I know, but what an item to consider! What if it were my body that was supporting the life of another being, that being you? How would I do things differently? How would I respond to the changes in me, the increasing weight, the drain on my energy? I'd probably get tired just as early as Beth does. And I'd probably worry and wonder if I was doing it right.

May 1

I feel left out. Beth gets to be privy to your growth and change all the way along. I get to hurry to her side to witness, from a great distance, the echoes and reverberations of you going on inside her. Many fathers I have known have had that kind of relationship with their children *after* the birth as well. I plan to be a different kind of father.

May 3

This is just a hypothesis. But let's just assume here that the lower back and pelvis pains I've had for the past week and more are somehow sympathetic pains for Beth's childbearing responsibilities. It's like I want to support her so much in carrying you, that my back hurts. It hurts more than hers does now.

June 1

Now get this. Me, a real new-age, nurturing-father type, feeling uninterested in you and your growth. The newness has worn off the thrill of watching your movements ripple across Beth's abdomen. At least two times in the past two days, I've been talking with Beth and she's interrupted suddenly to say, "Watch this baby moving!" And my sudden impulse has been to *feel* interrupted and say, "Hey, Beth, pay attention to me, not the baby." But Beth finds it difficult to listen to anyone else when you are communicating with her through movement.

I think those feelings I have are partially due to my envy of Beth who is able to have such intimate conversations with you. I really am the outsider. Is this how the battle between one parent and a child for the other parent's attention begins? If so, then I am declaring a cease-fire. I don't want to compete with you for Beth's attention; I want to magnify and support her attention for you. But I won't deny my own needs either. So let's agree that we'll each take our turns to both give and receive attention from Beth. All right? All right!

June 17

We returned to prenatal class tonight. The parents of a seven-week-old boy were there with their baby to tell us about their labor-birth-parenting experiences. Seeing a living tiny baby brought this whole thing into perspective for me. Yipes! You really are going to be born and be a real live person!

June 24

I had a lot of feelings during prenatal class tonight. Feeling isolated from Beth in her doctor visits, feeling irresponsible that we haven't practiced relaxation and breathing techniques enough, feeling ignorant not knowing what to do in class to support Beth in pushing practice and in labor positions. I sensed that this image I have of an informed, prepared, assertive birth consumer, able to get what I really want for your birth, was slipping away from me. Yukky stuff, all this.

I decided to share these feelings with Beth on our way home from class. Our talk was very enlightening because of Beth's reassurance that the most important thing is for me to just be there for her.

I've believed for most of my life that I have to be "doing something" to be accepted. Just being there for someone else never has seemed sufficient. There is a powerful internal contradiction going on inside me between Beth's just needing me to be with her and my own compulsive urge to be the active one, to tell jokes, to sing a song, to "do" everything just right. "Just be there," she says, and that's what I will be thinking of as your birth approaches.

July 15

Another busy prenatal Thursday. I arrived at our midwife Heather's house ahead of Beth today, and she and I talked a while about the birth and how Beth was doing. Then Heather looked at me and said, "And what about you, Tom? How are you doing?" That was neat. I felt really valued and included at last. To have someone take the time to listen to me about this pregnancy was very reassuring.

July 26

I had a rough night's sleep last night. Oh, the thoughts my mind tossed around for me while I tried to go to sleep! I remembered romantic encounters with girlfriends from the past and other adventures, like late-night bar-hopping with the guys, as a single male. I've been married nearly three years now, but even that joining with Beth has not transformed my life the way that you will in less than a month.

August 8

We went for a walk at 8:45 P.M. and regular contractions began. As we walked, I recorded the contractions in this journal, and it made me feel valuable, an important part of the labor process. When our walked stopped, so did the regular contractions. We phoned Heather, and she suggested we get some sleep.

August 9

We drove to the hospital and checked in, 24 hours after Beth's water broke. Because her contractions were still weak and irregular, the obstetrician wanted to admit us to the high-risk section. Beth would have none of it. She already felt nervous enough about this birth business and did not want the extra stress of being labeled high-risk. They admitted us into one of the regular birthing rooms.

As the hours passed, the number of tubes connected to Beth increased: First an IV tube with the petocin drip to stimulate contractions. Next a fetal heart monitor attached to your scalp. Then a tube into Beth's uterus to measure the intensity of her contractions. And finally a catheter. A few hours later, Beth asked for an epidural which left yet another tube. Prenatal class had simply not prepared me for the shattering feeling of seeing Beth immobilized on her bed by these unwanted, but necessary, intrusions of technology. What was happening forced me to shift gears rapidly from "natural childbirth" mode to "high-tech" mode without using a clutch. My one ray of hope through this cloud of gloom was your strong and consistent heartbeat.

After ten hours in the hospital and only a slight increase in dilation, Beth asked one of the doctors, "Isn't there another way to bring this baby out?"

This hospital's policy was to support vaginal birth in every way possible. They were using most of those means with us.

Eight hours later, the doctors finally decided a Cesarean would be needed. I gathered all my childbirth-educated, assertive-birth-consumer grit and declared to the nurse, "I want to be in the operating room to see my baby born!" The nurse replied, "Well, of course! Fathers should certainly be there to see their babies born!" So much for that issue.

August 10

And so off we went to the operating room. It was now 6 A.M.,twenty hours after our admission. Beth's epidural was increased, so that she could remain conscious during the operation. I sat on a stool next to her head. I chose to keep my head below the small screen that was across her chest, talking to her rather than watching the surgery. Then, at the precise moment that the obstetrician was lifting you out of Beth's womb, I raised my head to look over the screen.

The first thing I saw were your eyes: one was open and the other half-shut. Your expression seemed to say, "Where am I, anyway?" The doctor lay you on Beth's leg to suction off the mucus. My head bobbed up, down, and sideways as I tried to peer between all the busy medical arms attending to you to see if you were a boy or a girl. I caught sight of your little penis and said to Beth, "We have a son!"

You were then given to the pediatrician to do whatever it is pediatricians do with three-minute-old babies and then you were handed to me. You were wrapped snugly in a little blanket and your eyes were bright and alert. My heart melted. Tears welled in my eyes as I welcomed you into the world and held you close to Beth so she could kiss your face and greet you. You were born large (9 pounds, 5 ounces), long (21 1/2 inches) and very healthy. Praise the Lord and let us all three now get some much-deserved rest. We have worked hard.

> Tom Zink works in family recreation and parent education. He and his wife Beth Hewson have one son, Jesse. "The most important thing about me as a father is that I love the role. I take pride in being a nurturing, playful, firm, loving man with my son, and I have chosen to make time for myself as a father in the midst of my career."

Pregnancy and Sexuality

Michael Rossman

I don't remember much about the pregnancy, less because it occurred long ago than because it took over Karen's body rather than my own. My one sharp memory, ironically, is of the way it *did* take my body over: from the fourth month on, Karen might as well have been a pillow, for all the sexual response I could summon up for her.

There was nothing awry between us that I knew of. Lovers for six years, we had come together in renewed passion and commitment to make a child, and we were doing just fine. I felt all depths of comradeship and tenderness for Karen as we snuggled on lazy afternoons. But the flare of desire had vanished as never before. And what surprised me was less this than how natural that lack of desire seemed.

If I felt any guilt, it was not for my sexual disinterest as such, but rather for not feeling guilty about it. For it was clear, as Karen confirmed without complaining, that my neutrality didn't answer her needs. It wasn't so much that pregnancy shook her senses of self-image and self-assurance as that it reinforced them. Freed of contraception, focused on her body's sensations and changes, feeling more deeply *woman* than ever before, and with her genitals excited by the growing pressure of her womb—why, Karen was simply avid. We had some luscious play before her body's changes became unmistakable, and tripped me into mine.

After that, she might as well have tried to seduce a stone. I felt for her and wanted to support her. On the infrequent times when desire did stir at least in response, if not by itself, I was grateful. I pleasured her some regardless and otherwise left her to her own devices. I realized that I might have done more, but I didn't know what. We'd never faked things with each other, and my body was telling us both quite clearly that what I was feeling for her was not a lover's desire but some new state—call it protector (as I had rarely been) and guardian of the nest, of my lady the mundanely wondrous vessel of the planted seed, or whatever—a lovely state, but one in which my asexuality took us both by surprise.

I wish someone had confirmed for me that it was okay and normal to feel this way, and even to explore the feeling positively in the face of Karen's evident needs. But my talking with other men about our experience of pregnancy never quite got to these depths. It was all the more complex because my feelings for other women were unchanged, persisting in a separate domain until the last few months, when I pulled back into the nest completely.

If I did not feel greatly conflicted about it all—and I did not—this was not only because I was sure of my feelings for Karen but because something had happened. By the third month, as Karen's bodily changes became evident and the abstract facts fermented into substance in my dreams, I began keenly to feel myself caught up in an organic flow beyond my control, as if I were being swept onward in a river. I felt engaged with Karen in something more intimate and more mysterious than we had ever known; I felt myself a hostage to history and fortune and the world—more deeply, nakedly, and gladly than I'd ever been. And as the months of pregnancy passed, other evidences beyond the physiological accumulated, showing us both as animals in the grip of a biological force.

For me, the main action—which took up most of my energy—was economic. It was not metaphor alone that left me feeling like a pack rat, scurrying out from the nest innumerable times, prospecting the country to stock and prepare for the child. I hustled my tail off traveling wherever I could get work to build up a bulge so I could stay home after the child was born. I envied Karen the bodily experiences of pregnancy and birth; but I envied her as much her transport, so much more immediate than my purposeful pack-rat hustling and my own final nest preparation, as I hammered in the kitchen and watched her wander dazed and holy.

As for Karen, feminism must deal with what I witnessed during the last month, for I think it runs deeper than ideology or even social programming. For weeks she who had been at best a shiftless seamstress moved around our small cottage in a daze, sorting out pieces of cloth, sewn into garments or raw, sorting and re-sorting them into categories, bundles, neat piles in drawers, in corners, on chairs, for all the world like a nesting mouse. I'd come upon Karen in the bedroom, going through a pile for the nth time; she'd start, look at her hands and recognize what she was doing, and just nod and grin at me in sheepish marvel. She'd come have tea, and then find herself back at it as soon as her mind got unfocused from purpose. By the last week or so, when the kid was overdue, I think she was off somewhere in her mind or spirit at least half the time.

The sexual complexity did not end with her pregnancy. After the birth, my passion returned in a flash: I had my old dear lover back; it had been so long. But *she* was confused now. Nursing the child, given over wholly to this rich, sensual relation, she found it often impossible to shift gears back into the familiar sexual groove. My frustration was too comic and symmetrical to be a problem. But it must have been six months before we got sex straight again.

Michael Rossman is a writer and educator in Berkeley, California. He and his wife Karen have two children, Lorca and Jaime. He says that, fatherly speaking, "love, purpose, testicles, and genes" are the most important things.

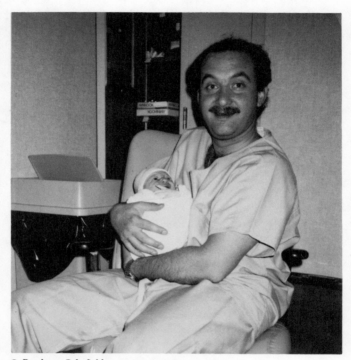

© *Prudence Schofield*

Chapter Two
Pregnancy: Unplanned

Second Child, Second Doubts

Robert H. Pruett

When Mary walked into our backyard, where I was swing-blading our knee-high grass, and said she was definitely pregnant again, I experienced an inward gag, as if an emetic had been induced through my heart. I felt hard, like tempered steel or stone. I said nothing, dropped the swing blade, walked inside, and left her standing there.

It was May then, and the respite from teaching that I enjoy each summer was imminent. I knew that this summer would be another period of transition, demanding, like the last. Our first child was only nine months old, and I still hadn't adjusted to him; nor had our marriage. A year after Jess was born, I was still trying to stabilize my life, still feeling completely original emotions, still going through a period of spiritual preparation, and still asking myself, is this really happening to me?

I was having doubts about my ability to be a father at all when I was jolted with the news that I was to be a father again. Over those next several months, anger, guilt, resentment, uncertainty, and ambivalence became part of a daily vigil I had to endure while caring for my born child—an experience I found more frustrating than satisfying. Our children will be only fifteen months apart. The news, therefore, was a kind of double-barreled version of first-time fatherhood.

The second pregnancy was completely unexpected. Even though Mary is an R.N., her conjectures about the likelihood of another child so soon after the first sailed over my head. I refused to accept it even as a vague possibility. But there was a grinding, gnashing feeling in my solar plexus and a distress around my heart when I secretly allowed myself to consider it. I *knew* another child would destroy our marriage, our financial stability, and my emotional health.

After our first child was born, I had felt antagonized, harassed, and confined. I wanted to run away, as the French painter Gauguin had run, give up my job and family, chuck it all and take up residence on his carefree South Sea island. Simultaneously, when I looked down at that tiny reproduction of my face, I knew that I could not. The mixed feelings I experienced then, I experienced again when the news came of another birth; but, to be candid, the second time there were more negatives than positives.

When Mary missed her period and the possibility became a reality, I felt compelled to suggest the inevitable solution. We had never discussed it: it was something other people did—friends, neighbors, people in housing projects, people who go to free clinics. To us it was just theoretical, political platform rhetoric. I assumed that Mary felt as I did, that we were both just hesitant to say it out loud. I had hinted more than once; Mary would sit silent and pensive. I assumed, naturally, that under the quiet, calm exterior, she was mulling over the same solution: an abortion.

But when I finally suggested it, I knew I had transgressed, that I had stepped on hallowed ground. Still, I felt no regret: it was double-edged, like so many other feelings I had during those months and still experience to this day. I remember thinking at the time how presumptuous of me it was. Who was I to be asking this woman to abort her child? Still, I knew it was the only solution. Pehaps I couldn't comprehend the meaning and the feeling of carrying a child. But neither could my wife understand the male experience. She fought for her point, I for mine; she for the female function, I for the male. I felt that she was imagining a fairy-tale fantasy where the family lives in a cocoon of joy and pleasantries, where there's a white picket fence and swing, and the father comes beaming down the driveway, carrying a leather briefcase, all aglow with pride, to sweep up his three children.

I felt that she wasn't facing the truth about our suffering relationship and what we had been through with one infant. I couldn't understand how she seemed to have forgotten the previous year so easily—the loss of sleep, friendships, social fun, time alone, freedom to travel.

Yet somewhere deep inside, I knew that she intuited something I missed as a man; I felt self-deceiving, as if I were denying an instinct. I knew I was afraid of growing up, admitting that I was thirty-four years old. As insufferable as those months had seemed, as hectic and demanding as parenting was, we had established the bond every parent creates with his or her child. And that bond somehow makes all the interrupted sleep, missed films, and dirty diapers worth it.

Meanwhile, abortion became a dirty word. I rarely broached the subject. When I did, Mary was still as inflexible about abortion as I was about the child. I had never envisioned myself as a father at all. Now I was to be the father of two.

All the assumptions I had about my wife's so-called feminist views were dismantled one by one. I discovered that she believed in the freedom to choose abortion, but for her it was not a viable solution.

I fought with a tremendous guilt and experienced a constant battle between my selfishness and a selflessness that was expected of me as a father.

While I had become accustomed to relaxing when I came home from work, sitting mindlessly before the television or losing myself in a good novel, I now had to keep a keen eye on our son, who was trying to climb the kitchen table or destroy the pots and pans. My wife had had a full day of it; now it was my turn.

The days and weeks passed. At least on the surface, I was no nearer acceptance of this second child than I was when I was first told the news. Inwardly, I passed through phases like the moon—a quarter, half, full, then quarter again. When full, I was full of optimism. Hopeful. At those times, I felt that perhaps I was imposing unrealistic expectations on myself. At the quarter phase, however, I sunk to the depths of cynicism and distaste.

Running away was an alternative I considered more than once. At the hospital where Mary works, she made friends with someone who had decided to run. He couldn't adjust. She told me that it was good to talk to him, to find out how another man was dealing with the same circumstances. He was leaving for the Bahamas the next Monday. His choice hit home. I thought about running for a long time. I argued with myself, with Mary, even with the counselor whom we began seeing. But running was both too easy and too difficult. I loved my son too much to give him up.

I think new fathers are misled. The media has created an ideal image where father comes home in a cloud of pride and greets his lovely wife who's made up and dressed to beat the band. The real husband, like myself, comes home annoyed and easily provoked at the slightest request from his real wife, who has had two hours of sleep and still drags around in her housecoat.

Our marriage certainly had its flaws, and the havoc of those first months after Jess was born, and even before, had begun a transformation in our relationship. Facing the second pregnancy in addition to the burdens of growing marital strife made for a precarious future. The marriage counselor idea came up as a consequence of both, and my reaction to that was also mixed. I felt that any third party, particularly another woman (who happened to be pregnant with her second child), couldn't be objective, nor could she improve our circumstances. I was frightened about the spiritual accord these two pregnant women would share, to my loss. But I consented to meet with the counselor, and when I did, I told her why I had hesitated: that I felt I would be an outsider and that I would be uncomfortable. Our counselor, it turned out, was incredibly empathetic. She let me talk, and over the next several weeks as the three of us met, we worked to solve the numerous problems that had developed. It was the beginning of a transformation of my own sensibilities.

I told them both one evening that I had come to the point where I knew nothing could be done about the pregnancy, that I had never stopped respecting Mary's refusal to have the abortion. I accepted the inevitable. I felt that I should direct my energy toward things I could change. So many other concrete problems needed our attention.

My feelings had changed, but not as a quick impulse. The mountain of ice didn't suddenly turn into an avalanche of penitence. It was a gradual evolution of a new perception prodded by time and the inevitable. I realized that I had actually talked to someone about my fears and doubts and that this person did not think me perverse. I came to accept my own ambivalence and anger and understood the consuming self-reproach I had been living with.

For me, fatherhood was, and still is, a trip to an amusement park where you encounter a combination fun house and house of horrors. I don't know if there will be a laughing clown's face or an alarming darkness around the next turn.

I'm passing through another transition now. Soon I'll be watching the clock in the labor room again and, shortly after, coping with the garish light at the 2 A.M. feeding. But I'm not lying to myself or falsifying emotions. I know that it's all right when I scowl or feel bewildered and confused, since negatives often make the positives more intense. And I know it's not an emotional aberration to dream about running to Gauguin's island, even if I'll be right here tomorrow.

Robert H. Pruett teaches and writes in Richmond, Virginia. He and his wife, Mary, have two sons, and a third child on the way. Of parenting, he says, "I'm still a beginner. Every day is a test of my patience, capacity for learning, and willingness to get in the sandbox. To be a good father for kids you've got to stop being grown-up. I see myself as a lifelong apprentice."

The Birth of the Father

Christopher Origer

When the announcement came that we were to have a child, it was as if an enormous lid had slammed shut on my past, and I wondered whether pitying myself might be more appropriate than rejoicing. I was then working part time to attend college full time, preparing myself for an eventual career as a writer. Suddenly it seemed that all my efforts were in vain, that I would stumble into the bread-and-butter circuit sooner than expected, that I would have to accept exteme compromises. Graduation? Impossible now. From this moment on, I imagined, my family would take excruciating precedence over all personal ambitions. And so, on the day of glad tidings, this is how I perceived fatherhood: a gigantic snake about to squeeze the life out of me. What lunacy!

Margaret and I were young, ambitious students when we married. Barely four months after the wedding, she came home after a visit to the doctor with a stunned look on her face.

"I'm pregnant," she said.

"That's impossible," I declared.

It wasn't fair. We had vaguely planned to have a family after college, at a convenient time "in the future." I was annoyed. Before I could even adjust to the news, people around me began echoing my own feelings.

"Well, congratulations, er—I thought you two would wait," said one.

"Was it an accident?" asked another.

"Did you mean it? I mean, to get pregnant?" said another so-called friend.

Whether pleased, amused, or insensitive, their comments were intimidating. Margaret had mixed emotions, since she assumed this would put an end to a blossoming teaching career. For the first few nights after the "joyous" news, I sat up, consoling both of us and trying to make sense out of what was happening. *Didn't mean to have a child so soon*, I thought. *Not about to admit it to anyone else, though.* Secretly, I was resentful of this intrusion into my life, but instead of admitting it publicly, I heard myself justifying the child.

And yet, despite the great blow to my pride, which is what it really amounted to, we never considered not going through with it. Both of us believe in God, and we didn't want to mess with his work. I reluctantly accepted our fate, figuring that in the end everything would work out.

The first few months of the pregnancy dragged along. Sometimes I didn't think about it at all, and other times, particularly after an exasperating workday, it was foremost in my mind. But as time went on, I discovered that not all my feelings were negative. A side of me that I had tried to suppress was secretly enthusiastic; I had a sneaky feeling that having a child might be a lot of fun.

I suppose every man wants a son, and I was no different. I began to visualize a real child. It was pleasant to imagine the things we might do together: lie under cool shade trees in summer and watch the grass grow; climb mountains and see the world beneath us as the birds see it; read children's stories aloud. It would be a chance to relive the best parts of my own childhood. The delightfully warm sensation of falling in love came over me again.

After admitting the possible satisfaction of having a son, I accepted my new role and started preparing for the rest of my life. I read books and magazine articles on the subject. I discussed my prospects with other expectant fathers. I attended parenthood classes. Eventually I started telling people that, yes, I was going to be a *father.* The uneasiness that had swept over me initially wore off. Now it was only a matter of time.

But a few months before Margaret's delivery date, several friends took me to a bar for drinks. It was Saint Patrick's Day and lightly snowing. Everyone in the place was either drunk or making sloppy attempts at it, and here I was, happy and satisfied, without even raising a glass to my lips. Looking back on that scene, I wonder whether the toasts my friends made to me were to celebrate my gain as a father or to pity their loss as my friends. One friend, in particular, had seen nothing but tragedy in marriage. Too many of his close friends had come together only to be separated in the divorce courts. He had never married and he claimed he never would. At first we argued playfully, with each of us in a different camp. Then he caught me off guard.

"The birth of the child," he pronounced solemnly, "is the death of the father." Then he stepped back to see how his blow had fallen.

I saw worry on his face. I imagined confidence on mine.

"Why must one live and one die?" I said. "There have to be compromises, but I'm not going to cease being who I am." *I hope,* I thought to myself.

"Ah, but you will," he said. "They all say that. But the change is so gradual that you don't even notice it."

Even after we left the bar, I kept hearing his words, delivered with the mock lucidity that too much liquor can produce. Perhaps it was all true; perhaps I had been deceiving myself.

The moment of truth—the beginning—finally came at two o'clock on a dark, rainy morning in May when sensible people are snoring lustily. After so many days, hours, seconds in limbo, the verdict was delivered: "A girl!" Suddenly, it didn't matter that she was not a boy. Flesh of our flesh and blood of our blood—was this who I had so feared? Kristen was no longer a nameless, faceless child, but a tiny daughter resting in the crook of my arm. I was delighted.

After visiting hours ended on the morning of the birth, I stumbled home from the hospital, pulled down the shades, and crawled into bed, alone. The sheets were laced with my wife's familiar scent, and I thought of her with our daughter, in a hospital a world away from me. As I lay there, scenes from the delivery room flashed before me. Reliving the event, I again saw the confusion, the short bursts of pain, the warm tears of gratitude, the laughter. All the months of preparation had been for that terrible, wonderful moment. I drifted off into a deep, comfortable sleep.

Hurrying to the hospital the next morning, I felt eager to greet my new family. I remembered my friend's threatening words of a few months earlier and I laughed. If this was death, then why was I so happy?

Time has told its tale. Nine months have sailed by since Kristin became a part of my life. I have run an emotional gauntlet and emerged unharmed and wiser. We were promised sleepless nights, dirty diapers, and unwashed dishes, and they came. But considering everything, that period will always be written in my memory book as the best time of my life.

There has been little interference with our careers. Margaret went back to school after a semester's leave of absence, and I never stopped attending. With both of us still in college it has been necessary to divide up the household work load. I take care of Kristen while Margaret is in classes, and vice versa. After graduation this will probably change, but for now it works very nicely.

Changing diapers and feeding and caring for the baby is not as bad as I had imagined. I'm still able to get all my work done. Kristen and I have a routine. If she's crabby when I'm at my desk, I pull out the backpack (one of the best things ever invented) and strap her in, and off we go around the house. Sometimes I read or write standing up with her looking over my shoulder. In fact, as I write this last part, she is sound asleep on my back.

Occasionally I think about my friend John's words—the birth of the child is the death of the father—and I smile. The idea behind his statement has become such a cliché—associated with everything that marriage and family connotes to the roving spirit, including imprisonment, loss of individuality, and so much more. I believed in this imagery, for in the beginning I felt threatened. Well, I have changed, and I have been changed, but I am still me. And that's that. In fact, I am not quite sure where I would be right now had we not been blessed with such a warm, loving daughter, but I suspect that I might still be finding excuses for not having a child.

I cannot speak for others, but for myself fathering has been an elastic experience. Kristen's birth was a beginning for me, a further definition of myself. To a two-dimensional life, she added the third dimension. And I lost nothing more than my fears. What started out to be the birth of the child wound up as the birth of the father. I am grateful to her for so much. She has taught me what the wisest of sages failed to teach: how to love. As Robert Frost once wrote,

> Two roads diverged in a wood, and
> I—
> I took the one less traveled by,
> And that has made all the difference.

The road less traveled is sometimes the harder and sometimes the longer, but it is not the arrival that is most satisfying to reflect upon. It is the journey itself.

> The husband of Margaret and the father of Kristen, Christopher Origer lives in Valley Falls, New York, where he is assistant registrar in a history museum. "I have learned to be more patient and sharing of myself. That I am willing to take the time to listen and learn is significant to me and important for a father."

POSITIVE IMAGES, © *Jerry Howard*

Chapter Three
Adjusting to Fatherhood

Barrage

Douglas Worth

the constant weight, building
exhaustion

at 5 a.m. thumbs, pins and needles
the feeling you've got his arms on
wrongside out

the point when the quivering buzzsaw of his rage
spewing frayed nerves, grates bone—
when song, when even mother's breast
is no solace, the light gone sour. . . .

"I keep thinking this will all be over
in a few days
so I can get back
to my life."

at the cleaners, remarking
"Well, it's only for the next eighteen years."
the white-haired, smiling lady replying
"Don't kid yourself, Mr. Worth—my boy's
thirty-four next week."

Douglas Worth is an English teacher. "I try to write as deeply and clearly as I can about my experience of life and the world around me. I try to celebrate the miraculousness and complexity of existence, as opposed to what I perceive as a trend in contemporary art to be negative and despairing." He and his wife, Karen, have two sons, Colin and Denny.

The Eve of Postpartum

Rick Fisher

We had done it! There she was, all purple and slippery, turning pink; complete with fingers, toes, and other necessary parts—a real baby. Faithful attendance at Lamaze classes, reading hundreds of volumes ranging from conception techniques and prenatal massage to newborn swimming instruction—it had all paid off. We had a daughter.

Safely strapped, buckled, and snapped into her new car seat, the little bundle slept contentedly as we drove home—four miles per hour, on the shoulder of the road—from the hospital. The house was welcomingly warm and clean; the bassinet and stuffed animals were in place. Kristina signaled her pleasure with her new surroundings by yawning drowsily.

Lisa and I prepared proudly to celebrate Kristina's homecoming. At about nine, our normal dinner hour, we ate lobster pie and drank champagne. Our celebration was followed by tape-recording our memories of the long labor and delivery. Another bottle of champagne and calls to family and friends filled the remainder of the evening. Kristina was being an ideal baby, nursing quietly and then sleeping. It had been an exhausting, exhilarating experience and, as was our custom, we turned in around midnight, pleased that our habits and life style would obviously continue in spite of our new addition.

It was almost 1:00 A.M. when Kristina first aroused us from a deep dream state; a brief hunger call, no doubt. I leaped to the bassinet to bring my darling to her mother and then admired her as she nursed. She was soon contented and drowsy as I laid her back in her bed. A warm feeling of accomplishment flooded over me. Sleep came quickly.

At 1:50 A.M. Kristina needed a bit more to eat, or perhaps just the comfort of our presence. Again I moved to her side, seeing to her diapers and checking vital signs. This time she didn't settle down right away. I knew that such a perfect child could never be an annoyance; I would simply reason with her and project a calm, sleep-oriented aura.

By 3:00 A.M. a decision was made that our newborn probably wanted to sleep next to her elders. I carefully placed her between us in the double bed, letting her snuggle and nurse at will. We whispered what an improvement this was over the hospital nursery, with its anonymous plastic cribs and twenty-four hour nurses.

The new solution proved effective, except that I could not sleep for fear of rolling over on her in my exhausted stupor. She was quiet and happy, though, and this knowledge made the next few hours easier.

It must have been after 5:00 A.M. when Kristina grew hungry again and obviously bored with all the lying around. Although she couldn't do much besides lie flat on her back, somehow we knew that a good rocking-chair session was in order. But first the diapers. A quick change was beyond my limited experience; I finally managed to fumble a fresh one onto the general area, using masking tape instead of those dangerous safety pins. This will cheer her up, I reasoned; it didn't.

The first morning light found us in the living room, each taking a turn in the rocker while the other sought sleep on the couch. With one red eye open, focused on the squirmer just in case, I welcomed the new day. It was then that the words of a friend/father formed between the numbed synapses somewhere deep in my midbrain, echoing persistently off my semiconsciousness—"You'll never sleep again." You will never sleep again!

At nine, as Lisa and I stared shakily at each other over coffee while Kristina slept soundly in her bassinet, we realized with crystal clarity that we had truly become parents.

Rick Fisher is a sculptor living in Santa Fe, New Mexico, with his wife, Lisa, and his two children, Kristina and Eliot.

Feet to the Fire

Daniel F. Schnurr

I am a thirty-seven-year-old father of a three-year-old. I have master's degrees in social science and in library science. I have been a VISTA volunteer, dorm father (for twenty teenagers), a history teacher, a feed mill laborer, a student and head of maintenance at a Quaker Study Center. I am presently a reference librarian at a college in New England; and I have never done anything more difficult than to parent.

By the time my wife and I decided to have a child, after nine years of marriage, I had found a job I enjoyed, sown many of my wild oats, and worked at becoming an adult. In short, I felt that I was really ready to be a father. In preparation for this new aspect of my life, I did all the right things. Even before my wife became pregnant, I read extensively about pregnancy and childbirth. My wife and I discussed what we wanted and did not want to happen during pregnancy and delivery. We chose a team of obstetricians who both supported prepared childbirth and allowed full participation by the father. In our Lemaze class, after listening to numerous embarrased answers to the question, "Why did you come to this class?" I could honestly respond: "I want to be here." In a word, when our daughter arrived, I came to the delivery prepared.

But what I had not prepared for was the fact that after two days in the hospital, Havalah came home to live. I did not know how to bathe her, change her, or support my wife during breast feeding. Suddenly, after all my work and self-congratulations, I faced what seemed to be an overwhelming responsibility: this little bundle of energy had come to stay. Coupled with the joy of having fathered this baby, I faced the reality of trying to parent her. I needed not only to cope with her whole new life but to build my new life as a parent. Slowly, my ambivalence became undeniable. On the one hand, I took my Polaroid pictures to work and nodded in agreement with the comments "cute," "alert," "long fingers," "your eyes." In the evening I watched her nurse and snuggle down to sleep in her handmade cradle. I wallowed in the part I had played in the creation of this unique new being. On the other hand, I felt alone and frightened by the everyday realities of helping to bring to maturity this child who was, night after night, waking me up—sometimes every two hours. I had never been so tired; the baby was turning me into a zombie. In the early weeks of Havalah's life, I often found myself outside her door begging her to go to sleep. Desperate for sleep myself, I stumbled through the first two months of her life.

As Havalah got a few months older, I felt more and more the need to have some quiet moments with my wife. I swear that child sensed every time we sat down to eat. One evening we planned an elaborate meal to coincide with her usual nap period. Just as we got the meal on the table, she started to cry. While I watched our meal grow cold, I felt my anger rise. This baby kept intruding on the simplest acts of my married life. Although Virginia nursed her at the table so we could at least eat, it was hardly the intimate meal I had wanted. During this ill-fated supper, it took all my "years of growing up" not to back out of my role as parent. Instead, I did the mature thing: I calmly leaned over to my wife and said, "I am going upstairs now and throw myself out the window."

At first I tried to convince myself that this parenting business would become easier as Havalah developed more skills and became more independent. But as she learned to do more things, I discovered it was usually more convenient and always faster for me to do it for her. Although I wanted her to do more and took pride in her accomplishments, I suffered from her constant admonishment, "Hava do it 'helf.' " Picking out what clothes to wear took forever, going to bed took forever.

As a man of Teutonic heritage, I live by routine. However, what sane man can remain the rational parent after acting out this 2 1/2-year-old's nightly ritual? Three readings of "The Little Engine That Could": "She was a happy little train." Three "ring around the rosies" with duck, Raggedy Ann, Mommie, Hava's baby, giraffe. Three "jump over the pillows." Finally, close the door and answer the following questions:

Havalah: What did Mommie and Doejoe (that's me!) do?

Reply: Goofed.
(We failed one time to snap her pajamas correctly.)

Havalah: What did Havalah do?

Reply: Threw up.
(Three months ago she did that for the first time.)

Havalah: Who came last night?

Reply: Jack Frost.

Havalah: What did make him go away?

Reply: Father sun.

Havalah: Have a nice nap.

Reply: You too.

Cute? Yes. As a story to tell friends, great. At eight o'clock at night, after two months of the exact same routine, absolutely no variations, boring.

With each new skill she learns, I must develop a new set of parenting skills. I never seem to catch up. I am never prepared, and I am always paying a certain price. For instance, when we started to toilet train Havalah, mothers and grandmothers the world over reassured us that there was nothing to it. I entered this new phase of fatherhood with genuine enthusiasm. No more diapers! I thought with glee. Well, she got the hang of it, and for weeks every time I took her (sans diapers) in the car I felt minor panic: Would she have to piddle in transit? *Would* she piddle in strange surroundings? Or most dreaded, would she have an accident? Once in the parking lot of Bradley Airport, she said, "Hava piddle." I discreetly pulled down her pants and we left a puddle behind us. Quiet, serene meals? True, we had no crying. Instead, we had a potty chair next to the table so when Hava screamed "poop, poop" we could snatch her up.

We have finally moved out of the twos into the threes. I believe the experts call it "the helping stage." How many adults spend half an hour Friday night organizing for *help* on the Saturday morning waffles? While I weed my garden, she helps me by crushing the tomatoes, picking the green raspberries, and pulling up a complete bean plant in an attempt to pick one by herself. When she helps fix something, she wants to paint, she wants to hammer, she wants to do all of it. Everything she does is such a great discovery for her that it is hard not to feel proud; it is harder still not to wonder whatever happened to the time when I could work at things in my own way and at my own pace and have them come out the way I wanted.

It has taken me three years of living with Havalah to come to what now seems like an obvious conclusion: she is her own person, she has her own personality, and she will be heard. It should surprise no one that when a new person moves into your home and starts sharing your meals, your space, your chores, your leisure time—your life will change. Yet somehow, it surprised me. Perhaps my romantic ideas about being a father got in the way of the reality of parenting. Fortunately, for me, my romantic notions were not entirely unfounded; and by enjoying those times, I have found renewed energy to meet the quiet heroics of parenting.

Daniel F. Schnurr is a college librarian. He and his wife, Virginia, have one daughter and a second child on the way. "With all the ups and downs of any relationship, I believe it is my love for my daughter which makes fathering possible. Before she joined our family, it was impossible to imagine life with her; now I cannot imagine living without her."

Postpartum Obsessions

Don Lessem

Can fathers suffer from postpartum depression? I'd say so, if what I feel after the picture-perfect birth of my daughter is at all normal. When exhaustion finally prompts me to leave Paula's hospital bedside, I sleep fitfully on a friend's couch, twisting clichés in my mind; "I haven't gained a daughter, I've lost a wife" is the worst of them.

Hiding in this anxiety I know is anger—anger over one who would demand much attention from me, and appropriate affection that I might otherwise have received from Paula. These thoughts are the hardest for me to acknowledge. I remind myself that this child didn't ask to be born. More clichés. I made my bed; now I must sleep on the couch.

When I arrive in the morning Paula looks rested, I haggard. She describes the unqualified love, the closeness she feels for the child, and I am jealous again. She's held this baby within her for nine months; I'm just getting my hands on it.

I'm not at all sure how I feel about all this. I've always believed emotions are there to be avoided, and if I'm not a textbook anhedonic I at least give Woody Allen a run for his therapeutic money. Since this is, however, one of those anxious times that brings emotions perilously close to the surface, I decide to survey my feelings, all the while uneasily eyeing the tiny bundle swaddled in blankets and stocking cap.

This is a marvelously, dare I say it, miraculously formed little creature. Tiny fingers, bright swollen eyes, toes as small, uniform, and smooth as corn kernels. But is this thing human? Is it mine? I have a litany of terms of endearment for it already, but they all have a mocking or inanimate quality to them; eggplant, pumpkin, meatball, goober, goobie, gooberatamus, beanbag, McBaby, donut, Dumbo, cry-baby, moonface, goonface, Lady Di.

When I'm not name-calling, I'm still referring to Rebecca—that is her name—as "it", a nine-month-old habit that is tough to break, but one I am resisting. What if I never lose the habit? Where's *its* dress? Who's *it* going out with tonight?

More questions. What's on Rebecca's mind? Not much, I reckon. I've read a bit on newborns, but nothing to persuade me that she thinks, dreams, or even sees clearly. Just as alien are the things she does that we don't. The pediatrician has been around and put her through reflex tests: lowering her swiftly to make her "Moro"—splay her arms and legs in an unhappy-looking startle motion. There are other tricks I put her through myself, feeling the grasping strength in her toes and fingers, the rooting reflex activated by a brush of the cheek or, strangely, by a touch of her palm. Still more curiosities: rub the outside of her soles and her toes splay; press her feet to the ground and she does an ungainly walk. Most of these traits will disappear in weeks, but they constitute an amusement for me now, as I play with my own guinea pig. I used to wonder how Piaget could observe his children with such objective distance. That seems less mysterious to me now. She is a stranger, my daughter, and she is strange.

When will it change? When will I feel that overwhelming love that every woman I know was ready to dole out unstintingly from the moment of her child's birth? When does the instinct that psychologists call bonding strike men? A male friend and father of two says paternal love engulfed him suddenly after three weeks with his child. I wonder if it will strike me when Rebecca first recognizes me. Or when I can see myself or Paula in her.

Meanwhile I am lined up with all the other proud fathers on the nursery breadline at the end of visiting hours, waiting to receive my order. I am a bit ashamed of my pride. My contribution to the making of this child was truly microscopic. Delight, amazement, would be more appropriate. But it is my pride that swells when the pediatrician says her neck control is exceptional and that sinks when a relative likens her to a red raisin. It is that same pride that has me pointing her out in the nursery to a twelve-year-old stranger passing by, that has me handing out chocolate cigars, phoning distant relations.

One of my minor fears immediately after the birth was that I wouldn't be able to pick out my baby from the nursery lineup of screaming newborns. Now it seems absurdly easy to me, only hours after the birth, far easier than remembering the five-digit password that gives me access to her. I can pick out Rebecca's scream in the nursery as quickly as Paula can, and I hope that my facility of visual recognition is a sign of awakening parental instincts. I could use a sign.

What I get, though, is a treat, the chance to watch a demonstration for mothers on bathing the baby. This is not, judging from the absence of males, fit work for fathers. But the terminology used would be appreciated by them. "Hold its head like a football," says the businesslike washerwoman, ignoring the raucous cries of the spheroid infant in her hand.

When we leave the hospital—and Paula is as eager as I to escape the twenty-four-hour activity on the floor and a marathon monologue in the room, I rely on Paula to fill the primary parenting role, a quick turnabout from the would-be father who wanted an equal share in bringing up baby. Now that I'm shaky I look to Paula. If she can't do it, as the football cheer goes, no one can.

Now, months after these postpartum concerns have faded, I see Rebecca with eyes that are constantly, delightfully clouded in a protective, admiring gaze. I can't imagine any child more wonderful nor any parental love stronger. Which is what, I suspect, all mothers and fathers feel. Some of us are just slower to get there.

> Don Lessem is the author of five books, including *The Worst of Everything*, to be published by McGraw-Hill. Of fatherhood, he says, "I find it difficult, still, to think of myself as a father rather than a son, but even harder to imagine life without children, for they are my greatest source of pleasure."

© Bonnie Burt

Chapter Four
Fathers and Daughters

To My Daughters—On Names

Gerald M. Tuckman

Carry on my name?
My name's my own,
struggled for
and found,
sounding only
like itself.

I give you that name

to use as a pillow
if your bed is hard

to chew
when you're hungry

to wrap around your shoulders
in the cold

to absorb the first few tears
of loss

to form a letter of your own name,
if you will.

Carry on my name?
No need. The seeds
have been
sown, and so
I'll watch you
grow your own.

Gerald M. Tuckman is in real estate investment. He and his wife, Jan, have two daughters, Emily and Leah. "My daughters see me as an integral part of their lives. They can come to me in happiness and sadness. I am involved in their discipline as well as their creativity and fun. We are able to learn and share together."

A Very Old Daddy

Gordon Baxter

Although there is not much written about it anywhere and you never see an artist's depiction of God laughing, I suggest that God does have a great sense of humor. I base this on what has happened late in my life—that I, who have had fifty-seven birthdays, am the father of a little girl who has had three. Notice that I didn't say I'm fifty-seven years old and Jenny is three. Such calendar counting can be both inaccurate and misleading. Diane, who is the wife and mother of this folly, says that the reason Jenny and I get along so well is that regardless of the fifty-four-year spread between our birth dates, Jenny and I are approaching the same age. Diane is thirty-nine, going on Methuselah.

If you had seen Diane's and my wedding pictures, you would never have been able to write the captions without a program. Diane is about the same age as my oldest daughter. My mother-in-law and I look about right for each other.

Through Diane's constant prodding, I was making creditable progress toward learning to give up "men's rights." In fact, I was beginning to enjoy the novelty (privately) of this foxy little broad thinking of us as equal and fellow humans. Then one night she hit me with this: "I want our baby."

"What? And ruin my playhouse?" Instant recidivism.

"We are not playing house," she said, as I raved on about having done my share of all that. Then she closed the issue with one of those one-liners you never forget, "Would you deny me my womanhood?"

My fear that I would no longer be the sole focus of her attention was justified. I miss that and am still adjusting to the loss. As an expectant father I desperately needed information on what changes to expect from a wife who is suddenly thinking for two and the second person is inside her. Of course, all that seems trivial when Jenny looks up at me, reaches out her arms, and says, "My daddy . . ." I can't imagine anything I would give in exchange for those moments.

The bonding to Jenny was Diane's doing, and at the time it seemed like the most ridiculous ritual I had ever been dragged into: Lamaze classes, with all those drum-taut young mommies rolling around on the clinic floor, waving arm fronds into air scented with their counted breathing. All the husbands looked at each other with sheep's eyes, and their added embarrassment of "Who is ole dad over there?" even kept me from the fraternity of men in maternity.

But before Jenny saw the first light of day, I knew her. First I had to share with Diane the courageous decision to have an amniocentesis test. The sonogram was more gentle, enabling me to hear the deep rhythmic whooshing of a mother's heart entwined with the running footsteps patter of our child within her. "My, what a strong heart . . . oops, she rolled over." Later, we would all admire the sonogram photos: "Such a fine head, see, right here" And months later in the delivery room, I wanted to meet her. Although I have seen men in combat in two wars, I have never seen such human bravery as a woman panting in childbirth. Then they handed me this little human, and my eyes met the triumph in Diane's. My heart filled up and brimmed over, and it's been that way ever since.

At home I took the predawn shift, the morning picnic time with Jenny. With a quilt on the rug before the glass wall that overlooks the forest and creek front, I would take Jenny to my own bosom and feed her. She quieted to the beat of my heart, and we would gaze long into each other's eyes. Diane would find us, glued together with a bottle of formula, curled up in dawn's light. "You two," she would softly murmur.

Diane and Jenny are the center of each other's universe, but I am a part of it. My special thing is that I could quiet the infant when her belly was knotted with colic. We would softly sing and slow dance at night, and I could feel her gradually relaxing, hear the change in the moist breathing in my ear, and we never lost the talking with our eyes.

In one of Diane's books, I read that until a child is about nine years old, most of life—the best of it—is just a game. I would have to agree. Jenny and I have the "Going Down the Hall to Bedtime Waltz." We have the "Let me see if I can put all those pigs in this sack," for "Putting On the Socks Time." And when she comes in screaming with a stubbed toe, there is "Kindly Old Doctor Toe," who quickly cleans off his desk top, spreads a towel, has the patient lie quietly for some examination and hugging, then goes out to the shop and comes back in with the saw and pliers.

Jenny knows where her mother keeps the gold stars, and if I have been a good boy, she will drag up a chair, climb to that shelf, and get a star for me to wear on my own forehead as she often does on hers. I wear it, too, all day, in public.

"Where'd you get the gold star, Bax?"

"I been a good boy."

"I bet you have. Har har de-har."

Why should I tell them that this is an affair going on between me and a three-year-old? It's hard and surprising enough for me to understand. Believe me, there was nothing in my life script to suggest that one of my best and closest friends, as I neared sixty, would be a little twirp with a bouncing ponytail the color of copper wire, and astonishingly clear, wide blue eyes that, ever since they first opened, have been trying to encompass all the knowledge of this world. It is through these new eyes that my own, which have seen too much of hurricanes, wars, and bars, are seeing the world again—innocently—as if for the first time.

This is not your easily explained, common variety grandfather attachment—the old gaffer strolling the park with a toddler clinging to his finger, both of them having the time now to slow their pace to discover the face of a wildflower. I have grandchildren. Some in junior high school now. I was never this close to them, nor, I deeply regret to say, to their parents.

Oh, the follies of a young father. I never had time to bathe a little bottom, nor feed a baby to sleep, watching dreamy eyes slowly close as I held a solid little bundle of warmth in the circle of my arms. I was too busy. "I'll make friends with them after they grow up and get to be humans." I'm still trying. "There is woman's work, and there is man's work. I won't have any babies, you won't bring home any paychecks." That was our contract. She had beautiful babies, and each one took its space between us. I never missed a paycheck. Sometimes when I was fired, I would not come home until I could reassure her that I had another job for tomorrow. For long times I moonlighted, fronted a hillbilly band, and ran the roads at nights after a solid day of broadcasting. The first litter must have associated me with "Shh-hh, your daddy's sleeping."

Today we have a child who has only been on this earth a little over thirty-six months but is an open and fearless person who might stroll up to your table in a restaurant, all pinafores and pigtails, say "Hi," and start a friendship with you. I take her with me every chance I get. I don't consider it baby-sitting; I just enjoy her company and the new language she gives me.

"What's the matter, Jenny, sleep too hard?"

"No, I've got a grumbly mouth."

There is some bittersweet in all of this. I'll probably never see a thirty-year-old Jenny. I'll be in my seventies if I ever walk her down the aisle to marriage. (Wouldn't you hate to be the young man who comes a-courting this redhead and has to put up with her weird old daddy?) Actuary tables do not favor the male members of my tribe. But there is solace in knowing that Diane and Jenny have each other, and I see no end to the delight in life that these two ladies shall share with each other. I have sometimes asked other May-December daughters how they remember dear ole dad. I wish you could see the glow as they recount a girlhood much as the one Jenny and I are now enjoying. The special love of a very old daddy and a very young daughter is not common, but not all that unusual either.

Jenny will drop whatever project she is working on when we meet at the door tonight for our high ceremony. Then she will say, "My daddy, will you come play with me?" (I have noticed that we both use the more elaborate "My daddy" and "My daughter" when addressing each other.)

And it is easy to play dolls. You just pitch your briefcase aside with your shoes, lay down on the floor by the dollhouse, and get into the conversation. Dolls talk just like ordinary people, but are not as restricted as to what they can do. Just moving a hand in the air with engine sounds can become the swiftest, most beautiful plane, moving through clear skies with all the whole world laying there before you.

Gordon Baxter is a writer and commentator for National Public Radio. He lives in Beaumont, Texas, with his wife, Diane, and daughter, Jenny. He is the author of *Jenny 'n' Dad*, which was published by Summit Books in 1985. Short excerpts from his book appear in this essay.

Little Things Mean a Lot

Mordechai Rimor

Fatherhood? Obligation? Lineage? Offspring? Such words soar abstractly high above my emotional comprehension. The only times such words have meaning for me is when they are tied to specific events, or during actual interaction with my daughters. Let me illustrate this in the following images, moments, and events, chosen not at random.

I remember well the day my older daughter turned three months old. My wife had to go back to work, so we had to let the baby stay for several hours each day with a hired sitter. The first three months with the baby were intense, absorbing, and energy consuming for my wife. As for myself, they were not too exhausting. On the contrary, I was not very involved at first and only gradually did I feel the beginnings of a conscious attachment to my daughter.

It was not a long drive from our home to that of the caretaker. On that clear and windless morning, we carefully wrapped our daughter in her tiny clothes, and drove her to the baby-sitter's house. I felt a little sad, but mostly only detached. Together with my wife, I was immersed (or I immersed myself purposely) in the details of the arrangements. The last thing I remember is the baby lying on her stomach in the middle of the cover of a large bed. We soon left for our respective jobs.

Then a painful thought gripped me. This delicate and newly blooming human being, who was given uniquely to my wife and me, was in the hands of a strange woman. I slowed and stopped. An agonizing pity gripped me. A part of me—a physical, delicate, and breathing part of me that I had been given to keep—had just been discarded to a stranger. My small baby, I thought, I need you near me. Yes, it is I who need you. I imagined her lying there on a stranger's bed, with her helpless eyes moving slowly from new faces to new forms. A sad and heavy pain pierced me. How could I do it? I felt that I, and only I, should be with her now, to comfort her, to protect her. I could not leave her, my delicate baby. At that moment, she was my baby first, then my wife's, and then ours. For myself, I felt I could not possibly let her stay there.

A mounting resistance to the situation rose in me. The feeling became so strong and personal that it was uncommunicable. I did not feel the urge to share my feelings with anyone. That evening I told my wife that I could not let the baby stay, at her age, at another person's house. Instead, I proposed to stay at home myself each day for several hours (my working hours were not that rigid). My wife agreed quickly. She had had similar feelings that morning.

Another bonding event occurred when my daughter was about four. We were invited to her close friend's birthday party. After two or three hours, the grown-ups were busily chatting among themselves, talking about their important issues, and the children were noisily busy in the other rooms. During the party, my daughter came to me with a rather sad face and told me that two of the girls were reluctant to play with her. I gave her the usual answer and, satisfied or not, she returned to the other children.

Then, a little later, I happened to pass my daughter in the corridor. She did not notice me. Her small face seemed rather desolate. Her wide eyes had a hurt and faraway look. She was looking forward, as if searching for help, but at the same time knowing that there was no help for her. I felt a pang in my heart. I wanted to reach toward her, to take her in my arms, to put her little head on my shoulder, and maybe to put my head on her shoulder, and to tell her: "Yes, my little child, my poor little child, I know it hurts when others do not like you. I feel the same hurt when I am rejected, by looks or by deeds. I know you feel lonely now and abandoned. It is not a game for you, I know. It is for real. I feel the same sometimes. You are so much like me."

But instead I stood there, following her with my eyes, feeling her sadness and being hurt by it and for her. I did not reach for her. Maybe because my being hurt for her was so deep at that moment that I became frozen. Maybe because I was embarrassed to put my head on her shoulder in front of all the people at the party. And maybe—and this, I think, was the main reason—because I knew that I could not help her at that moment. She had to carry her emotions by herself. She is a separate human being. Feeling hurt is a part of her life.

In your world, my little child, you are sometimes by yourself. Each of us has his or her own two legs to stand on—shaky sometimes, but better ours than others. It hurts me to see your struggles, but you are growing, my child, in your own world, growing in your sadness and in your happiness. I will watch over your achings, and I am ready to comfort you whenever you will come and reach for my comfort.

Another image comes to me. It has repeated itself rather often, much to my enjoyment. I was sitting in my armchair one gray Sunday afternoon, looking out the window, doing nothing. I then noticed my daughter coming slowly toward me. I looked at her and she, without looking at me, laid her head tenderly on my chest, put her thin arms around me, and said quietly to me or to herself: "Oh, my softy." Slowly I gathered her in my arms, her cheek resting on my chest.

We sat like that about five minutes without uttering a word, and I felt rising in me the warm and delicate feeling of being needed and of having a lot to give, and of a mutual need toward this small and hesitantly blooming daughter of mine. I felt as if I were in a "bed of warm rosebuds," holding my own daughter. Her eyes were open and she rested her head upon me, as if gathering comfort and love. Emotionally and physically I felt that I was someone special she could always come to lean on for comfort, with or without reason. For me, her resting her cheek on my chest and my holding her in my arms was an act of mutual covenant, trust, and respect, which has been established between us for the last five years of our sharing her life. We need no words to express this. It was her act and my feeling that expressed it. After a few more minutes she raised her head and, without looking at me, turned and went back to her activities.

Much to my delight, this enjoyable, sweet, and humane act of complete trust has come to repeat itself every couple of days or so—the "Oh, my softy" and the resting of her cheek on my chest. I once asked her why she calls me by this particular adjective, "softy." Her answer, in the usual concrete style children use, was that my shirt is soft. (It is not.) But then she added, "and you are much softer than Mommy." (As you might guess, Mommy is much softer than me.) Then I knew that she meant what I (and probably she) feel when she comes to me like this. It is only between us: the tender and delicate mutual trust we have for each other, and my offering all-embracing warm human assurance on which she can always depend.

A final image, this one dealing with my other, younger daughter. It took place on the day of her birth, right after the moment she came into life. The morning began like any other Saturday. The delivery was short but painful for my wife. I, standing there aware of the many things occurring in the room, tried to be of help. As usual in such a situation, I felt on the one hand a little detached, as if I were observing my wife and myself; on the other hand, I felt a primary wave of excitement mounting in me. After an hour or so, the baby came out. After wrapping her in a white blanket, the nurse immediately put her in my arms. I was probably the first one she looked upon.

She lay there in my arms, watching me intently with unblinking eyes, contracting the tiny muscles between her nonexisting eyebrows. I looked into her eyes and then it happened. I felt myself slowly sinking into her gaze, transferring, loosening, and identifying myself with her open eyes and with what she was seeing. The feeling was powerful, primary, and new; vaguely the first words from Genesis arose in me in an unordered fashion—the strong, heavy, well-remembered words: "In the beginning God created the heavens and earth. The earth was without form and void, and darkness was upon the face of the deep; and the Spirit of God was moving over the face of the waters. And God said: 'Let there be light'; and there was light."

There is one more feeling I would like to share. Almost every time I watch my daughters playing near me, especially in a physical way, an unusual feeling takes hold of me. I do not identify with the big smiling male whose offspring play at his feet, although I do expect to feel like this, looking at their tiny bodies and my own big one. On the contrary, I feel small and open. I feel as if the three of us are learning independently how to be dependent on one another. Through the full-lipped smile of my older daughter and the caring and playful look in her big soft eyes, I see the budding human being learning to care for and love her own children and her man. Through the adoration and echoing laughter the younger sister gives the older, I see the beginning traces of a human being learning how to be voluntarily and happily dependent on another person.

And me? I feel so warm and small. I feel that a once-in-a-lifetime unique gift has been bestowed upon me freely, without my having to do anything in return. Together, the three of us were brought to life by a warm and humane act. I myself have been created flesh and blood as have they. They did come from me, but they are not mine. Each of us is independently open to the other, all by and through the same act of creation.

Putting these images, memories, moments and feelings into words has given them a categorized hue. Curiously, when I read them now I feel that they have somewhat changed their meaning. Trying to describe these images makes me feel as if I live on two levels, the same levels I feel each time I hear my daughters call me "daddy." One is the known level, public and common. For are there many more frequently used words than this one in everyday life? The other is my primary, intimate, wordless, and emotionally shared time with my two daughters. At these special moments, "daddy" is my proper name. I, and only I, am defined by these two human beings. And they, and only they, are defined by me.

> Mordechai Rimor is an Israeli psychologist currently working at Northeastern University. He and Rivka have two daughters, Ruthi and Nurit. "I sometimes feel, especially with my daughters, as if I live in two worlds. One is the everyday and known level of words and movements. The other is wordless, uncommunicable, and emotionally experienced. Only through certain smiles, looks, or touches is the second level transformed to the first."

Bedtime with Sarah

Jerry Howard

It is bedtime, actually well past normal bedtime, and I have finally unscrewed myself from the evening's multitude of excitements—feasting, cat baiting, playing tricycle tag—to attend to this ritual.

"Sarah, it's time: let's go to bed now."

"NO."

Sarah is overstimulated, and she knows the situation offers her leverage. Because I am not Mommy and we are not at home, the standard rules—tested nightly under the most ordinary circumstances at this age—seem more honored in the breach here.

"Come on, let's brush your teeth and put on your p'jamas."

"Unh-UNH!"

Sarah stands her ground, all thirty-seven inches and thirty-five pounds of her, staring down this paternal Goliath with all the cheek of David. Her head wags slowly, her tongue flickers across her upper lip as she confronts me, girding for combat: "I WON'T!" she repeats, hissing through clenched teeth.

So the gauntlet is down, and I draw a breath. However amusing, this is a public act of insubordination and therefore unconscionable. There is an old tape inside me that starts to play: *Don't you speak to ME that way, do as I say at once because I am YOUR father and I SAY so.* Such lines were my father's undoing, and I check my temptation to repeat his error. While I hold her glare, I ponder my strategy—trickery, intimidation, negotiation, force. It occurs to me that her defiance is also a heroic act of will and courage, however misguided, and that it clothes a fine if unbridled spirit which I can either nurture or try to break by my action at these times.

So I say finally, with firm humor: "You have exactly ten seconds to get your small buns moving toward the bathroom."

The trace of a smirk flirts across her lips: "Or WHAT?"

She has called my hand, so I play the ace: "Or I will put you straight to bed without a song or story."

I have resorted to a threat, or a threatening promise, which has its dangers. If she holds out, I may have to act in a loutish manner that will be disagreeable to both of us. If I waffle, I will lose credibility and bedtime will be harder tomorrow. I take the risk because the bedtime story is essential to this ritual. Sarah has never ever gone without a story by choice.

She is also adept at this game, and craftier tonight than I anticipate. She replaces the defiant glare on her face with a bored expression and parries, "But Daddy, I don't even *want* a bedtime story tonight," in a tone of voice one might reserve for someone annoyingly dull of wit.

Checkmate.

I can think of only one more ploy.

"Well, Sarah. I'M tired so I'M going to brush my teeth and go to bed."

"Oh, All right Daddy, I'll follow you up in a couple whiles after I put my dolly to bed."

Teeth brushed and faces washed, we are downstairs undressing: shirt is off, pants off, undershirt and panties stay on, sneakers stay on.

"You forgot to take off your sneakers."

"No Daddy," she explains breathlessly, "I need them on 'cause I am going to run a VERY long race in my dreams so I don't wanna take off my sneakers BEFORE I go to bed, only AFTER I finish running."

Her shoes are not dirty and our sleeping bags are not precisely clean, but the request strikes me as highly irregular. I remind myself that consistency is the hobgoblin of small minds; I recall my distaste for dogma. The request is *still* irregular: I will be sleeping next to the sneakers and will inevitably be kicked by them during this very long race. I say so.

"No Daddy I promise you I won't, please Daddy . . ."

"If you don't take your sneakers off this moment I will eat you."

"NOOOOOOOO."

"DAH-DEE," she yelps with exasperation, "I am a person and you don't eat *persons!*"

"Are you sure you are not a pork chop? I think you are a sausage."

"NO I am a SARAH!"

"Shhh, there are people sleeping upstairs."

The sneakers are off and have been set on the hearth of the mammoth stone fireplace beside the sofa bed in the middle of this rustic living room, where flames lick the crackling pile of oak logs. We lie side by side for a bit, two friends, staring up at the Big Dipper through the skylight, talking of stars. The day has been long. I am feeling grateful, humbled by the magic of our rapport which began again so easily after our absence. My fears of what might happen, my notions of what divorced fathers ought to do, have dissipated swiftly as we have passed time.

Sarah continues to amaze me with her beauty and ingenuity, her perception. It strikes me sometimes that we both wear father-daughter masks, that this comedy we play together is just a temporary act on a larger stage. There are times when Sarah seems to know this too; I suspect that we have worn other masks together before, in other lives. And we share moments, even now, when our masks come off and we find each other face to face.

"Daddy, I'm not sleepy, I still want to play s'more."

"Hush, it's late, I'm tired."

"Daddy."

"What."

"I want to play horsey on your tummy."

So she climbs on my stomach and I tense it while she bounces, gently at first, holding my hands as reins; then more vigorously, trotting, cantering, while I bounce her, bucking from my bended knees. Her hair splashes about her face, ruddy in the light of the fire. We look into each other's eyes and bounce harder; the longer we look the more we bounce, the more we laugh and laugh. Our eyes are welded together, hers are huge black saucers moist with joy and dark fire.

I am transported, beyond Daddy, beyond Jerry, beyond space and time. We are Goddess and Stallion galloping through galaxies; we are lovers in the garden, and the universe is ours.

This intimacy is suddenly too intense to bear. I understand the imagery, and stop. The implications of this frolic are clear to me, and I feel a mean shame. Fathers are not supposed to do these things with their daughters. I am overcome with sadness, and my eyes flood with tears.

Sarah, too, stops her bouncing without a word; she leans forward to caress my face softly, as I have seen her do only with little kittens. I lift her from my belly and arrange her beside me on the bed curled, her back to my chest like a large and small spoon together. I kiss her neck, and whisper good night in her ear.

"Daddy?"

"Yes dear."

"You are a good horsey and a very good Daddy. I love you."

I am forgiven. I forgive myself, for the sin I have not committed. I drift off to sleep, forgiving our fathers for the petty threadbare sins they have visited upon us, pain that still lies deep in our collective minds.

> Jerry Howard, forty-one, a writer and photographer primarily concerned with relationships between homo sapiens and the landscape, contributes regularly to a variety of magazines and periodicals. Looming larger than size on his own personal landscape are daughters Sarah and Elizabeth. As a consequence, he is forced to dwell often on that relationship as well.

© Carol Palmer

© Bonnie Burt

Chapter Five
Fathers and Sons

Humping Curious George

Wm. Palmer

My three-year-old son makes love
to Curious George. Before he naps
he lies on top of the soft monkey
and rides,
his bony butt in bleached-out blue underwear
pumping off an urge he doesn't understand.
But who does?

I didn't think it would start so soon.
Our baby-sitter, Molly, a fundamental Baptist,
says he has the largest penis of a boy she's ever seen.

It doesn't seem abnormal to me.
But nothing seems abnormal;
everything is eccentric sometime.
Take me for example: I can't urinate
in front of anybody, not even my son
(unless we're outside at night when it's raining).

I was ten, I think, when I discovered
the urge to stick my finger
in my navel.
My legs would tingle
as if glass mobiles were inside them
with wind blowing.
I'd lie by the TV,
watch Ed Sullivan,
my hand inside my pajama top,

legs tightening.
I'd press inside the hole
as though probing
for a diamond.

Around midnight I wake my son
to pee, so he won't wet his bed.
He often has a three-year-old erection.
And he can control it.
He shoots fast and straight, not like me.
I usually start by forking
into two streams that dribble beyond the rim.
That's why I sit down like a woman.

Maybe I am drying up,
growing brown fur inside.
I don't want to interfere with Curious George.
I like his red grin,
the red cap flapped up on his head,
when my son jams him inside his underwear.
My wife tells him to stop it
because he is stretching out all of his underwear.

Yes, he is stretching out all of his underwear.

Wm. Palmer is an assistant professor of English at Alma College
and the father of Brenden, six, and Ean, who is three. He and
his wife, Bonnie, live in Alma, Michigan. "I like my three-year-
old son patting my back when I hold him. It's as if he is holding
me—trying to comfort me. I appreciate small concrete moments
like this."

On Common Ground

Michael Goodwin

At the risk of sounding corny just as the World Series gets under way, I confess that I believe baseball is one of life's treasures. Growing up in a small, isolated Pennsylvania town in the 1950's, I received from the game not only the simple summer pleasures of friendship, competition and exercise, but also an early sense of the opportunities of the outside world. Except for the fantasy of far-off places provoked by the melancholy whistles of freight trains rumbling through the night, baseball, with its exotic roster of cities and states, constituted perhaps the biggest window on the world I had for many years.

By the time I graduated from college, however, other interests and new friends had squeezed baseball out of the way. The game's timeless rituals suddenly seemed endless and pointless. But I'm in my 30's now, and baseball has made a comeback with me. The reasons are two: I've rediscovered the inherent beauty of the game, and I've been able to share it with my son.

Scott is 7 now, and we've been playing baseball in the park—I pitch, he bats, I chase—watching it on television and going to major league games for three years. I took him to his first game when he was 4 and I was a newly single father searching for a way to entertain him, to pass on what few male secrets I knew. I thought I would start with baseball, which is what I knew best. It didn't disappoint. The fun I've had explaining the game to Scott and watching him enjoy learning it matches, even supersedes, the fun I once had playing the game. We've had some great times wrapped around baseball and hot dogs, and his delight very much reminds me of the times my father would pack the family into the car and drive three or four hours to Philadelphia or Baltimore to see our favorite teams play.

But Scott and I get more than fun out of baseball. Little by little, and certainly without our planning it, the game has come to play a significant role in my relationship with Scott. Somehow during the last three years, the national pastime has developed into the first private place we've had together, a common ground where our naturally disparate lives mesh smoothly. A good relationship of any kind is not possible without a shared passion that knocks down the walls that separate people. Baseball does that for us.

The irony has not escaped me: My son and I communicate best while we sit in the middle of 30,000 people watching young men in cleats and knickers hitting a white ball. Our conversations begin about hits, runs and outs and, 20 minutes later, can focus on God, divorce and school. A friend who overheard Scott and me discussing baseball promptly labeled it "male bonding," which sounds too clinical. But there is no denying that the game has opened some inner doors for my son and me.

That's not to say we have nothing else to do together. We ride bikes, bowl, go to movies or museums, often with friends. But the pleasure we get from these activities often seems short-lived, while baseball, with its long season and day-to-day results, has continuity. And that is especially important because our time together is limited. Sometimes when we've not seen each other for a few days, I sense there is a little distance between us. Baseball—playing it, watching it or just talking about it—usually closes the gap.

There were hints it would turn out this way at Scott's first game. It was about 6 P.M. on a hot August Saturday in 1981 when we boarded the subway for the ride from Manhattan to Shea Stadium to watch the New York Mets play the Cincinnati Reds. Scott was 4, and on the train he kept asking, "Are we there yet, Dad?" I feared that we would no sooner get there than he would want to return home. I expected him to be bored after one inning and cranky after two and that we would spend more time in the subway than at the game.

I had chosen the then-hapless Mets over the Yankees in the hope that we would be sharing the stadium with a small, quiet crowd. So much for planning. It turned out that the promise of postgame fireworks had lured 45,000, the largest crowd of the season, into the stadium. For the crowd, the most memorable moment occurred when the game was delayed because some of the fireworks went off early, shrouding the field in smoke.

But for me, the real action was in the stands, or, more precisely, on my lap. The $5 seats I bought from a scalper for $10 each were so far from the field I thought we were back in Manhattan. We tried them briefly before I pleaded with a grandfatherly looking usher to find me a better seat for my son's first game. The usher nodded in sympathy, said he would help—then asked how much I wanted to spend. The few dollars I tipped him was enough for only one good seat.

But sitting on my knee was no trouble for Scott. Once he could see the field, he was in love with the spectacle, if not the game. The lights, the bases, the crowd, foul balls into the stands—every aspect fascinated and energized him. He laughed when I pointed out that the Mets' pitcher, Mike Scott, had both of our first names. His smile grew wider with each purchase— hot dog, soda, ice cream, team pennant, second hot dog. Happiness at a baseball game costs about $40. But what fun we had! Scott hardly knew what a Met was, yet he squealed with delight as we tried to keep time with the clapping

© *Andrew Brilliant*

and chanting of "Let's Go Mets." His eyes sparkling, he followed my lead and stood to cheer the final out as the home team won. Never mind that the fireworks hurt his ears and I had to carry him out of the stadium, tears making shiny clean streaks down his dirty cheeks. That detail didn't spoil our glorious night.

We've been to about 20 games since, and we've never had a bad time, even when the home team lost. Scott understands the game remarkably well by now. He freely offers his opinions, on who is and who is not a bum. We enjoy ourselves so much that, sometimes, I fear I'm turning him into a clone of myself. I make a secret promise to expose him to new adventures before long, get him interested in new things.

And yet, what the two of us have in common is limited. He doesn't share my interest in politics, and I'm not much on cartoons. We're lucky we feel the same way about baseball.

Michael Goodwin is the City Hall bureau chief for the *New York Times*.

On Being Picked Up

Andy Solomon

"I'll pass. I always do," said Jeff, one of my college students. He was a cocky "rich kid" who refused to do his work.

"I'm perfectly willing to work with you on your papers, go over your drafts and make suggestions," I told him, "but if you don't put in more effort I wouldn't bet on your moving into English 102 next semester."

"I'll be there," he retorted. "My dad'll just give the college some money for a new library wing or something and it'll be all right. Can I go now?"

That night at home, my first and only child, Marty, turned five months old. He was, then as now, the greatest joy in my life. The marriage was nearing its end, and Marty's mother was no longer the lover she'd once been to me nor the friend she's since become. School, despite the occasional Jeff, made me happy, made me feel I was taking part in the growth of many young people. But Marty raised my life to a higher level.

He was still in the paradise stage, the time when he scarcely knew where he ended and the world began. In his misty consciousness all was here and all was now. He was the center of a cosmic unity, like a mystic, and through Marty's eyes, I could glimpse a little of what Adam knew before his fall.

Marty's fall from paradise was not yet to be, but another milder fall was about to take place.

He sat in the middle of his playpen babbling and gurgling, drool seeping from the upturned corners of his mouth. In front of him was his red Happy Apple. He wore only a Pamper.

The room was dimly lit, the only light coming from the lamp behind my shoulder. I let my eyes drop back to the Joyce Carol Oates story in my lap, and before long she had me completely engrossed. It must have been five minutes later that I heard the shriek.

I looked up. There had been no alarm in the shriek, nothing to jump up for. It was, instead, a shriek of joy, of conquest. Marty had used his pudgy fingers and the mesh of the playpen sides to draw himself to a standing position. I had never seen him stand on his own before. His face had an incandescent smile which I foolishly sensed seemed to say, "Look, Dad! Look what I did by myself!" Such a look must have flashed onto Icarus's face as his wax wings bore him skyward.

"Way to go, Marty! You did it, son!"

But he had not done it for long. Hardly was "son" out of my mouth when the smile faded from his face. The triumph was momentary. Standing by himself was new territory, and it was beginning to slip away.

I started to stand. It was clear what was happening. His left hand lost its grasp on the mesh. The toes on his left foot turned upward and outward. The smile was completely gone now, and a new look, not panic but puzzlement, came into the shiny blue eyes as large as quarters. He tottered bravely, not willing to give up the achievement without a struggle. But one foot was slipping, and the battle was hopeless. I started to lurch toward him, but something stopped me.

My son was falling on his Pampered butt, and I wanted to be there to catch him. I didn't want to see him fall, see him lose the battle. I wanted to catch him and pick him up again, hold him up and cheer him on. But something stopped me.

I saw my student Jeff. I saw Marty as Jeff in eighteen years. What had Jeff's dad done when Jeff fell in his playpen? Picked him up? Paid someone to pick him up? Jeff was falling in school and was confident his father would be there to pick him up. If I caught Marty and picked him up, when would I stop? At a year? When he started school? When I died? If I caught him, it was clear to me, I would catch him for the rest of my life. I can't recall any time in my life when it was harder to sit down. But I did.

Marty fell with a soft thud. He surveyed his damages and found them negligible. He again put his fingers in the mesh. He stood slowly, more cautiously, now knowing some newly gained territories are easily lost. He stood longer than before. It was the right foot that lost its steadiness this time. Again a thud, but now he laughed.

I watched for several minutes. Marty stood six or seven times and then went back to gurgling. In two weeks he was standing regularly and for as long as he liked. Without anyone's help, he'd learned to stand up on his own.

An associate professor of creative writing at the University of Tampa in Florida, Andy Solomon has one son, Marty, who is ten. "I became a single father just after Marty turned two. The most important thing I've learned about fatherhood is that a child grows best when you're cheering him on rather than telling him how to live; I can't chart Marty's path, but I can walk it with him so we can turn and smile at each other along the way."

Scott's and Julie's Daddy

Mark R. Belsky

Fatherhood has been a growing experience replete with love and pleasure as well as responsibility and anxiety. The births of my children, Scott, five years ago, and Julie, two years ago, have mellowed and matured me. Just as they began to grow and develop so, too, did I begin to grow and feel like a father. The feelings I have for each are unique for they are two different people. Since Scott was the firstborn, I have had more time to establish a relationship with him.

I often feel a pleasant warmth when I look at Scott. I am so proud of him and enjoy watching him interact with children as well as adults. There is so much I want to tell him, but he needs to discover these things for himself. Most of all I enjoy hugging and kissing him. I am describing the love I feel for Scott. It is different from the love I have for my wife, parents, and siblings. I helped create him and have nurtured him since birth. But more than that I see part of me in him. At times I feel what he is feeling and anticipate his reactions. It is wonderful how close to him I can be. I have discovered a special bond between child and father for which I am most grateful.

The love and pleasure we share is very satisfying. Playing basketball and building with blocks are among the things we enjoy doing together. He tries to please me when we play and enjoys my positive reinforcement. One of his favorite activities is to gather his parents and whoever is visiting to be the audience for his "play." He dances onto the living room floor and sings songs that he makes up as he performs. Our applause when he stops brings a bright smile to his face. It is wonderful to see his pride in his accomplishments. I suspect he is making the transition naturally from doing things to please his parents to doing things to please himself.

Concern over this transaction and similar issues make the fatherly role perplexing. How to be a good father is neither written nor conveyed in the oral tradition. Instead it seems to be learned by trial and error! As I have searched for the "right thing to do" in difficult situations, my thoughts frequently have shifted to my own father's behavior toward me as a child. There is no ideal father, but I admired my father's strong suit, which was consistently offering love and support. I did not appreciate his short temper and inflexibility. I reminisce about how he responded to me in similar circumstances and try to repeat the actions I approve of and avoid his unpleasant responses. He was a very good father to me and I want to improve on the model he was without losing the good parts. I love my father and trust Scott loves me as much.

A typical challenge that I confront is the daily list of "should" questions. Should I let Scott stay up late to play with me on the computer, or should he go to sleep at the expected time? Should I play golf today, or should I spend more time playing with Scott and Julie? Should I stay late in the office to catch up or should I leave early to go home and have dinner with the children? There is an endless supply of these dilemmas each day. I don't think my particular decision in each issue is as critical as being consistent in my philosophy and responsive to their needs. My children have learned that their father can make mistakes and that certain issues are negotiable.

One major dilemma is dealing with the second child. Julie is now two years old and an integral part of our family. Not only did Scott have to make an adjustment to her arrival but so, too, did I. Giving enough time to both children is the challenge of challenges. I am aware constantly of Scott's perception of what I am doing with Julie, or rather not doing with him. He competes with her for my attention. I try hard to keep him happy and support his needs as well as give Julie love and attention. Having them three years apart alleviated some of the strain. I can encourage Scott to do things with her that I do, such as feeding her cereal and pushing her on the swing. This leadership role is attractive to him, as it makes him feel special.

There are times when I am tired, my patience is limited, and I can be very short tempered with Scott. My wife, Nancy, has taught me to explain to Scott that I have feelings too and that he should be tolerant of me. The first time I discussed this with him it amazed me how understanding and sensitive he was. I learned from him that it was okay to feel like an ogre—that I was entitled to it!

I have decided to devote enough time to my children so that they will know me while they are growing up. I do not want them to be deprived of this contact because of my busy professional life as a physician. This type of commitment must be a choice because it is too easy to be "too busy." I enjoy this commitment to my children because it feels good to me. Their greeting makes each of my workdays end in a special way, as they meet me at the door at night with a jump into my arms and warm kisses and tight hugs. As they grow older I know I will miss this.

The biggest realization of fatherhood has been the endless responsibility. It begins with the economics of providing food and shelter for another member of the family, but it is much more complicated. I feel responsible for bringing this young man into the world and giving him a positive direction. I want him

POSITIVE IMAGES, © *Jerry Howard*

to be warm and loving, as well as confident and content. I want him to have my good attributes and improve on my weaknesses—not very different from my own expectations of improving on my father's.

I am probably most anxious about being a good and loving father, although I am more confident now that I am seeing Scott develop into a young person whom I like as well as love.

Being Scott's daddy is a very important part of my life. I am thankful for the happiness he has given me, for it is a satisfaction I could have found only by being a father.

> Mark R. Belsky is a physician specializing in surgery of the hand. He and his wife, Nancy, have a son, Scott, and a daughter, Julie.

A Letter to My Son

Gerald W. Lewis

"The Child is Father of the Man."
—William Wordsworth

Dear Aaron,

It is now a few weeks before your new brother or sister is scheduled for arrival, and I feel the need to reflect on our lives together thus far.

It has been just over four and a half years since your conception. I remember well how your arrival filled me with great joy and hope and a touch of apprehension. Since that time, I have grown increasingly comfortable with my role as father. However, my reminiscences of the pre-Aaron years have taken on a special nostalgic sentiment.

I daydream about a time in my life that seemed to be exciting, relaxing, free from responsibility and concern. I see myself as having had ample time to work, to play, and to relax. I had a little more hair with a little less gray in it, lots more energy with much less stress, and I did not worry about impending periodontal work. I could sleep late on the weekends. I was a young married man embarking on an exciting career and able to embrace everything with endless time and energy.

And then you were born. Nothing has limited my freedom, influenced my attitudes, or intensified my feelings as much as you have. Nothing has caused me as much anxiety and anguish, as much concern and conflict as you have. And nothing else has helped me grow, appreciate my world, and experience deep-rooted joy more than your presence in my life.

There are times when I sit and look at you with awe and

amazement. You are my blood, a being created directly from me. I study your expressive face, your fine little fingers, your growing muscles, and your ever-expanding gestures and words. You pull me out of my grown-up world and plunge me into the realm of fantasy and make-believe—a world full of Bugs Bunny and Spiderman, jungle gyms and parades, bedtime stories and good-night snuggles. You slow me down to see things I have grown blind to, like anthills and skywriters. You coax me to think about things I don't really understand and to answer questions like "how does the music come out the record, Daddy?"

You take me back to zoos and amusement parks and places I haven't been for twenty or more years. I ride the merry-go-round, feed the elephants, get nauseous on the Whip and hold my nose in the monkey house, all with a bittersweet sense of déjà vu. To rediscover and reexperience childhood with you, my son, is indeed more precious this second time around.

Then there are the other times, when it seems that you have removed most of the spontaneity from my life, reduced my world to routines, and pushed me into another generation. The impulsive late-night forays for Chinese food have now been replaced by staid evenings planned two weeks in advance, and dependent upon the whims and social crises of the thirteen-year-old baby-sitter.

Your keen internal radar seems to keep you on guard for any potential marital intimacy. You are faster than a speeding bullet and more intrusive than a locomotive when you sense the acute danger of your mom and me talking intimately, snuggling, or loving without your presence and active involvement.

There are evenings when I return home exhausted from work and recoil from your demands for attention. If only I could lie down and watch you play and enjoy you from a distance. Or if only we could lie together and talk quietly. But on these nights it seems that only piggyback rides and pillow fights will satisfy you. These evenings are disconcerting for me, because what caring father would prefer to crash on the couch in front of "Star Trek" reruns than devote time and energized attention to his son? You could not possibly understand that, at least not until you have a child of your own.

Aaron, the evolution of becoming your father has been tough to get used to and it is difficult to fully describe. In the course of a weekend, I can go from contemplating life and disability insurance, to rereading cartoons and comic books. The contrast of these types of experiences used to feel like emotional whiplash, but I am now steadily gaining ease as the myriad aspects of fatherhood become better integrated. You have aroused within me a greater sense of my own vulnerabilities—that I am finite and limited. I worry that I will fail you in some significant way, that your current childish adoration will fade as I disappoint you, and that my current idyllic dreams will diminish as you disappoint me. Will I be a decent Little League coach? Will you refuse to sail with me? Will we maintain an open and honest relationship?

Against this sense of vulnerability stands a contradictory feeling of power. I recognize a strong and primitive protective instinct, which is almost impossible to describe. You are my blood and my future and the only person whose survival is more important than my own. I am not a very brave man, but I would face anyone or anything that threatened your well-being.

There is another dimension to fatherhood that I have discovered through you. My Dad has become your Pappa. And when we are together and I sit in the middle of our three generations, I get a profound sense of where I came from and where I am going. It was not so long ago that I sat as the grandchild in a trigenerational picture. And with a hopeful eye to the future, I see your Dad someday becoming someone else's Pappa. This sort of existential insight brings with it an ever-increasing awareness of my own mortality. It is a fulfilling and frightening reality.

In closing, I want to thank you for helping me realize intrinsic potentials of which I was mostly unaware before your birth. You have encouraged me to mature and become a man in the true sense of the word.

I love you, Aaron, and will always be proudly,

Your Dad

A clinical psychologist, Gerald W. Lewis and his wife, Joanne, have two sons, Aaron and Jacob. "I'm doing the best that I can to be the son, husband, father, and professional man I hoped and dreamed I might become. Who knew that it might be impossible?"

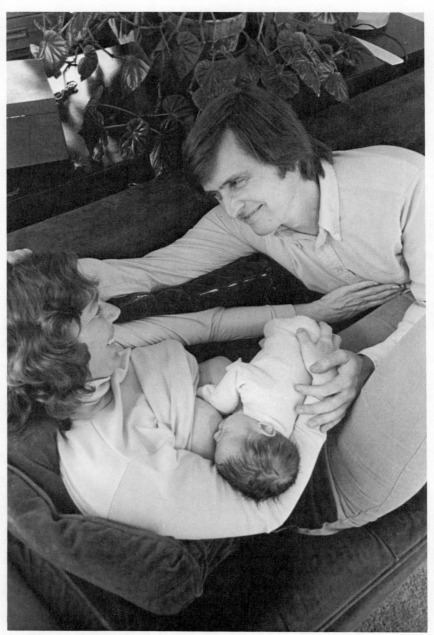

POSITIVE IMAGES, © *Jerry Howard*

Chapter Six
Fathers and Mothers

Becoming a Father

Christopher Vecsey

The fact is, I never wanted children. For years I resisted the arguments of my parents and the overtures of my wife, Carol Ann, to reconsider, and I avoided even a general discussion of the topic.

My male friends agreed with me, and we buttressed one another's objections to fatherhood, saying that children would inhibit our freedom, squelch our sex lives, destroy us financially, and tear apart our friendships. We saw fatherhood as a lifelong sentence to boredom and fatigue, and refused to be gulled or shamed into changing our lives. We chose to be twentieth-century spacemen, soaring in our own orbit without the deadweight of dependents.

My female friends didn't do much to change my mind. Some sought careers or graduate education; they were not going to let children jeopardize their futures. Others had raised families and regarded their decades of motherly service with undisguised disgust. "Have children?" they asked. "Why?" Now and then an acquaintance announced her pregnancy; the stoniness of my response forced her almost to capitulate in apology. I didn't desire children and I didn't rejoice in other's children.

My two elder brothers and my two elder sisters, all with offspring, might have stood as models of parental happiness. My parents, who raised the five of us with love and strength, might have shown me that it can be done. But I could still remember how, as a child, I lay in bed on Saturday mornings, pretending to be asleep, to avoid my mother's frustrated scolding downstairs. The notice on the kitchen table once read: "Mother at the End of Her Rope." I could still remember as a teenager when my eldest brother told me—in the midst of a daughter's tantrum—"Never have children. You'll regret the day they were born." What to my mother or brother were only passing outbursts, were to me the bulwarks of my resistance to fatherhood. By the age of thirty, an argumentative academic, I was telling my mother and father that I had better things to do with my life than "making babies." They were calling me, in return, a "premature fossil, full of dust and empty of empathy."

In part my refusal to father children derived from my own familial conditioning. I was the youngest of many, with a solar system of siblings rotating around me, the sunny young son. One sister taught me to tie my laces; another taught me to dance. One brother treated me to ball games; the other treated me to summer camp and fancy clothes. I taught no one; I treated no one. Almost never did I baby-sit, and I never learned to care for or about a baby. Nieces and nephews were competition for my central stage in the family circle ("I'm the only clown in this circus"). Even as a young adult I did not wish to undergo a personal Copernican revolution and find myself to be a planet among the other planets, revolving around a new family star.

With no practice at nurturing, I worried about my competence. When I read stories about battered babies, I saw myself as a potential brutalizer. Could I prevent myself from hurting a baby whose cries were preventing my sleep or flouting me in public? I could not convince myself that I could love a child and be the kind of father I thought a father should be. I felt that "to father" a child meant more than providing sperm, fertilizing an egg, and then abandoning the infant to the daily care of mother and others. I accepted the feminist idea that to be called rightfully a father, a man must learn "to mother." Fathering should be an ongoing, not an ephemeral, task. I believed this as an ideal, yet I doubted my ability to match my values. I knew that fathering was a sociological as well as biological responsibility, but I could not conceive of myself in the role of an infinitely nurturing father.

I had a long-standing love affair with my wife, with whom I shared intellectual interests, household chores, intimate confidences, and a house that served us and our friends as a refuge. I feared that a child would cause our marriage to disintegrate, chasing me into my study or out of the house entirely to get any work accomplished; putting an end to Carol Ann's professional goals; dividing our tasks into isolated units of labor; disaffecting her attention; and driving our friends from us. Our fortress of a home might become a prison from which I would contemplate only escape. I had seen households fall apart under a baby's weight, so I dreaded the possibility for my own.

I had broader reasons that reinforced my determination not to have children. I believed that the world was unfit for future human habitation. Bringing a child into a world threatened by overpopulation, ecological mayhem, and nuclear devastation seemed to me a cruel and immoral act. I did not want to have children of mine facing what I perceived as a probable worldwide holocaust. Perhaps these were but rationalizations to validate my refusal to procreate; however, they seemed to me a cogent argument.

Carol Ann remained unconvinced by my reasons, and although sensitive to my aversion, she continued to hope that I would change my mind. She adored children. She liked them sweet, she liked them sassy. She liked to hug the cuddly ones; the aloof ones she liked for their independence. When they visited our house, she pulled out toys for them, and she joined their games at their own homes. Carol Ann wanted children of her own because of her overflowing satisfaction with her own life. As a girl she knew that she deserved and would always receive affection. As a woman she trusted unswervingly in her ability to show affection and produce offspring bathed in her love.

Without ever complaining or threatening, her persistence forced me to ask myself if my refusal might cause her suffering. I felt justified in my own position because I had warned her for years that I would never tolerate a child. At the same time, I was denying the woman I loved what seemed to me to be her greatest desire. In the process of maintaining our unencumbered, uncomplicated love, I ran the risk of destroying our love, because in the end she might resent my refusal and become bitter over her lost chances for motherhood. We were now in our early thirties, and we were running out of years in which to continue our standoff. Without changing my mind immediately, I decided that I must entertain the possibility of conversion and perhaps grant her greatest wish as a love-gift.

For a year I contemplated fatherhood. Carol Ann and I discussed it constantly. I kept a journal to record my thoughts. I observed my friends with their children. I tried to change my mind. The process was slow and not entirely rational. I wavered periodically. I allowed myself to be swayed by romantic images and by the euphoric testimony of my new friends who were parents. Finally, I did not so much negate my reasons against childbearing; rather, I repressed them, at least temporarily. For a while I tried out my fathering potential by visiting the house of a recently divorced mother of young children. The smallest boy engaged me immediately. We fixed his makeshift kite. We wrestled and hugged. We sang songs and read books. He was great fun, but I soon tired, leaving with the sense that fatherhood was a nice to place to visit, but I wouldn't want to live there.

I watched around town. I saw one of my older friends pacing the shady streets with his nine-year-old daughter. They had ice cream on their cheeks. They carried twigs, stones, and leaves to build bricolages fashioned after their dreams. With these two in mind, fatherhood became a possibility to me: a father could love his child and could love his child's company.

Some of my friends became pregnant. I eyed them, with their great round frames, like billowing ships at full sail. Compared to them, certain childless women I knew seemed like dessicated driftwood: all limbs and angles with no life at the core. I asked one pregnant friend to describe her feelings, close to delivery. She conveyed to me an inspiring experience of human completeness. She said, "I can feel sad, on an intellectual level. I can recognize a situation before me as one that causes sadness. I can even say to myself, 'What a sad case.' But the sadness doesn't reach into me. I feel invincibly full of life." With such testimony, with the image of childbearing as a fountain of fullness and renewal, I couldn't deny my own wife—and even myself vicariously—the chance of a lifetime to carry and deliver and raise a child.

Still I had not overcome my two greatest doubts: in myself and in the world. None of the experiments, none of the images I had accumulated in a year's time, had persuaded me that I could become a loving father. In the end it was necessary for me to make a leap of faith in myself, without any concrete assurances. I said to myself that I would love Carol Ann, and perhaps my love for her would spread magically to the child. Equally, I could not convince myself that the world's distress was illusory. This was not a good time in human history to be born. Having no assurances regarding either myself or the world, I still went ahead and became a father, fueled by my commitment to my marriage and my double-legged leap of faith.

Once Carol Ann became pregnant and the initial celebration of friends and families subsided, I came to some realizations and some surprises. I realized, as I read the newspapers, that we were part of a mass movement. Most of our contemporaries, with their backs up against their biological clocks, were having children. We baby boomers were a herd of buffalo—marching for civil rights, playing folk music, donning Nehru suits, and "living together in sin"— and I ran in the middle of the pack. The parenting fad was as manipulated by social forces as jogging or born-again religiosity. I was almost embarrassed to be part of it.

My surprise came from the reaction of some friends. Those who had recently lulled me with the melodies of family joy now chuckled and clucked malevolently at my upcoming "eighteen years of servitude to a monster of your own creation," as one wag put it. They advised us to enjoy our last days and nights of sex: "You'll never know coitus uninterruptus again," one smirked. "Then, by the time your kid grows up and leaves, you'll be too old and tired to care." Another snidely remarked, "You think the Vietnam War lasted too long? Fatherhood is a dark tunnel with no light at the end." The more upbeat know-it-alls told me that 51 percent of parenthood was fine, but the rest was terrible.

By the time of delivery, my faith and my fears were in combat. My joy at witnessing the birth of our son was undermined by my anxiety upon carrying him into our house the next day. Despite all my preparations, I felt thoroughly unprepared for this unexamined, invited alien. When we lay him down to sleep between us that first night, I felt the terror of falling into dark, unexplored territory.

What did I discover? That this baby was born too soon. Don't ever let your doctor sell you the notion that your baby is late. They're always too early, years too early. Not only did it take weeks for my son, Christopher, to stop his frantic sucking and clenching, but years would pass before he could exist on his own. For the first few years my son's ability to survive would depend totally on the care of other humans—his parents and other adults. I suppose that we exist, our species persists, because our parents or their surrogates accept the responsibility for our lives. Carol Ann and I had decided early on that we would not lock him up in a playpen; we would respond to his cries in the night; we would have him sleep with us as long as he wished. In her new and happy role as mother, Carol Ann flourished; I accepted biological responsibility, my duty of kinship, and it almost crushed me. At times I thought of him as a parasite, siphoning my life resources (so much for renewal), at other times as the most exacting overseer a slave ever had. I resented mightily his constant demands on me for his sustenance. Christopher had one main skill for survival: he cried. His cries alerted me to some need—hunger for food or drink, or for human contact—arousing intense emotions in me to stop his crying and satisfy his needs. I despised his cries and would do virtually anything to stop them. Unfortunately, he frequently needed what I was not—his mother—and no amount of rocking and cooing could appease his appetite. There were times, I admit, that I dropped him onto a bed in furious frustration, causing him to cry the louder. On these occasions our struggle with each other was fierce.

Some people might say that a helpless infant excites their pity. For me it incited contempt and a mood for violence. My contempt for his helplessness was contagious, infecting my attitude toward my wife, so associated was she in my mind with the child. One night they were both asleep in bed. I was sitting in a chair, enjoying the silence after a day of squalls. I looked at the two lumps in the shadows, one little, one large, and I wanted to suffocate them both. So much for love's magic.

I had hoped that a child would invigorate us; by being with a baby we would restore our own childfulness. Instead, we became more cautious, anxious, scolding, and demanding. Our personalities and bodies aged markedly during the first two years, and I became authoritarian not only toward our son but in other areas of my life. I had heard that parenthood meant seeing the world afresh through our child's eyes. I was too busy watching after him to experience the world anew. Parenthood meant for me a narrowing of my vision, a hardening of my character, as I catered to his cries.

His demands interrupted (and in some cases ruptured) our relations with friends and—more traumatically—with each other. Mutual sex became a rarity. Carol Ann was exhausted (though exhilarated) from nursing for over a year. During that time she never once slept through the night. Christopher awoke chronically and almost never let us relax together. One night we decided to let him cry. He did, for two hours, until we rescued him, and ourselves, from our callousness and his tears.

Fortunately Christopher was capable of more than crying. And if his cries infuriated me, while arousing my sense of responsibility, his smiles bound me to him with a devoted passionate love. He smiled at me: nice, no-tooth laughs. He reached toward me with his little, wrinkled hands. I liked his liking me, and I liked him for himself, so full of life. He had no idea what to do with his existence, but he wanted life without hesitation, and I loved him for it. In the next two years I doted on this most loving, lovable boy. He was smart, engaging, playful, and I took great delight in his cognitive and physical progress, even while resenting his demands.

I loved the boy—no jealousy here for my wife's affections. What I hated was everything surrounding him. It wasn't just the shit and pissy diapers, although changing him was always a battle of wills that often made our life mean. But an infant can't be resented for excrement. Rather, it was the paraphernalia of babydom that disgusted me: the off-key music boxes that changed tempo as they unwound; the chewy, orange, rubber dog-heads; the plastic rattles and mirrors; the tube-metal highchairs; the carrying sacks; the jars and blocks; the books and the baggage. First they lurked in the corners of our rooms. Then this accumulation of junk and necessities took over whole areas of the house and filled up our car on trips.

Even worse, Carol Ann and I had to talk about it all: which product was less despicable than the other, how they washed, and how they rusted when they didn't dry, how much they cost, and where to dump them when they outlasted their use. For the first two years of Christopher's life, we were more boring than we had ever been in our lives. I stopped writing my journal shortly after the birth, because I didn't have time to record my thoughts, and I'm not sure I had thoughts anymore. They surely never surfaced in conversation. Every moment of my waking life, it seemed, was suffocated by my fatherhood. Furthermore, I couldn't face my disappointment, my despair even, in realizing through my journal that I had made a mistake and was facing this unrelieved night of treading water in the ocean of responsibility. I was drowning; at times I was certain that I had already drowned.

Certain scenes from the first two years stay with me. In the summer of his second year I spent mornings looking after him. One day I was trying to pick raspberries in our garden, and he would not stop pulling at me to get my attention; then he cried for me to lift him up whenever I put him down. I couldn't even pick a goddamned bucket of berries with him around. I dragged him to the sandbox, where he threw sand at me and bawled when I stalked away. On that day I planned suicide.

When he was almost two, we were staying with friends, and I was trying to change his diaper in their bathroom. His screams angered and embarrassed me, and when Carol Ann came in to help I turned on her viciously, pushing her out the door. I couldn't stand changing and fighting with him, but I hated worse her interference, which only certified my incompetence. I resented our diminished sex relations; I resented her assistance; I resented her for our child. On that day I made plans to abandon them both.

The irony of our situation was clear. I fathered a child to act upon my commitment to my marriage; the love-child was leading us toward divorce.

But divorce did not come. I didn't die. I didn't disappear. Instead the conditions of my fatherhood changed. Christopher grew more independent, spending long stretches of time by himself in his sandbox, or building castles of blocks, or reading his collection of books, or giggling wildly with other children in the playroom. He made his first syllogism. He toilet trained himself. He went to a day-care school five mornings a week. The two-year pattern of absolute dependence was over.

At the same time I arranged my schedule to be out of the house more often, decreasing further my burden of responsibility for him. I withdrew to my study in order to work, such as to write this article. In effect, I compromised my ideals about infinite fathering in order to become a good father within my capabilities (leaving Carol Ann, I admit, with proportionally more work). As a result, when Christopher and I are together—when I read to him, when we explore the zoo, when we tumble in the snow or splash in the lake, when we down our ice cream or snuggle in bed—we are happier together. I can love him well only if I have a life apart from him.

When people ask me how my fatherhood measures up to my previous expectations about it, I have three things to say. First, that many of my fears—about the loss of freedom, spontaneity, sex, and friendships—have been either realized or exceeded by the reality of parenthood. Second, that my son—not the abstraction of "a child" but Christopher himself, incarnate—is more of a joy to me than I ever anticipated. And third, that my hope to perpetuate the intensity of my marriage through parenthood has turned ironically—but not tragically—on itself. Christopher is the present passion of my life, the obsession of my daily thought and conversation. Carol Ann and I have become less singularly crucial to each other, as our boy has changed and filled our lives.

When people ask me to make summary or conclusive statements about my first three years of fatherhood, words always fail me. So, I do what any self-respecting academic would do: I quote someone else. A friend of mine, a mother, once said about having a child: "It's the best thing that ever happens to you, and it ruins your life." Alternating between drudgery and delight, I often think she is only half right.

> Christopher Vecsey is an associate professor of religion at Colgate University. He and his wife, Carol Lorenz, live in Madison, New York, with their son, Christopher.

Fatherhood: Continual Changes

Michael Mrowicki

Being a parent has profoundly altered all my relationships—to my wife, to our parents, to my friends, and to myself. The birth of my child has put me in contact with instincts I never knew I had. For example, I've never felt protective toward anyone before. In fact, in this society—with its emphasis on rationally getting ahead—I rarely used my instincts.

Before Grace was born, it wasn't easy for me to focus on my priorities. Well, it certainly is now! I am continually making adjustments for the responsibilities I've accepted and acting on my priorities. It's this focus of time and energy that has been the common denominator in any of the many changes in my various relationships.

My wife and I, for example, have gone through significant changes in the last year. Before our daughter was born, Ann was starting her third year of college, while I was finishing up the eighth year on the same job. Now, she's got a full-time-plus job, and I've left mine to work free lance so that I can have more flexibility to help her.

Also, since the baby was born, Ann and I have grown much closer. We depend on each other more, and it's enhanced a special intimacy that I think was precipitated by the home birth of our baby. All through the birth, we didn't need to talk in order to connect. Feelings are hard to convey and always seem to lose so much in the translation. Since our daughter's birth, though, my wife and I seem to have reached new depths in our ability to communicate spiritually. Our concerted effort in raising our child seems to have further added to our appreciation of each other. As new parents, our lives and relationship will never be the same, but they seem to be growing better.

There is another aspect of our changed marital relationship that I would like to share—the sexual one. Postpartum, we were both usually too tired for much extracurricular activity. My libidinal urges were soon much stronger than my wife's, however. While she experienced a somewhat decreased libido, there were times when I felt a distinct desire to repopulate the entire Western Hemisphere, or at least to die trying! Thank goodness, my wife is a very understanding person. Thank goodness, too, these times do pass.

There were definitely some tense moments, when it helped to have a sense of humor. On one of the rare occasions when my wife and I were both sexually inclined, baby had concluded an extended nursing session by, angelically, falling asleep at mother's breast. As she put baby in the cradle, mother threw me a rather lascivious smile. We embraced, and just as it seemed we were getting intimately comfortable, baby made it known loudly and in no uncertain terms that she had a need greater than ours. At that point, there was nothing to do but to laugh. As a matter of fact, I recall laughing all the way to my cold shower.

Our friends seem to accept the changes in me. That is, the friends who really matter. Since Grace's birth, my circle of friends has, well, not so much grown smaller as grown tighter and more selective. I just don't have the time for loads of people outside the family, as I used to. If a so-called friend can't understand that, I'm sorry but we're probably both better off. On the positive side, we have defined who are the close friends, and who are mere acquaintances.

Another group with whom my relationship has changed greatly is the new grandparents. Where there once were furtive rumblings and frequent dissertations about life choices, there now are two sets of smiling, doting grandparents, all with arms outstretched to hold the latest addition to the family.

As for dealing with the people where I work, my schedule has been somewhat different, and certainly more flexible, than that of many other fathers. When we found out that we were to be parents, I decided that I'd like to be a bit more free from a disciplined work schedule in order to help out more. Also, I thought that I would like the opportunity to watch my child grow from a closer perspective than that of the distant father-provider. Since then, I've left my regular job and free-lanced in various ways. One of my regular employers is a man who has a child only a few months older than mine. It is therefore not difficult for him to empathize. In this regard, I think I am fortunate. I have often heard of less fortunate fathers whose jobs, or employers, are too demanding to allow them any flexibility.

It stands to reason that any changes in me will force changes in my relationships. I've found a new meaning in self-denial. Whereas my personal interests were once concerned only with myself and my wife, there's now a new life that always depends on me. What this boils down to, in terms of other relationships, is that you get what you give. And I now try to give much more to my family and to indulge myself less.

Sometimes, there does not seem to be enough hours in the day. It is not always easy having a baby and her demands. But since the birth of my daughter, my relating to those around me has taken on a brighter tone. It hasn't been difficult to see the benefits that arise from being a father. It's so easy to feel sorry for myself because of losing a night's sleep, or missing a chance to have some people over because of a fussy baby. Then, all Grace has to do is smile. It's as if the love I've been pouring out is being mirrored right back. And it's all worthwhile.

Michael Mrowicki lives in Putney, Vermont, with his wife, Ann, and two daughters, Maria and Grace. "Between working at a day-care center as a substitute, gardening for myself and others, playing guitar, and writing, I earn a living while still managing to be an active parent. It's been vital for me to be able to pursue my various interests in order to offset the stress of being a full partner in child rearing. We've effected a modest life style that's facilitated this. It has become evident that no financial gains could substitute for the spiritual and emotional riches we've come to enjoy with our children."

Even a Child Couldn't Keep Us Together

Greg H. Osgood

FATHERS' BOOK: How old were you when you and your wife, Ellen, decided to have a child?

Greg Osgood: I was turning thirty and Ellen was six months older.

FB: Were your ages a factor in your decision to have a child at that time?

GO: Yes, we had been married about three years, and we thought that Ellen should have a child then, before her body got past the right age for one, before she ran any risk. That's basically how we decided.

FB: Once you decided, did everything proceed smoothly?

GO: Not exactly. We had both been angry at each other for some time but did not talk about it. One of the ways the anger showed up was that we had no sex. When it came time to try to have a child, I thought that things would get better between us, that we would be able to make love, and that the whole thing would be good for our marriage. But Ellen was so compulsive about "having a baby" that it no longer felt like making love. It was just "Let's see how fast I can get pregnant." It was cold and to me it was very hurtful. After not having sex for such a long time, I was thrilled about the prospect of having it again and expected it to be loving, caring. Instead, I felt like I was this fucking machine or something, and I wanted to put her off. I felt exploited, brutalized.

FB: How did that affect your desire to have a child?

GO: I'm not certain. I knew that I wanted to have a child, or children, sometime. There was a period when we were first married when I felt that I wouldn't be able to take care of a child, that I wouldn't know what to do with one, because I couldn't even take care of myself. I wondered how in the world I could teach a kid to handle life when I couldn't handle it myself. You see, I had career conflicts then that I was trying to resolve. But by the time we finally began trying to have a child, I was attempting to be more positive, feeling—yes, I could raise a child.

FB: What happened when your wife became pregnant?

GO: The pregnancy *seemed* great, but all during that time I felt that the decision to have a child was more Ellen's than mine. I felt that Ellen just needed me to screw and had no other use for me. During the pregnancy she didn't want or need me to participate. She didn't want to read about pregnancy with me; she didn't want to practice the breathing techniques with me. We were happy when we weren't talking about the pregnancy, but as soon as we did, things had to be her way. She didn't want to listen to anything that I had to say.

FB: It sounds as if you wanted to share in the pregnancy, but she didn't want you to.

GO: Exactly. I felt that the pregnancy was *her* thing. That feeling extended into the birth itself. I did everything I could. Looking back, I now realize that she really wasn't listening to *me* count with her during the birth; she wanted to hear what the nurses had to say. She didn't even want to hold my hand. Having me with her didn't make her any more comfortable. Being with me made neither the pregnancy nor the birth any easier for her.

FB: You felt superfluous?

GO: Right. It made me furious at Ellen, and eventually at our daughter, Cathy. When Cathy was first born, I wanted to help and to take care of her a lot; I was attached to her. But I grew less and less involved as the marriage got worse and worse and, as I increasingly perceived Cathy as being Ellen's, not mine.

FB: When Cathy was born, did you have time to spend with her?

GO: I stopped going to graduate school and began a full-time job when Cathy was born. Unfortunately, the job didn't work out. There were long hours and a great deal of pressure. So I didn't have time to take care of Cathy and on my meager time off, Ellen had to nurse her. What I most wanted on my time off was to improve the relationship with Ellen. In the evenings I would come home and ask, "Honey, what do you want to do tonight?" I would suggest going out and doing something together. Ellen would say that she was too tired; she was not at all interested in going out. So I felt rejected. She would take care of Cathy which meant that I would be left alone, trying to think of ways to amuse and relax myself.

FB: Did you resent Cathy because she was the reason that your wife did not want to go out?

GO: Yes, and I also resented Ellen's relationship with the child. It took her away from me. She *never* wanted to go out! She just wanted to stay around the house, taking care of Cathy, nursing her, and watching television.

FB: Were there other areas of conflict?

GO: Well, we disagreed about discipline. For example, should you let the baby cry? Also, I was jealous of breast-feeding: I couldn't nurse. After half a year, when we switched to a bottle, I was happier. I enjoyed feeding Cathy. On the whole, though, as my relationship with Ellen soured, I became less interested in Cathy. I began associating my anger toward Ellen with Cathy, almost as if Cathy were Ellen! If Cathy were a boy instead of a girl, maybe it would have been different. Maybe I would not have thought that a boy was Ellen's as easily as I thought a girl was hers. It wasn't looks, merely sexual identity. I see a daughter as being more likely to pick up traits of Ellen, which I don't like, than a boy would be.

FB: Do you think the birth of your child precipitated the breakup of your marriage?

GO: The birth of Cathy added to the already existing tensions and troubles within my marriage. It did not precipitate the breakup, but it did help reveal more clearly to me how we differed and disagreed in so many ways.

FB: Would it have happened anyway?

GO: Very likely.

Greg Osgood is a pseudonym.

POSITIVE IMAGES, © Jerry Howard

Chapter Seven
Fathers and Grandfathers

Son of Love and Rage

Denis O'Donovan

The son comes before the father,
    before the rays slant still farther into the forest,
      before the stone blossoms into moss,
        before the woman calls from beneath the covers,
          that slow liquid call that says
            all that needs to be said.
The son waits for the father
    to walk slower now like a discarded toy
      that leans still farther into the garage
        while things grow over its surface.
The son sees the father,
    alternate stripes of sunlight, neglect, sunlight, neglect,
      aluminum then bronze grown green. He takes a closer look,
        only half involuntary, from the thin corona of hair
          to the corrugation of crabbed and flabby flesh,
            corrupt in holding on, corroded in letting go.
The son imagines the father,
    sees his own conception like a puddle in the beam of his eye.
      Almost by accident not being, not being the particular one
        he is, not being this son to this father.
The son goes against the father,
    half not wanting to, half for practice, he needs to know
      in an emergency he can pull the line either way.
        He does not yet want both ends in his own hands.
The son mourns the father.
    Even before it is time he counts how many dreams smashed
      like accidentally dropped grapefruit stack themselves up

between those patient eyes waiting in line with the
raspberries already growing moldy, the take-out
chicken uneaten when the fever rises.
The son honors the father
by taking something, anything, seriously. It is necessary
to feel embarrassed about doing it well or badly
and to be unable to imagine not doing it.
The son knows the father
through the woman, and sometimes forgets her and remembers
him. If he lies long enough with any woman,
she reminds him of the father.
The son remembers the father,
how it was, then, before he could imagine being anything beyond
being his father's son. He dreams now of the grandson
secretly growing hidden fingernails and even more
hidden teeth and most hidden of all the sperm
that struggles upstream toward blue eyes.
The son buries the father
a little each day. When they come to find something
to put in the ground, the real father will be gone.
The son becomes the father.

A resident of Boca Raton, Florida, Denis O'Donovan is a widower with three adult children and two young grandchildren. He is a professor of psychology at Florida Atlantic University. He writes: "After my wife's death, someone said, 'I guess you can handle it because you're a psychologist.' I said, 'I can handle it because I'm a poet.' " His first poem was published in 1945, his first feminist research in 1959.

Pieces of a Puzzle

Allan Lenzner

When my father's first son, my older brother, was born, my father was thirty-two. When I was born, my father was thirty-four. When my first child, Benjamin, was born I was forty-three. Forty-three. Thirty-four. Father and son. Like most children I had no concept of what it meant to be a parent. Until Benjamin was born.

There were two comments that friends, themselves parents, made when they heard Laura was pregnant. One, "You'll never be alone again," was a rather provocative statement for soon-to-be-parents, but one that we did not take all that seriously. How could we? The other was, "You are about to experience the greatest change in your life. Not even marriage can touch it." Well, it stands to reason that if the first turned out to be true, the second had to follow, yes?

Yes. True. Both true. In spades. Doubled. Tripled. And so were the comments that followed after Benjamin came home from the hospital. I remember one in particular. "Are you ready to send him back yet?" Cute. Friends. Had my parents' friends been like that? Commenting on my brother's birth? On my own? On that of my younger brother? And if they had, would the thought have flickered through either of my parents' minds, as it did for a split second through mine, to answer that question affirmatively?

Coming home from the hospital on New Year's Day, high, higher than I've ever been, higher than my own writing can transport me; carrying Benjamin from room to room, showing him the Hudson River, paintings on walls, Laura's tapestries; calling friends downstairs, Benjamin's home, you want to come up and see him? Uh, Allan, last night was New Year's Eve, we came in kind of late, how about later in the day? Looking at my watch, only ten-thirty in the morning; high, higher than I've ever been, putting Benjamin down to sleep, the house peaceful, as we imagined it; later a moan, a cry, Benjamin awake, crying, hungry, Laura feeding him, then putting him down, Benjamin still screaming, Laura and I realizing that in the hospital he would be in the nursery now; Benjamin crying, ear-shattering screams, mouth wide open, rounded perfectly for projecting voice, audience in last-row balcony hearing every note; walking Benjamin up and down, up and down, first in my arms, then over my shoulder; Laura spelling me, up and down and around while I prepare a dinner planned for three days: eye of the round, roast potatoes, salad, 1970 Croizet Bages; Benjamin still screaming, Laura frantic, what's the matter with him? The roast cooking, walking Benjamin, the telephone ringing, five o'clock, can we come up now? Benjamin crying, Laura crying, my stomach in knots, angry, frustrated, how do we get him to shut up? Laura sobbing, they can come up if they want to see a crying mother and child; roast beef finished, Benjamin still crying, Laura holding him, me cutting roast, saying to myself, to Laura, to Benjamin, to no one in particular, still angry, frustrated, not at all what I had expected of myself, now I understand why my parents had a nurse; Laura between sobs, you wouldn't want a baby nurse, would you, you wouldn't want somebody else looking after him, would you.

My parents had a nurse who performed many of the daily tasks for my brothers and myself when we were first born. But later when my younger brother was about two or three my mother took over those responsibilities. And when I think now—after only five months—of the energy expended by my mother, I am in awe. In awe. And I have never been in awe of my mother before. In conflict, but never in awe.

What I didn't know anything about but have heard since Benjamin's birth: how hundreds of cloth diapers were washed in pots on top of the stove; how there was no diaper service until my younger brother came along; how there were no Pampers, no strollers, no Snuglis, but a large and comfortable carriage. How there was no breast-feeding ("my milk dried up"), only bottle after sterilized bottle of sterilized formula.

And later what I knew about and took for granted: my mother rising at six or six-thirty to squeeze—squeeze by hand—fresh oranges, slicing the orange in half, inserting it into the top of the juicer, pulling down the plunger, orange juice spurting out the snout, slowing to a trickle, repeating the chore until four—count them—four large glasses of orange juice were made on how many mornings? Hundreds? Thousands?

Of getting us off to school; making our beds after we left; cooking dinner when we returned; helping with homework; putting us to bed and then putting up with us once we were there. In awe.

My two brothers and I tearing our apartment apart, playing football, destroying beds, breaking windows, scuffing walls; making wire coat hangers into makeshift baskets, fitting them over closet doors, using an old tennis ball or a pink rubber one, dribbling, smashing into doors, bureaus, elbowing brothers, rushing to hospitals, sutures; my mother in her room lying on her bed, reading? sleeping? thinking? going mad?

I can remember my mother complaining of headaches, saying to no one in particular (my father was a dentist, not yet home from either the office or his club where he played bridge and drank), "I have a headache. I'm going to take a codeine," my father, I assume, having prescribed the anodyne; my mother—a junkie? Perhaps. And if so, if in those years of dealing with the energy of three sons, to say nothing of a husband who drank, only years later— when we were all grown and gone our ways—joining AA, my father to this day not touching a drop of alcohol, if so, if my mother was hooked on codeine, I say now, so what?

Both my parents are still alive. I am thankful for that, just because I have had the opportunity to understand and enjoy being with them now that I have my own child. I can understand, fit pieces of puzzles together, things I could not comprehend before. I think I can understand better why all three of us went to summer camp for two months at such an early age. It wasn't just that they were sending us out of the city for the summer. Or that it would develop certain skills and enable us to make new friends. Whether they were aware of it or not—I certainly am, but only 37 years later—it was because they wanted those two months to themselves. I can appreciate that now. I never did before. And I can understand why we were sent at 15 to boarding school—not only because it would provide us more of a challenge, new friends, an entrée (so my parents thought) to a better college, but also because it gave my mother and father more freedom. A return perhaps to whatever spontaneity they had before Robert and Allan and Terry.

And if there are moments, particularly in the evening when Benjamin is crying and I am exhausted, the evenings when I have told Laura that Benjamin is all hers, moments when my patience is at an end, when I understand the potential of child abuse but not what it is in me that puts up a hand palm out, a policeman at a crossing warning me to stop, withdraw, only the thought cascading through my head; if there are these moments within me then I can understand those times when my parents' patience and energy was at an end also, and I and my brothers were spanked, thrashed, strapped, with ugly glances, frightening words. My mother and father. I understand.

And I am thankful my parents are still alive because I love them and am able finally after 43 years to tell them that. To tell them I love them before they die. Benjamin's birth, as morbid as it may sound, was a benchmark not only for my own mortality for that of my parents as well.

Before Benjamin, I had never given much thought to my parents' death. The subject had barely penetrated my mind. And when on odd occasions it did, I would do anything to drive it out.

But now I reflect often on my parents dying. And while the thought frightens me, the fear of being abandoned surging through my body, still when that fear subsides, a kind of voluptuous love, a longing, an ache never before experienced takes its place. I can only describe it as an overwhelming warmth and excitement filling me up. Filling me up, every part of me filled with this pulsating glow—an understanding that there are only two people in the whole world, in the universe, only two people from all the ones I have known who have always been there for me. For 43 years, whatever I may have been going through, broken bones, failures, successes, emotional shoals, supportive or not, my mother and father were there. Physically there. An infinite constant. The only constant in an inconstant life.

And yet only Benjamin's birth really made me aware of that. Of that one permanence. And I wonder if that is just one more cipher uncovered, another part of the puzzle revealed, another reason for Benjamin, a long cycle unraveling itself.

> Allan Lenzner is a writer living in New York City with his wife, Laura, and two sons, Benjamin and Samuel. He says, "The mystery of life is not death, but birth; and if there were no economic constraints, I would have an infinite number of children."

Hit First, Ask Questions Later

Ralph Holcomb

My father died about a month ago, just before Christmas. I flew out once, suddenly, in early November when the doctors said he was going to die within the day. Machines revived him and he lived through a second visit at Thanksgiving, when my wife and son accompanied me. The last time I saw him he was in the casket, skinny and wasted from disease. His face was a mortician's challenge: a few days previously he had fallen and bruised himself badly above one eye.

I didn't cry when he died and feel no need to cry now. I once believed that when my anger at him dissipated I would find love beneath. But now I only feel a little emptiness and a strong sense of relief. "It's finally over," I said to myself when I heard the news.

My earliest memory of my father is of him running with me across suburban lawns. I was no more than five years old then. He was happy, and happy to be with me. I felt the same. When he had the time or energy, we would play together. He often worked night shifts at the boiler plant, and so he would often be working or sleeping on afternoons and early evenings.

I soon learned that there was another darker side to him, a violent angry side that frightened me and that I think may have frightened him as well. I say this even though he was so comfortable with his child-rearing philosophy that he would jokingly say, "Hit first, ask questions later." We children even learned to laugh with him when he said it.

In my next memory I am about six years old. I was crying as I hid from my father behind the couch. My sobs gave me away. He pulled the couch away from the wall and beat me in front of the family. My mother pleaded with him (she was my defender until I could defend myself), and my older brother and sister looked shamefacedly at their shoes, quiet, knowing that if they spoke they would be next.

The next image is of my father beating me for what I believe was the last time. I was probably eight years old by then. I remember the offense: I had crossed the street without his permission. As a father myself now I can understand what probably happened. He was alone in the garage, working on one of his projects. He became too engrossed in his work, trusted my obedience too much, turned and found me gone. That is enough to send panic through any parent. That beating was significant because his blows did not hurt. I cried anyway to imitate pain and to escape him.

Shortly after this episode my mother began advising me about strategies for avoiding my father. She taught me how to bend our strict family rules without the appearance of any wrongdoing. My mother also told me about my dad. His own life was filled with fear and loss. He came from a large and poverty-stricken family. His mother died when he was just entering his teens, and his father died when he was eighteen. He entered the military before finishing high school. He had trouble expressing his love because his loved ones had been torn from him. All this I heard from my mother; my father was silent.

I never thought to ask my dad about his violence when I was young, and when I was older I refused to care anymore. I don't think my father thought of motivations anyway: hit first, ask questions later. He was guarded about his past, and the few stories he recounted seemed like they were out of an old school primer. I think he remembered his life as if it were a bad dream—the shadows passed over and he was silent again.

Another image from my middle adolescence comes to mind. I was testing out my naive liberalism by condemning Joe McCarthy, when my father began to give his own impassioned version of the communist conspiracy, ending by implicating the teachers at my school. He perceived the world as filled with danger, and people as trying to exploit him at every turn.

Some of his fears were well-founded. As I approached adolescence, my father had two heart attacks and was told to slow down or else. He had known only hard work and believed that physical exertion equaled manliness.

In my next memory, I am a lazy adolescent, 12 or 13. I feared and hated my father by then. Love had disappeared completely. We were in the garage, his kingdom, and I was his assistant on some job. I knew it was only a matter of time before some problem frustrated him to the point of flash anger, which would be my cue to slip back into the house to read. It was my second time out with him that day. In the morning he had been working on the car and suddenly became enraged, saying in a voice shaking with self-loathing that he couldn't see anymore, he couldn't hear anymore, he couldn't do anything. That afternoon he ordered me to do some minor chore for him. I was slow, and probably insolent in my movements (I was never insolent in words then). He blew up at me, threw his tools, and told me that I was useless for men's work and should instead learn "women's work," like doing laundry and making beds. This was strong language, even for him. I ran away to my defender, hurt and indignant. The following scene included me weeping, my father shouting, and my mother between us. There were other similar scenes, but in content they were always the same: my father shouting out his frustration at me and threatening me, my mother playing peacemaker.

I eventually learned to walk away from him, silent and filled with loathing, but at least without hiding behind my mother. Because his anger was unpredictable, I never chanced bringing friends over. We became strangers in the same house. I would sometimes bait him (as with the Joe McCarthy story) to see him break down into what I then called "temper tantrums." He lost all direct power over me by the time I turned 15, and I was never vulnerable with him again.

The moments of tenderness between us—and there were some—faded as any trust I had gave way to fear and then to anger. I moved away to college and then moved farther away to graduate school. We became civil to each other after a long while, silently agreeing to ignore the past. One time, when I was out for a visit, he and I were driving alone in the car. He was old by then, retired, and looking forward to some years of peace. He reached over and spontaneously grabbed my hand, saying he was sure glad to see me. I was shocked at this breach of etiquette and could only respond with mumbled platitudes. In fact I could not respond. There was nothing to bring forth. He was declaring peace, but I had left the field.

One final memory. It was our last Thanksgiving together when he was in the hospital, struggling against a stroke and diseased heart. It was harder and harder for him to stay in the present. Some days he traveled back in time or cried, some days he thrashed in anger at his fate. I volunteered to give him his shave and shower. As I held the mirror for him, he wept at his reflection. I rubbed his back in the hot shower and he moaned with gratitude. Throughout all this I was impassive, feeling the detached concern anyone would for a dying stranger. At one point, he looked up at me and asked through tears, "Did you ever think it would come to this?" I had no answer.

That same night, giving my own three-year-old son a bath, I tried to glean significance from this juxtaposition of events, but nothing came. I am not a poet. The water did not wash away memories. There is no absolution of sins and no feeling of transference from this stranger to my son.

An old broken man has died, but years ago I killed him in self-defense. He was a cruel, ignorant man while he lived, stingy with his love until the end. The effort to love or even pity him is too great, and I am too tired to hate him anymore. I have worked with and talked to enough other men to know that my situation is not unique. In a global sense he was a man shaped by his environment. In the end he seemed to love me when he no longer needed me to personify his ghosts. But there is not enough in that to provide forgiveness for the personal hurt and loss I endured growing up or to provide the basis for a new relationship.

Nevertheless a legacy exists, and it is my job as a parent to understand it. What did he give me? Insight by negative example, I suppose: how *not* to father; the tragic result of parsimonious love and blindness to one's feelings; the loneliness of a life filled with fear and ignorance. I also carry the seeds of his violence.

A long time ago I arranged my life so that I would repudiate the mistakes my father made in raising his youngest son. I am driven in an almost maniacal way to guarantee the cycle of abuse stops here. I have trained myself for fatherhood. I went into therapy for this. I studied life and books. I am creating my own definition of fatherhood, based on what I learn about myself and what I hated about that man in our house.

Although I live in confidence that overt physical abuse will never occur, it is the spector of "thoughtless" meanness that scares me the most, the kind of violence that comes out of the unconscious. When my father hurt me in his rough "play," I knew it was his violence coming out. His impulse was to see how far he could go. The other day I borrowed an indoor slide from the local toy-lending library. Ben loved it. Instead of leaving well enough alone, I used furniture polish on the slide to speed him up. The first time down, he flew out of control and landed with a hard bump on the floor. The incident may seem trivial, and I believe some fathers would dismiss it as a legitimate mistake made in an attempt to toughen their child, or perhaps that it was "all in good fun." In fact, I went against both history and common sense in order to see how far I could go to make a game more "interesting." It was *my* agenda to escalate the play; Ben had no desire to go faster. I labeled that subtle abuse a kind of physical meanness on my father's part, and I cannot now excuse it in myself or ignore the implications. I don't believe this is oversensitivity on my part. Ben knows who causes his fear and hurt, but he's still too young to understand why. Ben is afraid of the slide now, and it sits unused in the living room. All I can do is struggle to understand myself and my history, and learn from it.

I am wildly and passionately in love with my own son. This is not to say I feel no anger toward him, but rather that I work to focus my anger on behavior, and forgiveness is paramount. Nevertheless, as situations deteriorate over toilet training, meals, or bedtime, I can feel that same flash anger rise in me. It is the need to let off tension and frustration and gain control of the situation, and a signal that I want to ram my expectations down Ben's throat. I must remember that my father's violence and shaming grew out of his own unfulfilled expectations for me, which of course seemed reasonable to him at the time.

I am learning to ease my expectations and avoid the word *should* when referring to Ben's behavior. I am trying to identify dangerous times before they occur. At night when I am tired and desperate for some quiet time alone or with my wife, and Ben refuses to stay in bed, I can feel the anger rise to the point of explosion. It is my father in me—"hit first, ask questions later." The trick, which works when I can remember it, is to think creatively. I talk firmly and in measured tones with Ben, saving the irrational outburst for my wife or other sympathetic friends. Sometimes I exit the situation and let my wife take over (I do the same for her when she is at the breaking point). Laughing at my helplessness over the situation works wonders, when I remember, and brings me back to earth.

I am aware that nothing I can do guarantees my son will not someday reject me as I have rejected my father. My goal is to have no regrets: I encourage open communication, avoid go-betweens when there is conflict, and wrap our lives with love and mutual respect.

I suppose, analytically speaking, I am working out my own business on my son the way my father did with me. But we all do that in one way or another. In our own ways we all fight our ghosts from the past, and our ghosts are always there to trip us up. The trick is to understand and learn. This is certainly the most worthwhile struggle I can imagine for myself.

> Ralph Holcomb is a clinical social worker in St. Paul, Minnesota. He and his wife, Beth Flavell, have a son, Benjamin. "In both my clinical practice and my private life, I struggle to learn about the unique experience of men in this society. A fundamental part of that experience is fathering. I am dedicated to giving my own son the best fathering possible while at the same time understanding my own limitations imposed by my history."

© Mary Newhall

Chapter Eight
Work and Fatherhood

The Meaning of Life

Douglas Worth

at least that's the lofty title
of the poem I set out to write
this morning at 6:30
based on a dream I'd just had
that seemed to be saying it all

I'd just settled down in the kitchen
at my favorite writing place
the table by the window
with its two or three flowering plants
(the window still full of darkness
the plants looking half asleep)
and was sipping coffee and smoking
my second cigarette
having been interrupted
already a number of times
by Tiggy's comings and goings
(when he's in and wants to go out
his claws in your thigh let you know it
when he's out and wants to come in
he lunges at the screen door
and hangs there, spread-eagled, yowling
till someone takes pity on him)
but anyway, I'd settled down
and had actually written the title
and was zeroing in on my dream
when the swinging door swung open
and in walked Colin, my son

O shit! there goes my poem
I thought, but what could I do?
he's four years old, and I love him
and he loves me, in spite of the fact
(or is it *because* of the fact?)
that we're caught up together in this
incredible family thing
that tears along at a clip
of a zillion miles per second
most of the time we're awake
with rarely a thank you or please

so in he came, in his pajamas
all smiles, and wanting to sit
at the other end of the table
and spend some time with me

I told him about the work
I had to do, mentioned the poem
(he knows that I do that
though he doesn't really know
what poetry's all about
not that I'm so sure myself)
and said, "Why don't you go get a book
or I'll give you a pen and some paper
and we can work here together
wouldn't that be fun?"

but he didn't take to that
so we just sat there awhile
making faces and bits of talk
half serious, half silly
the way we often do
when nothing special's up
and he'd brought his twirly thing
we got yesterday at the circus
that lights up and makes a soft
low whistling sort of moan
when you pull the strings and it spins
so he was showing that off

and after a while, as it seemed
he wasn't about to move on
I poured juice and made him some cocoa
between hot and warm, with the spoon

left in the cup, as he likes it
and we sat and talked some more
about one thing and another
like why such and such is true
and how come this and that?
and what would you do if?
and can wolves or weasels jump
as high as a second-floor window?
and what do trees think about? `
and I could feel my poem
slowly circling the drain

well, at some point I made up my mind
and told him I had to work
and that he could go see Mommy
or play in the living room
his bedroom, or the basement
but, in short, that he had to clear out
all very calm and friendly
but firm, and he'd picked up
his twirly thing in one hand
and his other was rubbing one eye
when he said casually, "Dada
do your eyes sometimes start to water
when nothing's hurting them?"
I said, "Sure they do, sometimes sleep
gets gunky stuff in your eyes
and makes them water a bit
when you wake up and start to rub
                them."

then he said something else
I couldn't catch, but his voice
had gone a bit thick and wobbly
and he was trying to clear it
again and again, with no luck
and I was suddenly listening
and looking at him hard
and finally I said, "Colin
are you feeling a little bit sad?"

his reply was all gunked up
so I said, "Why don't you come over
and sit here on my lap
and we'll get all cozy and warm."

so he brought his juice and cocoa
without spilling a single drop
and we sat there, rocking and rocking
not saying anything much
sort of blooming, along with the plants
and then the window was light
and Tiggy was yowling again

so we let him in and went up
and I washed and shaved and got dressed
and he went in to see Mommy
and then I drove off to work
thinking I'll try that poem
during my free block at school
if I can remember the dream

I can't but I've still got the title
so this poem, if that's what it is
will have to do, and maybe
it's closer to the truth
about the meaning of life
(if there is such a thing) then any
a dream could have given me

Douglas Worth is an English teacher. "I try to write as deeply
and clearly as I can about my experience of life and the world
around me. I try to celebrate the miraculousness and complexity
of existence, as opposed to what I perceive as a trend in contemporary art to be negative and desparing." He and his wife,
Karen, have two sons, Colin and Denny.

Lawyer vs. Father

Frank L. Bridges

I should be a happy man. I have an attractive, loving wife and two gorgeous children who are active, well adjusted, and intelligent. I am a junior partner in a small Boston law firm with an extremely active practice and a relatively bright future.

But in reality, I am torn between the demands of work and the needs of my family—between my need to be successful and my need to love and be loved. Except for occasional feelings of satisfaction and joy, I suffer a regular cycle of anger, frustration, and guilt. I spend long days at the office and bring work home at night in an effort to develop a successful law practice. I try to be a loving, caring father, but while I am at work I miss the daily nurturing and growth of my children. I can never stay at the office late enough, and I can never come home early enough.

I spend most of my waking hours striving to produce concrete results, whether by writing contracts, resolving problems, formulating advice, or trying cases. I invest a significant portion of my humanity into it because in many ways I consider the fruits of my labors are the measure of me as a man. When I leave work, I do not easily dismiss the issues and concerns of my clients and all the conflicts and frustrations of the day. Practicing law could occupy my full attention at all times, and I tend to bring unresolved worries, conflicts, and issues home with me—spinning in my head. So adjusting to being at home is difficult. If I don't adequately make the transition, arriving at home is like having my wife and children come to visit me in the middle of the day at the office. It's like having someone tickle your ear when you are asleep: you are subliminally irritated and don't really know what is happening until you wake up.

I remember saying to one of my partners early one evening that I had to go home. As he hurried off in his own direction, he asked, "What for?" Fortunately, I guess I'm not beyond hope—I knew what I wanted to go home for. But it is still difficult to extricate myself from the office and its concerns. When I am able to, at the end of the day, I am often tired, drained, frustrated, and tense, looking forward to the pleasures of a warm, understanding greeting from my loving spouse, a relaxing dinner, a clean, neat home, and two happy children ready to roll and tumble with Daddy on the living room floor. In contrast, what I find is a tired, drained, frustrated wife (she needs adult interaction and I've had just about enough of it) and two children at the worst time of their day screaming at their mother or at each other. If I am lucky enough to be home in time to eat with Jamie and Matthew, it is a battle to keep milk in their cups, hands out of their food, feet off the table, plates and tableware off the floor, and voices below ten decibels.

More often, Jamie and Matthew have finished their dinner and are ready to have Carol and me brush their teeth and wash their faces, put on diapers and pajamas, read them stories and persuade them to go to sleep. I find myself yelling at the kids and at Carol, pushing to get them in bed or simply sitting and gazing at the seven o'clock news while a maelstrom goes on about me. The simple fact is that at that time of day, father, mother, and children alike all need to be on the receiving end of warmth, understanding, and caring—precisely the qualities that are in shortest supply. It is not a good time for concentrating on personal relationships. Getting through the first layer or two of "hellos" and "how are yous" and "what did you do in school today" is time-consuming, forced, and stilted. Meaningful contact is easy to avoid.

I remember a period of several weeks when I couldn't even get a hello from Jamie because my home arrival coincided with the daily airing of her favorite television shows. She couldn't tear herself away from them. It took a day or two of child psychology applied by Carol, and not just a little coaxing, to elicit a "Hi, Daddy." Imagine having your sense of fatherhood threatened by the Cookie Monster and Fred Rogers? The competition for my daughter's affection hurt my feelings—but it did get me thinking. I began to wonder how many times I had done the same thing to her by watching a movie, the news, a hockey game, or by being preoccupied with work.

Weekends apparently hadn't been great either. One Saturday at seven in the morning I was shaking off the warmth of my bed, anticipating a morning at home with the kids while Carol took a break. Jamie asked Carol, "Can I go with you this morning, Mommy? I don't want to stay home and play with Daddy today." I realized that part of the problem was that I hadn't learned how to pay attention, tune into the lives my children were leading. Jamie's affection for Fred Rogers can't be blamed on him or on the television. Most nights and even weekends I wouldn't have wanted to spend time with an irritable or absent-minded father like me either.

Recently, I was instructing Jamie that she couldn't have gum before lunch. She replied, "You're not the boss!" When I asked who the boss was, she said, "Mommy, of course." What she was really telling me was that I was not entitled to the privilege of setting rules. I realized that all the times when decisions are made and rules are laid down, I am not involved. Mommy is the boss because Mommy pays attention to doctor's appointments, car pooling, clothing, choosing what's for lunch, what to do about a tummy ache. Carol is the boss because she assumes the responsibility of being involved in our children's everyday lives. What is more, she is the one who is with them when important events happen. Often I am not. When Matthew says his first sentence, I'll probably be at work. When Jamie makes friends, learns about sharing, comes home from school with a new painting, I am at work.

The most difficult and painful lesson I have learned about being a father is that I need to be more than a provider. Work seduces me from my children as easily as honey attracts a bee, and being away provides me with an easy cop-out. I have a sense of what I want "being a father" to feel like, but when I am occupied with my daily concerns for my career and the financial needs of my family I close the door to the part of me that wants to tumble with my children on the living room floor. Being there is meaningless unless I open that door and become a participant in my children's lives. Paying attention requires more adjusting than putting work out of my mind.

I can't brag that I've been doing a great job of it, but lately I seem to be a bigger attraction than Fred Rogers and the Cookie Monster when I get home.

> Frank L. Bridges is a lawyer with his own practice who lives in Newton, Massachusetts, with his wife, Carol, and their two children, Jamie and Matthew.

Conflicts between Career and Family

David Ryan

At the end of my son's first year I was faced with a career choice that greatly altered my relationship, both with him and with my wife. I was offered a job that was professionally more rewarding than my current position, but that would greatly reduce the amount of time I was able to spend directly involved in child care. Accepting the position meant shifting my self-concept from that of a father who taught philosophy, to that of a philosophy professor who was also a father. In the first year I had taken great satisfaction in nurturing our son; in subsequent years I inevitably came to do less nurturing, while greatly increasing my pride and satisfaction in my work. This transition provoked mixed emotions in me. It gave rise to feelings of loss for the immediate intimacy I had shared with my son in the first year, but helped me gain confidence and happiness in my professional life.

Jason was born in May 1978 in Chicago. This was a fine time, because I had turned in my final grades two days before his birth and I was free of all obligations through September; even then I would teach only two days a week. This meant that my wife Alice and I had the freedom to share the birth and child-care experiences relatively equally. That year was one of the best in my life and the best year of my relationship with Alice.

The pregnancy had been a pretty unhappy time for both of us. I was ambivalent about becoming a father and anxious about the increased commitments and responsibilities. When Jason was born, however, all those worries disappeared. Whereas I had been uninvolved in the pregnancy, I was very active and supportive in the birth (from Lamaze breathing to dealing with unpleasant hospital personnel), and Alice felt that I was really there for her. The same feelings of goodwill carried over throughout the first year. When we came home from the hospital, Alice was weak and tired. I was able to keep the house running and help with the newborn Jason, and Alice acquired a confidence in me she had never really had before—that I would take care of her. That confidence and increased trust made a great difference in our relationship. The whole experience made me feel more emotionally competent and more deeply appreciated; I felt that I was being valued for qualities that were really important—supportiveness, warmth, consistency—rather than for more superficial qualities—being fun or entertaining or interesting.

For myself, the period following the birth was a peak experience. I loved holding Jason's little body in my arms; I was very proud of being a father; and I experienced great love for my son. Alice and I were both un-self-conscious about thinking Jason was terrific; and we loved spending the huge amount of time on him that a newborn requires. My affection for Jason was unambivalent, unguarded, and untroubled—an experience totally different from my emotions for Alice or other members of my family, or those of previous relationships.

During the school year following Jason's birth, my career was of secondary importance to me. I did my teaching, but I devoted much more of my time to Jason and our family life. Even though writing is an essential part of career success in my field, I did almost none at all then. I felt totally satisfied with the pleasures of fathering—the discovery of myself as a warm and giving parent, the satisfaction of being able to respond to Jason's needs, the physical pleasure of holding and playing with him.

In April 1979, the balance between fathering and career shifted. The new job I was offered at another university was terribly attractive to me professionally, but it would dramatically change the pattern of our family life. Whereas my current position allowed me to teach on a two-day schedule, which meant that I had a great deal of time at home, the new position would require my presence on campus all day at least four days a week. Furthermore, the college was in a remote part of upstate New York—a location my wife feared would be unbearable for her over an extended period of time. She had always lived in a large city and dreaded the thought of small-town life.

In deliberating about the choice, the negative considerations were in clear opposition to my career hopes. The conflict between fathering and career was easier for me to resolve than the problem about Alice's needing a city environment. I felt good about having spent a year devoting myself to family responsibilities and regret at the thought of spending less time with Jason. But I could not choose a life in which my career was forever subordinated to my family roles. It was important to me to feel that I had achieved some of my most central career hopes and that I had accomplished something professionally as a philosopher; and I feared that if I rejected the new job in order to remain more fully in our home, I would wind up very disappointed with my life. I also felt that the first year was the period of Jason's life when he would most need two full-time parents; in later years, a more equitable balance between career and family might be better for his emotional development.

After a difficult period of indecision, we decided to accept the new position. We moved to upstate New York, and our lives changed drastically. My working hours were greatly increased, and I was no longer able to be around the house much during the day. Some days I had no intense or exclusive time with Jason at all, although this happened infrequently; more often I spent about two hours a day with him, in place of the five or six we were used to. Inevitably Alice came to be the primary parent, and it was painful for me to watch Jason shift some of his emotional bonds from me to her. I had felt that we were equally close to him in the first year; but that was visibly untrue now. I came to feel more like a traditional father, seeing his children in harried minutes after work and before bedtime; and sometimes the time I gave him was less freely given than previously—time I might have preferred spending relaxing or reading the newspaper.

My wife found life in a small town as unhappy as she had expected, and ultimately she decided to move to Boston with Jason. We would see one another on weekends. I felt very depressed in the three months between the decision and the move. I felt that we were breaking up our family, and that I would lose touch with the fabric of Jason's life. I feared that I would come to seem like an uncle to him—fun when present, forgotten when absent. Perhaps these fears seem a little exaggerated in hindsight, since I would be separated from Alice and Jason only three or four days a week. Still, I found the decision a very painful one.

In retrospect, the choice I made between total family involvement and career satisfaction has been more absolute than I ever imagined. I now see Jason on long weekends (Friday through Monday), and even though the time we are apart is relatively short, I feel it as a loss. I miss the regular, close, warm feeling the three of us had as a family in the first year. I am afraid that Jason will come to resent my absence and will grow away from me. These fears make me feel guilty—didn't I bring all this upon myself by choosing career needs over family? On the other hand, the time I have with Jason is now more intensive and given very freely, and I take pleasure in his excitement at seeing me after an absence of three days. Despite my fears, I feel that our relationship is now fairly secure and healthy. I know that it is different from what it would have been had I not made this career decision; but I think that the somewhat greater distance between us may be better for him in any case. Even at two and a half years, he needs more independence than two ever-present parents might be able to give him.

In spite of my fears and guilt feelings, I would probably make much the same decision again. I realize that the kind of immediate intimacy the three of us shared in the first year could only happen in earliest infancy. We are all separate individuals, with separate needs and interests. It is probably best for all of us that neither Alice nor I finally sacrificed our most basic needs for the other's sake. Of course I would prefer a life in which no conflicts arose between family and career; but given the facts of our life, this outcome—painful though it is—was probably better than the permanent frustration of my career goals. Now at least I have the hope of preserving and enhancing my family ties within the context of a successful career.

David Ryan is a pseudonym.

Career vs.
The Paternal Instinct

Allen M. Spivack

I remember the instant it happened to me. It had been another hectic day at work. Events were fast-paced and the demands overwhelming. The intensity subsided for a moment, and then I threw myself back in my chair, let go an enormous sigh, and simply said, "What am I doing here?"

This particular day had gone well. All the pieces of my work world seemed neatly ordered, stimulating, and promising. Yet, my heart and soul were not involved with work in the same intense way they used to be. Now a big piece of myself was searching for the warmth and closeness of my son's caress.

It is unfortunate than many men like myself have to confront this same dilemma: family ties versus career satisfactions. I was beginning my career with all that it entails—establishing credentials as a professional, developing confidence in my skills, and preparing myself to make a mature commitment to a legitimate career.

Then a child arrived on the scene. And that child made the same demands of me—establishing credentials as a caring parent, developing confidence in my skills as a care provider, and discovering what the commitment to fatherhood really means.

When I began practicing my fathering, I found it a painful and exhausting learning process. I never knew what I was doing right or wrong, and was overcome with a tentativeness that I had rarely experienced before. I was frightened by the fact that my child was *totally* dependent on my wife and me. There were so many new fears, frustrations, and demands that I became very confused.

I struggled through these events for four, five, six months and one day realized that this child was changing my life, forcing me to challenge every priority. After all, what does a career mean when your child is sick and in pain? Who cares for decisions and big deals after caressing your sweet child and enjoying that wonderful newborn smell? How can you focus on work and meetings and that big luncheon when you've just left a child who asked you to stay because he was afraid?

As I prepare to leave for work in the morning, I don't rush out the door the way I used to. I linger to get a few extra kisses and hugs. I feel pained when I leave my son, watching him wave energetically through the window. At times, I feel like the great "betrayer of parental duty"—never available enough, having so little connectedness between his day and my own, trying to make up for lost time on the weekends.

I relish those days that I can sneak away from work a few hours early to spend extra time with my son. It gives me the chance to see his many sides, not just the one I experience when I return home from work in the evening. I remember my own father as a real presence in my life. Most days I would rush home from school, go downstairs to his pharmacy, and do some work for him. I knew he liked having me there. I was special to him and he had a wonderful way of showing it. He would ask me to sit next to him on a tall stool while he was filling prescriptions. It was my throne. That time gave me a chance to view my father in his full range of moods and manners. He let me see his "hard" and "soft" sides; they were both parts of his style that I learned to understand.

What does my son see of his father? Someone who barely manages to drag himself home at a decent hour. Someone who is tired, strained, and wound tight. Someone who needs to crawl in a corner for an hour to unwind. Someone who becomes the evening parent, appearing as the sky darkens and disappearing with the first rays of morning.

The very worst part of this evening fathering drama is my wife's recounting of the day's events and adventures. She tells me things about my son's day that make me resent working—stories of his activities, his conversations, his humor, and his affection. My own experience is very different. Instead of seeing my son function in the context of a whole day—with its ups and downs, highs and lows, and important transition times—I participate with him in daily "rituals of confrontation." We growl and grumble our way through the evening as I throw one threat after another at him. Who could expect much else from a person in my shape?

In the beginning, my situation as a father had less to do with the particular demands of my work and more to do with my role in our new family triad. I remember telling my wife when she first began breast-feeding my son that "I really don't have a natural place in my son's life now." My wife had an obvious survival link to this child—food. It forced her to adjust her lifestyle in many fundamental ways—her availability, her patience, and her sense of time. For me, there was no natural relationship and therefore, no explicit need to dramatically change my life and career situation. In fact, I felt so estranged from my wife and son and so uncertain of my place in our triad that work became more exalted than ever. It became my haven for finding meaning, for feeling a part of something, and for exchanging support.

After about six months of this struggle I realized that I had a role to play in my son's life and that I was a fool to miss the opportunity. I needed time to learn to father in a complete way so that I could relate in a loving and caring way to my child, but time didn't seem available—not if I had to work full time. The standard of "it's not how much time you spend with your child, it's how you spend the time that counts" is all wrong. Unless I was willing to make time available to my son (and lots of it), I would never learn to be a parent capable of providing quality time to him. That is the long and short of it.

When you work, the critical issue is time. The situation for me is straightforward: first of all, after many years of schooling and technical training, giving up a career and the idea of career advancement, even temporarily, for full-time child rearing may require an enormous economic sacrifice; and second, there is not much support out there to be a full-time father, although this factor seems to be getting better. I did manage at a previous job to rearrange my work schedule for two days a week. It gave me some extra time with my son and the chance to pick him up at school, talk with his teachers, and meet his schoolmates. It also gave the two of us some "special" time together at a different hour of the day, when both of us had more energy. I also took my son on some long vacations. Being his sole care provider for two weeks wasn't easy, but it opened up our relationship in ways that had long-lasting, positive results for both of us.

I have reached a decision point. Is the need to parent so strong a desire as to force me to abandon my career? And if so, how do I act on it?

I am frustrated with the state of my parenting role and want to really "give in" to my nurturing need. I want to discover my paternal instinct in the same way that my wife has discovered her maternal instinct. I've never had the time to look for it. I want to let the existence of my child fundamentally change who I am and who I wish to become. Consequently, I have decided on a role reversal. If Sherry can find a full-time job, I will stay home with our son.

In reaching this point, I have overcome a number of obstacles. Two are worth recounting. First, I used to think that I could be a "New Age" father, a man capable of maintaining a successful career, remaining an active community leader, entertaining friends, and being available to my child, spending quality time together as well as sharing all responsibilities with my wife. *I was wrong.*

Everything in my life had to change and adjust to my new role as father, including my career! It was nonsense to think otherwise. I couldn't talk about business deals and diapers in the same breath. Accepting the responsibility of fathering means reevaluating my priorities. I wanted to be a functional father, not one left unfulfilled and longing for a loving and caring relationship with my son.

Second, rearranging my life priorities isn't easy, but is certainly manageable. What is difficult is changing other people's expectations of both my priorities and my availability. Those "others" needed to understand that my life has become fundamentally different in both my mobility and in my relationship to my family.

The birth of my child was an event beyond compare. It's the kind of event that has the potential to change you as do few other things in life. I'm glad I've decided to take advantage of this rare opportunity. The changes have not been easy, but they have given me the chance to become a profoundly different person. Opening myself to my son, learning to give my love unconditionally has the power of transformation.

A simple thought crossed my mind the other day. I have devoted an enormous amount of energy and time to succeed in a new career. Now I have chosen fatherhood. Is not this choice of fatherhood worthy of the same commitment of energy and time? I can always find the desire and fortitude to create my career. With my children, I have only *one* chance and I don't intend to miss it.

> Allen M. Spivack is a house husband, part-time contractor, and student. He and his wife, Sherry Grossman, have two sons, Avi and Lev. "Clarity of values has always been a preoccupation of mine. I must have time to figure it out. When I resolve this, I act on it in spite of the consequences. I desperately try to learn the important lessons from my life experiences."

Chapter Nine
New-Style Fathers

One Half-Day Off a Week

Gerald M. Tuckman

I took off a half-day per week from work, starting the Thursday morning after my daughter was born. It was not an easy transition. For the first six months, I'd be home with my wife and child until about 1 P.M., changing diapers, cooing to my daughter, napping or reading while Emily napped, vacuuming the house, or going on a little outing. And then, suddenly, I'd have to switch gears—get into a shirt and tie, ride the subway at a time when it ran on an irregular schedule, enter a day more than half over, try to find out where my lunchtime staff was, pick up crises in progress.

When Emily was older and in nursery school, I began taking an afternoon off each week rather than a morning. How did it feel? Great, when I got into the subway on time, geared to pick Emily up at school. Incredibly pressured when there were lots of things that needed doing at work, that either couldn't wait until the next day or couldn't be scheduled for the day before. Tense, when I was late, standing at the subway, no trains coming, thinking of Emily alone at school, waiting. From the start, taking my half-day per week made me feel a little insecure at work. It weakened my professional role. This was especially difficult since a feeling of professional competence had not come easily to me in any case early in my work life. By Emily's birth, I had begun to feel my strength at work. In a way, that made it even harder to plan to take a half-day off on a regular basis. The discomfort with a regular daytime interval at home felt especially strong because I managed a small staff and they depended on me for direction. Still, I felt that the idea of taking time from work for parenting was reasonable and worth the effort. I needed to make trade-offs, and one of the major ones was a piece of my own comfort.

My half-day per week has become institutionalized in my life. When I changed jobs, it was part of whether or not someone wanted to hire me and whether or not I would accept the position.

A few days ago, my second daughter was born. I am writing this toward the end of my one-and-a-half-week paternity leave, after having dropped Emily and the rest of her car pool at summer camp. My half-day per week will continue. The time I've spent alone with Emily has bonded us in special ways, and I hope to do the same with Leah. Emily and I get into our share of struggles, but our joys come frequently and provide us with a great deal of pleasure. The intensity and involvement come with time as well as caring.

Gerald M. Tuckman is in real estate investment. He and his wife, Jan, have two daughters, Emily and Leah. "My daughters see me as an integral part of their lives. They can come to me in happiness and sadness. I am involved in their discipline as well as their creativity and fun. We are able to learn and share together."

Fathering: New Styles and Old Problems

Harry Brod

I've been a father for fifteen months now. Not long as these things go, but long enough to have already observed changes in myself from being childless to becoming a father, and further changes from my initial stage of fathering to the present, about which I have mixed feelings.

I suppose having been present at the birth of my daughter qualifies me as a "new-style" father. And yet I've grown weary of how often I'm asked if I was present at the birth, as if this has become the defining mark of the new father. I'm bothered by the implications of this question, because I feel in it a lack of consciousness of and support for the *process* of fathering. Traditionally, when one spoke of mothering a child, one meant a long, sometimes lifelong, process of giving nurturing care and attention. But when one spoke of fathering a child, one meant not an ongoing social process but a single biological event, the act of conceiving, of siring the child. When I am questioned about being present at the birth, I hear the event of fathering being moved up nine months from conception, but I still don't hear fathering being thought of as an ongoing social process. It seems to me that I still am asked about my past birthing involvement more than I am asked about my current child-rearing involvement; I am asked more about my past breathing techniques than about my present feeding techniques. But the latter is what fathering is really all about.

Sometimes I get the feeling people aren't asking about my current involvement because they don't want to hear the answer. I know the new-style father's involvement with his children in the eighties has received a lot of media attention, and yet I still think that people's feelings about it on a gut level are ambivalent. When I do spend a lot of time with my child, it sometimes is taken as an implicit criticism and challenge of the life-styles of those who hold to a more traditional division of labor in which men don't do much child rearing, even if I say nothing at all disparaging about them. And when I don't spend a lot of time with my child, I seem to feed fears that the new-style father is just a passing fad, that he still leaves the real day-to-day work to women when the spotlight is off.

Unfortunately, I'm finding that these fears are more justified than I like to believe. I'm less engrossed in the details of child rearing now than I was in the first heady months. At that time I was going to do it all. And since I teach at the college level, I was in a particularly fortunate situation at the beginning. My daughter's birth was in August when I still had a month's vacation left before starting work again. In that month, my wife and I shared everything, other than nursing, on a fifty-fifty basis: changing diapers, cleaning up, walking and rocking her to sleep. But when I returned to work, that arrangement ended, and since then my wife has spent much more time with our child than I have. Objective reasons account for much of the discrepancy in the amount of time I spend with our child: I have a job outside our home that requires a great deal of time and attention; my wife doesn't. Thus my wife is free to make a full-time commitment to parenting, but I can do it only part time. This has to some extent become a self-perpetuating cycle. Since our daughter has spent more time with her mother, she often prefers being with her mother, even when I am available. But it seems to me that there is more than simply an objective time constraint involved here. For my commitment to parenting is not only more part time than my wife's but also more partial. I don't seem to be as wholeheartedly involved with parenting as my wife is, even when the time is available. So I find myself not fitting the image I have of the new-style father—someone who is finding total fulfillment through his children.

I'm not sure what to make of this. Often I think that much of the new-fatherhood ethos is largely a social con game. Isn't it too much of a coincidence that at a time when society *needs* men to be more involved in child rearing as a result primarily of women's changing work-force participation—that at just this time large numbers of men are spontaneously discovering the joys of diapering and feeding infants? In fact, it's reminiscent of how the cult of motherhood emerged in the 1950s as a way of putting pressure on women to remain in the home and find their identities as mothers. Of course there are wonderful, unparalleled delights in being with children, but I feel no need to deny or romanticize that much of parenting is also boring and unpleasant work.

From one perspective, the differences between myself and my wife are simply legitimate personality differences. She apparently finds being with our daughter more personally rewarding than I do—hence her greater involvement. But again, this seems too coincidental. I know that the same pattern repeats itself in home after home. Women find more fulfillment in child rearing and so do more of it than men. Have I, and other men, been socialized out of being able to find the real joys in fatherhood? Or have women been socialized to imagine greater fulfillment in motherhood than is warranted, and are they ignoring the negative aspects and sacrifices it entails? Are we as fathers blind to the joys of parenting, or are women as mothers hallucinating the joys? And if either is the case, or if the truth lies in some mixture of the two, what is to be done?

As time passes, I find my own attitudes changing. I still do my share of the cleaning up after our daughter largely for the sake of my wife, out of a belief that we should be sharing the dirty work. And I still often find myself doing some unpleasant tasks for the sake of my daughter so that she won't grow up with restrictive traditional ideas about proper sex-typed behavior. Moreover, I believe that I should be doing my share of parenting in the interests of justice for the present and future generations, because I believe our gender division of labor is damaging to women and men. But more and more, I find myself wanting to be with our daughter for *my* sake, because I find that involvement with her is activating in me nurturing capacities and qualities previously unexpressed, capacities and qualities I find gratifying to observe in myself. Maybe it started at her birth. Like many men, I had been nervous about holding an infant, afraid that in my inexperience and clumsiness I might break or damage the child. Yet when she was born and given to me, the experience was so overwhelming that those fears dissipated immediately, and her small body felt safe and comfortable in my large hands.

I like the idea of having what are in a way self-interested motivations for fathering, though I think it's a positive kind of expanding selfhood, not a negative kind of acquisitive selfishness. There are many things that can be done well even if they are done grudgingly, but parenting is not one of them. Fathering for the sake of my wife or my child, without my real commitment, may enable me to function as a care*taker* for my child when my wife is away, but it doesn't enable me to be an ongoing care*giver*, and that's what fathering's about.

I feel the need to develop the capacities to enjoy my child more because I have come to see that the same aspects of male socialization that interfere with parenting work to my disadvantage in other areas of my life as well. As a male, I was taught to maintain a certain level of detachment and restraint, to keep my distance from others, to rely on reason, not emotion. I find now that these characteristics keep me from forming the kinds of intimacy I'd like to have with people of all ages.

Most of us have not had the kind of fathers we ourselves want to be. But I think most of us even as children knew what we wanted and what we lacked. When I feel the need to justify to myself my inability to meet my own expectations of myself as a father, (amid rising anger at my daughter for having brought my deficiencies so glaringly before my eyes), I find myself thinking "I didn't have it any better, and it didn't do me any harm." But actually, that's not true—I think it did do me harm. The lack of previous role models affects me at the level of motivation, not the level of skill acquisition. I can learn the nurturing skills I wish to acquire from women as well as from men once I make a commitment to learn them. But it's making that commitment that conflicts with inherited notions about what it means to be a father.

I once heard a man I know express the conflict faced by fathers by saying that in our society, he who fathers best, fathers least. On the one hand, fathers are still seen primarily as breadwinners, who earn the money needed to support the family. Even in families where the male is no longer the sole breadwinner, he's still expected to be the primary one. On the other hand, fathers are also supposed to be companions and moral guides for their children. But the father who is pursuing the former aspect of fathering has precious little time and energy left over for the latter. And even if I'm willing to do both, it's often too wrenching a shift of personality structures to switch from being the kind of competitive, aggressive male who succeeds in our economic system to being the receptive and nurturing male at home.

For me, the timing of becoming a father has intensified the conflict. The stage of life at which I am becoming a parent and thus in need of time at home is occurring at precisely the stage in my career when I should be working overtime if I hope to advance. Again, I feel conflicts about the extent to which I should be struggling to change my feelings. On the one hand, greater emphasis on parenting would make parenting more successful and rewarding. But on the other hand, I don't want to participate in my own brainwashing about what I *should* be feeling. Parts of me have been conditioned as a male to deny myself some of the joys of parenting, and I want to reclaim them. But I also want to accept those parts of me that are not enjoying the not–so–joyful work of parenting. I think the ultimate goal is to freely choose my levels of involvement in different areas of my life, taking into account the needs of others as well as my own. Before I'm willing to say that I'm really acting out of free choice and not simply acting out socially conditioned scripts about what I should value, I need to be sure that I have really struggled against the social expectations that impose values on me, whether it be the traditional style of masculinity that denigrates fathering or the new style that glorifies it.

Last month, another father and I went out to breakfast with our two fourteen-month-old children because both of our wives were busy that morning. We had a fine time with each other, our children, and passersby who smiled a lot. Our waitress even commented on how nice it was to see fathers out with their children. But I couldn't help thinking that even though we had talked about meeting in this way before, what finally got us to do it was the absence of our wives, rather than our own desire to get together as fathers.

I remember reading a letter several years ago from a son to his parents explaining why he was quitting law school to raise his child while his wife pursued her career. The letter was long and detailed, the kind that I thought a woman would not have had to write were the situation reversed. Her shift of priorities and full-time commitment to parenting would have been much more readily understood and accepted. We as a society need to be supportive of men's involvement with children and of their developing their nurturing capacities. I think this also includes supporting women who choose not to mother; otherwise men will continue to be seen primarily as substitute parents, rather than as parents in their own right. We still have a long way to go in offering men the kind of social support we really need so that we can fully validate ourselves as fathers, and so that all of us can be making truly free choices about the way we live our lives.

Harry Brod was born in Berlin, was raised in New York, and now lives in Los Angeles, where he teaches in the Program for the Study of Women and Men in Society at the University of Southern California. He is the editor of the *Men's Studies News-letter* and is active in the national organization of the profeminist men's movement, the National Organization for Changing Men. He and his wife, Maria Papacostaki, have one daughter, Artemis.

Fatherly Ambivalence

John C. O'Brien

I'm still angry—two and a half years after Meghan's birth—at all those people who didn't tell me the truth about parenthood. I listened to them as they spoke of little Melissa growing cuter and more sensitive by the day and of little Marc advancing at an alarming rate. Their eyes gleamed with reminiscence and their mouths grew smug with grins because of their children's most recent achievements. I rarely heard of obstinacy, manipulation, ingratitude, selfishness, or incessant demands, and when I did, these attributes were glossed over, tossed out with a chuckle and a casual remark: Daniel is such a boy, Erica is a real women's libber.

I was deluded into thinking that the rearing of children was the ultimate source of happiness and enlightenment, a fantasy trip through Disneyland and the world of Mother Goose. Sugar and spice were predominant; snakes and snails were easily handled. It was as if I had been a representative of a democratic government on a tour of a totalitarian state, guided through the new stadiums and factories but slipped past the poverty and hardship.

It was not long before I realized that I derived no inner peace from getting up night after night with a child frightened awake by nightmares. Excrement bubbling like lava from a sagging diaper onto the newly purchased carpet created no thrill. The draw on my energy, the lack of uninterrupted time with my wife, Maureen, and the loss of spontaneity and free movement produced sighs of despair, not of satisfaction. I had been duped and now was stuck for the next eighteen years.

In my naïveté, I would speak honestly about the exhaustion, the resentment, the diminished control over my own life. This, I soon learned, was blasphemy. Jaws tightened, eyes hardened, secret glances were exchanged, and nervous hands rose to cover shocked mouths when I expressed my impressions on the rigors of parenthood. My comments hung in the air like poison gas. No one wanted to touch them. No one could deal with their irreverence. I was swiftly becoming a flawed, self-serving heretic, threatening the sanctity of a long-hallowed institution. I decided to keep my feelings to myself.

Still, within me, the conflict went on. I grew guilty because of my insensitivity and selfishness. I feared the effects that my pitiable character would have on my daughter's future. Self-hatred germinated from my resistance to self-sacrifice. I began to doubt myself. How could I be such a weakling that I could not share my existence with an innocent little girl? How could I be so incomplete that a tiny addition to my household could force me to the brink of physical, moral, and mental bankruptcy?

Our jobs are intense and demanding. Maureen and I work especially hard so that we bring nothing home that will dilute our time with Meg.

Yet, no matter how hard I try to plan and prepare, there are exhausting days when work sucks my energy dry, when every person I've tried to help in my capacity as a counselor seems intent upon self-destruction. I spend those days desperately shuffling moods, redirecting energies, and opening lines of interaction. Gradually my shoulders develop a tension, my neck constricts, my eyes puff and redden with my efforts. By the time work ends, I am a bundle of exposed nerves and dull aches. I have aged ten years. Each bump on the road to the baby-sitter's home shoots an electric charge through my body, and I'm powerfully tempted to change direction, to head south to hole up like an escaped convict in a dingy, back-road Cape motel where no one would ever be able to find me. I would wake and sleep as I wished, read, eat, think. Each morning my possessions would be in the same places I left them the night before. There would be peace, simplicity, predictability.

But at the baby-sitter's a warm greeting from Meg shakes me out of my fantasy. She is smiling sweetly up at me, her hand placed gently on my leg, and again I'm thrown into a torrent of conflicting emotions. So I grit my teeth—what else is there to do?—and steel myself against the remainder of the day.

Once in the car, I reason with Meg that daddy is tired and will try his best, but, please, give me a break, will you, kid? I strain to calm my voice, but it is quivering with the effort, and Meg, because she is an emotional tuning fork, is becoming confused with the contradiction between my manner and my words.

At home she tries to solve this puzzle by spending every second with me. She produces piles of books with which I am to entertain her, demands a bath, flings a chestful of toys onto the floor in her search for a puppet that I am to manipulate. One moment she whines for a snack, the next for a walk in the yard. She wants to be comforted but will not be still long enough for me to meet her needs. Despite myself, my remarks to her begin to carry an angry tone that increases as she becomes more ill at ease. Finally, I'm yelling over a glass of juice tipped onto the floor or a ball chucked unintentionally at the dog, and Meg is given a hasty, rough, and tearful escort into her bedroom.

With the door slammed to contain her crying, I pace the living room floor, dragging angrily on a cigarette. Part of me is outraged by the audacity of the little cretin, while another part is incensed by my lack of understanding and self-control. Perhaps if I spanked her, the screaming would end. Or I could run crazily from the house and outdistance her wails. Should I skulk, repentant, back to Meg and console her with hugs and apologies? At this moment I need miraculous guidance pointing me to the correct course of action. I need an infallible judgment ascribing innocence and guilt to the proper parties. But the help I need never comes.

Evenings are given to cleaning, laundry, grocery shopping, and other chores in addition to paying attention to our daughter. By her bedtime, we ourselves feel overdue for sleep but force ourselves to sometimes read or, more often, slump in a stupor in front of the television. Maureen's eyes shut soon after she hits the couch. I snack and drink, snack and drink, simply to keep awake. I refuse to spend my entire day involved in obligations to others, but do not have the energy to use my leisure time more productively. Angrily, I shout "Entertain me" at the television, but all it does, night after night, is disappoint. I sit like a side of beef, my eyes growing redder, my mouth falling slack, until the inane images on the screen gall me into surrendering another day to sleep.

I know that my life style is possible because I have lived in this manner for two and half years. Meg's Saturday and Sunday nap times, and the few nights when we have energy, allow Maureen and I to talk uninterruptedly, catch up on events, make love, and reaffirm our relationship to some degree.

And there are moments when I experience enormous joy in being the parent of this humorous, curious, and rapidly developing child. When Meg was first born, I discovered a degree and kind of love so intense that its existence came as a fantastic surprise to me. It was unfettered, timeless, not contingent upon events that had—or would—occur.

Now, when I slam into the house after a fruitless day and Meg, all blondness and enthusiasm, skitters to hug me and kiss my cheek, I am reminded of my first contact with total love and revel in its return. She comes to me after naps, her wispy hair electrified in all directions, so that I can fit her tiny body tightly to mine and trace and knead the intricate bone structure of her back. When I watch her artfully piling blocks and singing a children's song in her garbled and slightly off-key style, she sometimes looks up to catch me watching and smiles with her whole being. She prepares endless supplies of pretend cakes and cookies for me to savor and teaches me, through her curious approach to life, new ways to view things.

And this is when I want to stop time, freeze the moment, so that I never lose the feelings of affection and wonder that seem to swell my insides with warmth. Yet, I also know that I will never be able to adjust completely to the lack of time that prevents me from walking undisturbed with Maureen through a deep wood and stopping for as long as we wish to appreciate a striking view; or from tenderly undressing each other in that deep wood to make love amid the patterns of sunlight and the rich, moist smells of the earth on which we lie. I grieve the loss of warm, dewy mornings spent reading lazily under a flowering crab apple tree. Most of all, I sorely miss the opportunity to simply sit and think, to roll whatever thoughts I choose around in my head, to sort life's pressures into perspective without having to lay aside a portion of my consciousness to monitor my daughter's activities.

I am certain that, when Meg grows older, I will be able to stuff myself under the kitchen sink to fix the garbage disposal and my mysteriously constructed tools will not be spirited away and examined. In the garden in spring, I will not have to leap from the potatoes I am planting to protect the onions I placed carefully in line the week before. I will walk the beach without stopping to inspect every shell and piece of driftwood tossed up by a storm.

And I know that, then, I will long for Meg's interruptions just as much as I bemoan them now.

> John C. O'Brien has been a house-husband for the past year and a half. He and his wife Maureen have two children, Meghan and Michael. "These days, I generally feel that being a parent is very much like traveling in Morocco. Although there is nothing innately wrong with my children (or with Moroccans, for that matter), it just seems that for the major portion of each day I've got someone at my elbow trying to influence me to do something I don't necessarily want to do. I've grown to realize that the healthiest method of handling the pressures of parenthood is to adjust to the reality of my situation so as to enjoy it as fully as possible."

Working It Out

Roger C. Sharpe

At times, when I look back, it's difficult to imagine just how much my life has changed and how different I've become. The career decisions and adjustments I've made over the years somehow seem unreal today, as if they all happened to another person.

Five years ago I took a job as editor of a national magazine. I began to write features as well as learn about this new field I had previously known nothing about. My workday stretched beyond office hours, as I tried to do more and more. Without really thinking about what was happening, I began to broaden my activities and my belief in what I could and couldn't do. Before I knew it, I found myself writing books and engaging in other projects I had never planned on, juggling two and then three careers. I thrived on my work and realized that the busier I was, the more productive I became; the two fed off each other. It was an existence of nine to five and then six to midnight and beyond, with even the weekends set aside for work. I knew I was on a streak and wanted to take as much advantage of what I was doing as I possibly could.

Things were to change, however, dramatically and unexpectedly. I had always known that all my work and sacrifice was never meant solely for myself. During the sixties I had faithfully watched "The Courtship of Eddie's Father" and always saw myself as Bill Bixby, walking down the beach with my son, being the ever-attentive and all-knowing father. Someday I, too, would have that experience.

I wanted a wife, children, and a career that allowed me to work at home at some point so I could spend time with my family. I didn't want things to be as they were when I grew up, with my father working all the time, not ever able to spend enough time with me and then dying when I was only fourteen. It would be different for my family. I would try to accomplish all that I could, as fast as I could, and then share those achievements and realize my dreams.

For five years there was one woman strong enough to persevere and accept my work ethic, as well as find a way to become a vital part of my life. There were no confrontations or questions of priorities, but, rather, the understanding that I had to do things one way or not at all. Everything was falling into place and Ellen and I got married, knowing that we both wanted to start a family as soon as possible.

Somehow, though, I never thought about how my life might be completely changed by my living with another person full time after having been in my own space for seven years. Work still came first, which Ellen accepted, since she understood that if I could do all that I wanted, in the long run we would both benefit and be able to enjoy the fruits of my labors. We planned our new apartment around the space requirements I had for my office at home, as well as for the new baby we were expecting. Amazingly, with all the classes, doctor's appointments, and shopping we had to do, I still found time to continue my multicareers.

Then Joshua arrived and the primary concerns of my world faded and were replaced by the wonder and magic of watching, as well as sharing, the life of this remarkable creation. I wanted to be there always, experiencing his discoveries and not missing a single moment. In the beginning it was easy. In fact, friends close to me were quick to point out that, for one thing, I wouldn't be able to spend an hour or two after work playing pinball at the local arcade, but that I would have to be at home helping out. Later, they would say, the novelty of my newborn son would wear off and I'd be back to the old schedule.

But I had a new timetable. I dreaded leaving for work in the morning and couldn't get home fast enough in the evening, even though I knew that Joshua was only sleeping and eating and not doing much else. The problem I encountered was with the broken sleep and the need to be "on" all the time when I gave Ellen a break from the ongoing routine.

I temporarily put my free-lance work aside and was willing to accept one career for the interim period. For me, being an active father was all-important, demanding an involvement that many of those close to me questioned as unnecessarily extreme and unyielding in its approach. I didn't believe in baby-sitters, whether family, friends, or strangers; nor did I believe in pretending that life doesn't change once one takes on the responsibility of having a family. I was willing to give up the movies and the nights out with friends in order to be with Joshua as much as I could. He wasn't someone to partially ignore or plan time around; rather he was the core of my life. Fortunately, Ellen supported and shared my perceptions of parenting.

As the months passed, and the amount of my productivity in outside projects diminished, it would have been easy to blame Joshua, resent him for the time he demanded, or even turn off my attention when I was home. I knew that, professionally, my life was at a standstill. I had a day-to-day career, but it wasn't going to get me a house in the country and an early retirement to write books. However, the choice I had made was a conscious one, maybe the only one I could make under the circumstances, and I was more than willing to shoulder the full responsibility for my decision. It was never really easy, going from overdrive to slow motion. I continually found myself fighting against the frustration and anxiety I felt in looking at how my life had changed while trying to combat my own internal war.

Admittedly, even now, over nineteen months later, I question my decision and the professional time I've lost. It's never a simple matter to accept things as they are and cope with the situation. I can come home tired from work and Joshua is there at the front door ready for playtime with Daddy. It haunts me that I'm not always capable of being attentive, and I wind up feeling guilty later on after Joshua is asleep. I somehow feel I've failed, let him down when he wanted me, and that I owe him something better from the few hours I am able to spend with him.

Other days I am there, totally, until he goes to bed, trying instead not to feel drained as I make my way to the typewriter in the hope that maybe I can salvage an hour or two of work before I collapse. It's a continual struggle, and I harbor great expectations of accomplishing much during holidays or long weekends, only to find that Joshua is there even more during these periods and is all-consuming.

I am always suffering with the knowledge that, as time passes, it becomes more difficult to get back on the work track. The self-imposed writer's block does little to offset the desire and, unlike riding a bicycle, one can forget the skills or at least lose the confidence, making it that much more painful and difficult a process to begin again. But I look at Joshua and savor the fact that I have been there for him, watching his growth and, I hope, having a positive impact on his development.

> Roger C. Sharpe is an editor/writer, currently a vice president for publishing in a computer company. He and his wife, Ellen, have two sons. "My boys and wife, along with the life we have created, are the constants. Any further professional success will come if it is meant to be, but at least I have discovered the balance I need to be effective in both of my worlds, professional and family."

Paternity Leave

John B. Ferguson

"Sixty Minutes" did a segment on paternity leave a few weeks before I was to stop work and begin to care for my daughter. Somehow this lent credibility to my plans. People I barely knew approached me, relaying information about the program. Could there be only a hundred people on paternity leave in the whole country? I doubted it, but several people assured me this was what they had heard on the news. I smiled. I enjoyed the attention. I told people how we had arranged the whole thing. I concentrated on explaining my hopes rather than my fears.

Paternity leave was never a decision. Of course I would stay at home with our child. My wife and I knew that even before Mary became pregnant, even before we were married. It was one of the things we understood about each other, one of the things that made us confident about getting married.

We planned our first child carefully. It would arrive two weeks after school ended so that my wife could finish teaching her junior high classes. We would both be at home during the summer, and I would not teach in the fall. I would have a marvelous time at home, and then Mary would take over in January. We would not both have to go back to work until the following year. Our savings would be depleted, but our child would have been well cared for during his or her most formative year.

Babies, of course, have never bothered to concern themselves with their parents' plans. Ours scheduled her arrival for the end of August. This suddenly made it more practical for my wife to take the fall semester off, and for me to take off the spring term. Fair enough. Everything was still all very abstract, and our newly adjusted plans still looked good.

The fall was exciting for me both because the baby provided new adventures every evening and because I was anticipating the end of the semester. I had a case of spring fever from about the first day of school. I don't think my teaching was as good as it should have been. I never settled down to a set pattern with discernible goals because, after all, for me the year was almost over.

Even as the beginning of paternity leave came closer, my ideals still outweighed my apprehensions. My time would be used to the fullest. I could write for two hours each day, read for two hours, work on carpentry around our old house for two hours, and clean a room every day. What a plan. What a vacation. A chance to do everything I'd ever wanted to do, but couldn't in the past because of professional pressures.

That the baby was not yet weaned, that my wife seemed to be exhausted every day, and that she didn't seem to find staying at home a great and enlightening intellectual experience were unsettling, but I was buoyed by the uniqueness of my situation. Colleagues would sidle up to me and ask if I was really going to baby-sit. I would look at them with disdain and explain very carefully that baby-sitting was hardly what I was going to do. There was so much need for intellectual development, both for the child and for myself. This was an opportunity to help form my daughter's character. This was what every man should do. After all, I said, who would want to trust the upbringing of his child to a mere woman? (A joke, I told my wife.)

I also began to acknowledge some fears, especially as the actual day approached. Some of them were based on concrete problems. Joanna refused to drink from a bottle. Period. She hated formula, was barely tolerant of expressed milk, and refused to consider juice. Friends told me stories of babies who never used a bottle, but went straight to a cup. I tried, but merely managed to pour several cups of juice down Joanna's front, much to her amusement. The pediatrician helpfully told us that he had never known a baby to miss more than two feedings before accepting a bottle. I did not look forward to her screams before she finally gave in. I had learned that the radial arm saw and the vacuum cleaner drowned out almost any noise she could make, but eight hours of vacuuming and sawing did not seem like a very pleasant way to spend our first day together.

Other fears were harder to define. Would the baby miss her mother? Would I remember to change her, to bathe her? Would I stay close enough to her to keep her from hurting herself, but far enough away to give her room to grow? Would I be able to give her the warmth and the comfort she needed? Would I talk to her enough? Would I be better for her than a neighbor hired to take care of her? Especially, would I be as good for her as was her mother, who could stay home if I continued to work? It was hard to express these fears, but they were real and raced through my mind as my leave came closer.

One problem solved itself two days before Mary went back to work. Joanna was left alone with a bottle of juice. Like a closet alcoholic, she picked it up and began to drink. She was not quick enough or smart enough to hide her accomplishment, and suddenly one of my main worries about the next six months was eliminated. That night she drank a bottle of formula and within two months weaned herself entirely. Now only my more abstract fears remained.

Monday morning Mary woke the baby up, fed and changed her, and left her happy in her crib. I slept until seven-thirty, enjoying sweet dreams of how pleasant the next six months were going to be. Joanna woke me up with her quiet singing and her louder demands for food. I spent the first day bouncing her and feeding her and talking to her and changing her. She seemed to demand a great deal of attention, and I was nervous about letting her out of my sight. I felt I had to sit and watch her while she played on her blanket. By the time she was ready for a nap, I was exhausted. I made another cup of coffee, sat on the couch, read the paper, and dozed.

When she woke up, she wanted lunch. Then I decided she ought to have a bath. We talked and played until she fell asleep again, and I put her upstairs for her afternoon nap. I picked up a copy of *Tuck Everlasting*, a children's book, and read most of it before Mary got home at four.

Mary was good. She expressed interest in my day. She wanted exact details of everything we had done. Much of what had seemed mundane a few hours before excited her and made me feel as if I had accomplished something after all. We were still a team. Now I was doing the important part of taking care of our family. I wondered if I had been as supportive of her while she was staying at home.

The things I expected to happen have not happened. I have not become the happy househusband finding great joy in his freedom. Neither have I accomplished a great deal. Sure, I've done some carpentry and some writing, but not much more than I did last year when I was working full time. I have not managed to organize my day as efficiently as I had hoped. I spend too much time anticipating the demands of my daughter, checking on her, washing her diapers, vacuuming the rug where she plays, and remembering to take meat out of the freezer for supper. I realize that I don't work very well without pressure. When I teach, I have a hundred kids demanding that I produce for them constantly. I have to meet their expectations or I would be wasting their time. At home the demands are much simpler. Joanna doesn't insist that I do something intellectually stimulating while she naps.

But something else *is* happening. There is a very subtle change in my role that is more important and more rewarding than anything I anticipated. I am becoming the authority on the care of my daughter. I am making the daily decisions about her care, and my wife has begun to defer to my opinion. I am the primary care person. I am the expert. I am trusted.

This may not seem like a very important accomplishment, but I think it is. During the fall, I had certainly made decisions and helped, but I was also checking everything with Mary. Is it time for her nap? Shall I change her? Has she had enough to eat? I assumed Mary knew the answers because she had raised five brothers and seemed confident in what she was doing. She was the mother. I lacked that confidence. I assumed I was "just" a man and not really knowledgeable about taking care of children.

My greatest reward is knowing that I do make a difference in the way my daughter is growing up. I suspect it will be impossible to distinguish the results of this attention ten or twenty years from now. Nevertheless, Joanna is becoming a different person because of my attention than she would have become if I were leaving her with someone else every day. And I am developing a fuller relationship with my daughter. What could be more satisfying?

A resident of Portsmouth, New Hampshire, John B. Ferguson is a high school teacher. He and his wife, Mary McIver, have two children, Joanna and Paul. "My children have made me alive again. They teach me new and amazing things every day."

Chapter Ten
The Two-Career Family

Giving Up Life as a Male Mother Figure

David Blasco

In my fantasy, I wheeled my twenty-two-month-old daughter down to the park, sat on the bench, and gabbed with the assembled moms while Erin made new friends in the sandbox. In my fantasy, I talked to the moms about kids, picked up some new ideas on what to cook Erin for lunch, and—who knows—maybe even picked up tips on how to cook it.

In reality, the moms sat on the bench and gabbed. Erin and I and all the kids played in the sandbox. In the end, I found I had more in common with the children than with their mothers.

Holding my wife Bonnie's hand in the delivery room while Erin was born didn't make me a mom. Caring for Erin every morning for sixteen months while my wife went back to work didn't make me a mom. Spending my days (I work nights) with my child while my wife worked made me a new-style father, perhaps. My dad certainly didn't do it. But my new-style father experiences did nothing to deactivate thirty-four years of training in being a man. Although I loved the role of father, that was always secondary in my mind to my ideal image of Mom.

It was easy and pleasant to show up at the park with Erin. As the only male adult on the scene, I was an instant celebrity. The mothers not only made me welcome in the park but gave me plenty of support for my decision to take an active role in caring for my daughter. I don't know how many times I heard a mom say, "Oh, if only my husband would do that."

I felt a bit guilty at raking in praise for doing things that most mothers must do without so much as a pat on the back. Actually, I was doing far fewer child-care chores than the other adults in the park group. All I had to do was watch Erin from 9 A.M., when Bonnie left for work, until a baby-sitter arrived at 2:30 P.M. to take over until Bonnie came home from work. Most of the playground group spent all day with their children. Most had more than one child. Most didn't escape family responsibilities in the late afternoon to drink coffee and jaw with friends at the office. I did.

There were other differences, too. I quickly discovered that the moms on the park bench weren't sharing tips about raising kids, as I had hoped, or about what to fix for lunch. These women already knew how to cook, and bringing up children (many are on their second or third) was no longer their number one interest. "I don't want to talk about babies," one mother told me. The park was recreation time for the moms, as well as for their children. Who was I to intrude? In other words, excuse me, I think I'll go make mud pies with the kids.

If mud pies were all there is to mothering, I'd be confident of success. But, despite all the praise I won at the park, I remained skeptical about the adequacy of my mothering skills. Usually, this was an advantage. When Erin would collapse face down, arms and legs pumping, lungs going full blast on the floor of an otherwise silent public library, I wasn't upset. She wasn't rejecting "mother love." Bonnie and I both assumed that Erin would look to her mother for the genuine article. So I could just laugh, toss Erin over my shoulder, and leave for someplace we'd both find more amusing.

Bonnie and I were in for a surprise, one that threatened our assumptions about the roles we'd play after Erin's birth. Bonnie expected to be a supermom, juggling a full-time career with many of the traditional jobs of a full-time mother. She would do all the cooking, all the shopping, *and* manage household finances. All I was expected to do was glorified baby-sitting. We ignored the fact that our differing work schedules gave me the benefit of slightly more of Erin's waking hours. We also forgot that, since the three of us were together only one day a week, Erin rarely had a choice of which parent to prefer. She had to accept mothering from whoever was "on duty."

Then Erin became sick while we were on vacation. Suddenly it was "Daddy, Daddy, Daddy" whenever she felt bad. When Bonnie rushed to help she was stiff-armed with a tiny palm. "No! Daddy!" Bonnie was crushed. Every guilt feeling she had about returning to work after Erin's birth was confirmed. "I didn't sign on to be number two," she said.

And I hadn't expected to be number one. As Bonnie moved to quit her job and put her career on hold in order to devote more time to our toddler, I found myself adapting quickly to the notion that I would become the primary provider for our family.

As Bonnie's job disappears, so does more than half of our income. Luxuries, such as dinners out and vacations, will probably disappear, too. It hardly seems to matter. Erin is the chief joy and interest in our life. Since my work schedule hasn't changed, I will have as many hours with Erin as ever and now Bonnie will be home to share them with us. The real loss to me is the financial independence families with two incomes can have. I've never been afraid of being fired. I've even quit jobs without having a new job lined up. I can't do that now.

I am the breadwinner. It is an old pattern, perhaps one of the oldest on earth. My father would be familiar with my feelings now. But my father never had the chance to know what it was like to be with his child much of the day. I've been lucky. I've had all that time in the park.

An editor for the *Miami Herald*, David Blasco lives in Fort Lauderdale, Florida, with his wife, Bonnie Gross, and their daughter, Erin. "Like all the other baby boomers, I'm confused as hell. But I still believe that somewhere beneath our infatuation with BMWs, spas, and personal computers we remember that we once made a sweet little stab at a better world. We were wrong to expect that we could have Peace, Love and Brotherhood overnight. But that doesn't mean we'll never have them."

Conflicting Interests

Donald H. Bell

My wife now works more than 40 hours a week, mostly in the afternoon and evening. As a result, I frequently must cut short my own workday in order to pick up our 18-month-old son from day care or to spend time with my older child. Often, I am also the one who is on call in case of illness, who prepares many of the meals and who keeps the house clean.

I have many fewer hours available for work than I wish, and sometimes I am too exhausted at the end of a day to resume my work when the children have gone to bed. I cannot pretend to feel comfortable about this, and at times I explode with rage or I withdraw into sarcasm and moodiness. There is no question that the rewards of sharing career achievement and child rearing with one's spouse are great, but the price paid can be high. It is a price, finally, that many of us never imagined we would have to pay, and therein lies much of the trouble.

Maybe we might learn—in the words of one departmental colleague—to give up the amenities of life in order to concentrate on the essentials, adhering not only to precise daily schedules but working late into the night (a major ingredient in the success of many men who seem able to combine the demands of work and family). We might, in addition, learn to exult in the career attainments of our wives, even if we must sacrifice some of our own professional ambitions. We might find the time, as well, to be with our children and to be involved as a matter of course in the necessary household chores. We even might learn to give up the anger and resentment that is often engendered by the need to do all of these things, and to do them well.

We might. But most of us, as yet, cannot hope to follow such a program, nor should we berate ourselves if we do not live up to the "superman" image. Despite the things we did learn from our own fathers, we usually did not find out how to balance full participation in work and in family. Now we are exploring uncharted territory, with all of the missteps and false starts that such exploration requires.

Still, if we think about it, we might ultimately come to gain from the new requirements in our lives. On the morning I was to begin writing this piece, my 18-month-old son woke up with a low-grade fever. My wife had a full schedule at the office, and this sick child clearly could not go to his baby-sitter. The only solution was for me to alter my plans and to stay home, where I diapered, played with, worried over and comforted a still-energetic but cranky baby. I could feel my bitterness and resentment boiling—for lost hours at work, for missed deadlines, for unprepared classes. "Men today," I found myself thinking, "really have a raw deal."

Then I discovered that my son had learned something new. For the first time, he was able to give a proper kiss, puckering up his lips and enfolding my face in his arms. "Kees Dada," he said as he bussed me on the nose and cheeks. No amount of gratification at work could have compensated for that moment. I found out another thing that morning, a discovery that came as a bit of poetic justice. I suddenly realized that in sacrificing my workday, I had learned a lot about how fathers might care for their sons. And I found that I had learned something further about what it means to be a man, something that goes beyond simply bringing home a paycheck.

Donald H. Bell teaches at Harvard University and is the author of *Being a Man: The Paradox of Masculinity.*

Sunday Afternoon Battles

Robert Roth

My son Brandon is only two years old; he's still in process, unresolved. I, too, am unresolved in my feelings about him and about his effect on my relationship with my wife. Though I would not wish to change the decision to have Brandon that Susan and I made together nearly three years ago, I do have doubts about the wisdom and ease of trying to raise a child when both parents have to work full time. Yet, wise or not, that is the situation Susan and I find ourselves in—for financial reasons and because we both need work identities to feel whole.

When we first had the baby, I looked forward to being a full-time father who would assume an equal role in caring for his son. I'd never been much of a macho type anyway, so I hadn't worried about my self-image becoming threatened. I loved holding Brandon, cuddling his body, singing for hours while looking deep into his brown eyes. Even changing diapers never turned me off. But I soon found that all the constant trivia of baby care could make me feel clumsy and incompetent. When trying to get diapers to stay on right, to snap on clothes frontward, not backward, to tie shoes so that they stayed tied, I was all thumbs. I felt inadequate judging a rash, a runny nose, or a cry. I still depended on Susan's assessments.

After a while, my image of myself as a man did indeed become threatened. I was proud of having such a lively, outgoing baby, and I loved taking him with me when shopping or showing him off where I worked. But I became increasingly unsure of myself, easily hassled. I was oversensitive to the way other men looked, often feeling grubby or awkward by comparison. I worried that they considered me unmanly, a husband controlled by his wife. I began to lose a sense of myself and wondered if it hadn't always been somewhat precarious.

To top it all off, I started to resent the baby, or at least the loss of independence his existence had caused me. This was the worst feeling of all: even my love for my child became questionable. I began to see that Brandon, despite his fragility, vulnerability, and neediness, could also be willful and fiercely insistent. At times his demands would seem so unruly and persistent as to become tyrannical. I began to see that for years I would be functioning far below peak efficiency. And I started to blame Susan for the situation I was in, to attribute my difficulties to her deficiencies. I fell back on all sorts of traditional, sexist notions. She was the mother, wasn't she? If the strain was becoming too much for me, wasn't it because she wasn't coming through? After all, I had taught my classes or taken care of Brandon and had still found time to do some food shopping and prepare a good supper for the family. Didn't I deserve some gratitude? I felt neglected and unappreciated. I wanted to get credit for being a helpful, capable father, but I also wanted to fall back on Susan as the final authority, the one who took on the burden of ultimate responsibility. Signs of trouble began to show up only a few months after the baby was born. During those crazy, bleary-eyed times when sleep often meant two- or three-hour spurts at best, Susan had become miserable and depressed at the thought of raising another child. Having raised my stepdaughter, Leslie— who is now twelve—to the age when she was old enough to be fairly independent, thereby giving Susan room to attend to herself and her writing, Susan realized that she was now starting the whole self-limiting process all over again. When she returned to work almost full time, she was caught in a dilemma between her concern for Brandon and her needs for herself.

Susan felt that she wasn't doing enough for Brandon, and yet she resented the demands we all constantly made on her time and attention. When she returned home exhausted from a long day at work and wanted a few minutes to herself, she was met at the door by a barrage of contradictory demands: not only did Brandon want to be held, talked to, read to, or played with, but Leslie had school events to report, and I wanted a chance to talk out my difficulties and experiences of the day. Susan began to feel she needed three pairs of ears and four personalities. And I in turn resented her irritability and what I perceived as her inattention towards me.

This was a difficult inner response for me to handle. I felt that as the man of the house I ought to be cool, in control, reassuring. But not only was I unable to reassure and encourage Susan, I myself craved that feedback from her. I knew that she worked more hours a week than I did, that in the morning she got up with the baby more often than I did, that unlike me she couldn't help but compare herself as a mother to many other mothers who didn't have to work outside the home. Still, I continually looked to her for recognition of all that I was doing. I would tick off in my mind all the traditional wife/mother tasks I had done—cooking, shopping, laundry, baby care—in order to reassure myself that I really was a wonderful husband and father. And I expected Susan to be grateful to me, as if all that I did was for her alone.

Moreover, my career—previously a source of self-esteem—was suffering, and for this, too, I resented Susan. Since I rarely had time even to talk to my fellow teachers, I could no longer play an influential part in departmental affairs at school. Before the baby was born, I had prided myself on taking time to rap with students after class or during the many extra office hours I voluntarily scheduled. Now whenever I wasn't actually teaching a class or doing another required activity, I had to be home. Even in class or at a meeting, I seldom had enough energy to be a lively, affable, alert teacher or colleague.

I also had fewer opportunities to chat in a friendly, relaxed way with neighbors or friends. Social engagements had to be few and carefully planned. Even a simple night out to a movie sometimes required written schedules, flow charts, and managerial genius. Once, when I hurriedly passed a neighbor walking as I drove off to get some shopping done with Brandon by my side, I immediately felt foolish and embarrassed because I had been too rushed to stop. Shouldn't I at least have offered him a lift? He's going to think I'm a weirdo or a snob, I thought. I had to shrug it off, but I knew I wasn't presenting myself as I wished to. And at such moments I blamed Susan! Somehow I felt as if she were keeping me down, preventing me from coming across to others (and to myself) as a capable, intelligent, successful man. And clearly Susan often felt a similar anger and resentment toward me. We were blaming each other for something neither of us could help.

During the week Susan and I saw little of each other, except at night when we were usually too busy or exhausted to talk much. And Susan often worked on Saturdays. So Sunday was our only day for relaxing with the kids and spending some quiet time together. But instead of giving us a chance to renew our relationship, Sunday often provided our only opportunity for expressing the resentments and frustrations that had been brewing all week. Consequently, Sunday afternoons became increasingly tense, sometimes explosive. And battles were fast becoming the rule rather than the exception. Susan and I became alternatively angry and frightened. At times we were desperate. Oh, we would occasionally try to talk it out, and sometimes we would even attain some understanding and mutual sympathy. But how often could we talk things out without being interrupted by the baby? I would find that I had let the mortgage payment slip past the penalty date, or Susan would find she had no time to prepare for a library program, or Brandon's whining would turn us both into tense bundles of irritability—and we would blow up at each other. Accusations and recriminations would fly back and forth. Within a week of a truce, we would usually revert to the same negative pattern that had begun to overwhelm us.

Our marital relationship had been reduced to a melodrama! I felt that Susan wasn't listening to me and she felt that I was withholding affection from her. She once described a dream she had. In it, I wouldn't hug her or hold her; I refused to touch her. She became angry in the dream and decided she wanted a divorce. Fine, I said. I was indifferent. But before we could attend to it, the divorce was interrupted by another crisis, a raging flood that took all our attention. Hearing the dream I felt upset that I was showing Susan so little affection. Yet I was angry, too, that she should expect this of me when I felt *she* was not really attending to *me*, not heeding my feelings and thoughts. Still, the dream enabled us to begin once more to talk to each other, to express our feelings, and to be heard.

I suppose that is how we're beginning to work our way off this crazy merry-go-round of chaos—by talking to each other. But the main healing agent has been something simpler than that—the passage of time. Slowly, we've learned to readjust, to evolve new selves. I've learned how to double-tie Brandon's shoes so that they stay tied, and to chat with him while I'm doing it. I've learned how to give my attention wholly to Brandon and still hold onto a remote island of independence within my mind. At times I can even be comfortable with the partial, hurried self I present to the world, knowing that these limits will gradually recede with time. And now when I find myself wanting Susan to say to me, "Thank you, Bob, for being such a helpful husband, for taking care of Brandon for me, and for shopping and cooking and washing for me," I stop myself, questioning the "for me." And I ask myself how long it's been since I've said to Susan, "Thank you for bringing home a full-time paycheck and still getting up with the baby and taking him to play groups and spending your only time off from work taking care of our son. Thank you for cleaning the house and making doctor appointments and buying clothes for Brandon and writing letters to my mother and sister. Thank you, Susan, for doing these things for me." I'm not happy that Susan and I both have so many demands on our attention that we often feel overtaxed and unappreciated. But I am happy that I have a beautiful, much-loved son. And I'm happy that I am able—at least at times—to put the whole situation into some perspective.

> Robert Roth is a college English teacher. He lives in New Jersey with his wife, Susan, their son, Brandon, and his stepdaughter, Leslie. "At my worst moments, I want desperately to make up for my life's lost opportunities through my son's achievements and self-satisfactions. At my best moments, I want to quietly share with both of my children life's unexpected pleasures."

POSITIVE IMAGES, © *Margurite Bradley*

Chapter Eleven
Single Fathers

Love In Breaking

William Johnson Everett

The news of separation
    let a heartached loneliness
    descend upon my son,
    now Absalomed among the branches of my
    love.
The age of manliness steps rudely on his tender toes
    as parenthood enshrouds an adolescent eye.
He helpless sponges up the blows,
    pounds on hostile fortune with his heart,
Looks down the darkened pathways
    where the father's love gives faltering light
    to stuttering footsteps in the gloom.
O Absalom, my son, my son.

A theological educator, William Johnson Everett has "tried to be an emotional as well as financial father—a doubly difficult task in divorce." He has been active in attempting to reform custody laws in order to guarantee both parents' bonds with their children in situations of divorce, and has three children—Eric, Aneliese, and Elaine. He is Director of the OIKOS Project on Work, Family, and Faith in Milwaukee, Wisconsin.

Uncle Dad

C. W. Smith

Years ago I called a college buddy I hadn't heard from in a while. He had divorced his first wife but had remarried. I asked him how many kids he had now.

"Just the one."

"One? I thought you had two."

"Aw hell!" he snorted. "You're thinking of the ones I had with Judy. They don't count."

A silence several seconds wide dropped between us while I pictured those two fatherless children drifting into space without a tether. How could a man discount his children's existence with the indifference of a claims adjuster?

But now that I've lived for the last five years outside the home where my daughter and son are growing up, I don't judge my friend so harshly. Maybe "they don't count" meant that since he had botched that job, he could hope for a better grade on a new project, offer "the one" as evidence of his reformation. If he had stormy struggles over visitation arrangements, or if he wasn't allowed to help decide who would be his children's doctors, barbers, teachers, or playmates, or if his former wife moved them to another city without consulting him, then I can see why he says "they don't count." When we feel our efforts produce only the frustration of impotence, then we cease trying.

That's a comforting thought. But then, as I seem to remember C. S. Lewis once saying, "An explanation of cause is not a justification by reason." I keep thinking about that.

My father is a pipe-smoking Presbyterian who speaks in witty one-liners; he taught me to stand when ladies enter a room and how to handle hammers, and once, when I was twelve, I saw him rescue a drowning man, a father, from a river and walk away without giving anyone his name. A hero.

That he would have chosen to divorce my mother and walk out of our house to live elsewhere was inconceivable.

Walking out of my own house twenty-seven years later, I knew I had forfeited the right to be so admired by my own twin son and daughter. But because my parents had not divorced, I wasn't aware of how devastating it might be. And didn't want to know—I could dream the damage to my children would be minimal by watching other fatherless kids go about their daily lives: in the age of divorce, this seemed to have become oddly normal; there were thousands of such children, and they wore no bruises I could see.

I saw nothing to stop me from being the good father I had always been. Aside from the months I commuted to another state for work, I had been around the house constantly. With two "first" children, both my wife and I had to keep diapers changed, bottles washed and filled. For the two years that my wife was a television reporter, I stayed home to write, changed vacuum-cleaner bags, separated darks from whites in the wash, shuttled the kids to school, and greeted them all at the door at the end of the day in an apron, a wooden spoon in hand.

I read the kids Curious George and Dr. Seuss books. Once, when a heavy snowfall closed the schools, we made an igloo in the yard using a cardboard box as a mold. (The defense offers this, Exhibit A, to show that this worm was a good, liberated father before he bailed out of his marriage; he regrets that the flaming hulk landed in a school yard.)

Giving them a hug or an off-to-school scuff on the head, crooning the bedtime mantra ("Good night/Sleep tight/Wake up bright in the morning light/ To do what's right/With all your might"), making cheese toast, cheering while running behind my cycling-novice son with one hand clutching the waistband of his jeans—these humble pleasures vanished the moment I decided to leave. To provide, to protect, and to guide—like a service club motto, these had constituted the dogma of fathering I had learned as a son, and I didn't know that performing these ritual duties was such good spiritual nutrition until after I had prematurely nodded to the waiter and the plate was whisked from under my nose.

My lessons began immediately. Gay and I agreed, I thought, to pad the shock to the kids with a spirit of mutual cooperation. The day we decided to announce that we would separate, I presumed that we would sit them down and break the news, over their heads, together. The words would come hard, I knew. Every speech I rehearsed sounded lame and false; I couldn't frame any phrase that would make my leaving a necessity that could outweigh their claim to the pain of it. But as the parent who had chosen to go, the duty was rightfully mine, and the difficulty would be part payment for my guilt. Facing them would be both manly and fatherly.

But when I pulled into the driveway late that afternoon, they were huddled together on the sidewalk at the curb, looking stricken, two nine-year-olds waiting for the Dachau bus.

At the front door I knocked on the screen (that seemed strange—hours before, the house had belonged to me) and went inside to say that I was taking the kids to eat before we had our talk.

Then Gay reported that she had already told them we were going to separate. "I hope you don't mind," she offered politely. "After all, it's our problem now." *So you go on about your merry way and don't bother about us!*

Yes, I *did* mind—it's one thing to confess you're a scumbag and another to have the news precede your appearance. Obviously, part of my punishment would be to be denied any strategy I might devise for my absolution, however meager. My guilt also said I had no right to be angry.

"How'd they take it?"

"Okay," she said, "considering."

I slunk back to my car. My kids were already in it. My daughter sat in the front seat. Gray coils of mud were clinging to the rims of her tennis shoes. I almost told her to get out and wipe her shoes off but didn't, not because it would have seemed petty in juxtaposition with the news but because I had, in one stroke, lost my moral authority.

We went to Burger King. White tile, hard plastic benches, everything colored in the hues of chewable vitamins. I can't remember what was ordered, but it all came in paper cartons and was cold by the time the first of us had decided to bolt from the silence by stuffing his mouth with something handy.

"So what do you think?" I finally asked.

Keith shrugged, which I interpreted to mean indifference or stoic acceptance. Now I know he felt helpless, numb, and utterly confused.

"Just a separation," said Nicole.

"Yes," I said, "just a separation." A legalistic truth: I was 99-percent certain we would be divorced, but that remaining one percent permitted me the luxury of cowardice. "I'll see you all the time," I added. "I won't go away." Another lie, strictly speaking.

Nobody had an appetite. I couldn't make myself talk about anything important, and that also discouraged talking about anything inconsequential— it would have seemed vulgar. *The* subject sat on the table between us like a Venus's-flytrap the size of a basketball we were each pretending was only a private hallucination. Not knowing what to say, I was unpleasantly surprised by my own relief that Gay had already "explained" it to them. I asked "How was school?" and "Did you do your homework?" knowing that no child in his right mind could perform any productive work after having heard such crushing news.

"How about some ice cream?"

They shook their heads.

"Aw, come on, surely you want some ice cream?"

Surely you won't hate me for the rest of your lives?

Most of the divorced fathers I know still hang on in some way despite the trouble and pain. We form a legion of what novelist Bryan Woolley has termed the Uncle Dads. Unlike traveling dads, we never will come "home" to any welcome or to settle a quarrel or to hear an appeal, and our children gnaw on the suspicion that we've rejected *them*; unlike stepdads, we live in another house, or even in another city, perhaps with other children whom our "real" children suspect are getting the best of our attention.

Some of us pop irregularly into our children's lives, bearing an irrelevant or even inappropriate gift, disrupting routine, asking that our children's plans be changed to suit our brief visitation or hoping to be included in their activities.

We console ourselves with the notion of "quality time," the divorced parent's fondest way of coping with guilt. "I'm a remote kind of person," said one divorced father who takes his sons to a cabin every summer for two weeks, "so if I was living at home with my kids, I'd probably be removed; this way, I tend to pay more attention to them. I think of using this time for them to talk about anything serious that they want to, but so far," he joked, "nothing's come up."

The truth is, though, that children tend to talk seriously only when it's their choice, and that usually comes when the surface of daily routine is glassy, unruffled. They're helping us to bake cookies or to paint a cabinet, and out comes, "Dad, were you ever in love in the eighth grade?" Or "Have you ever had a friend who was homosexual?"

When we're being honest, we admit that quality time is that rare moment when a stretch of ordinary time is interrupted by an unexpected burst of genuine rapport. To say "We will now have quality time" whether anybody feels like it or not is like saying, "We will now have fun, or else." We fear this truth: that the necessary preparation for quality time is quantity time, and that we can't give. Awakened by a nightmare that some disaster has befallen them miles away, or that they may be troubled by something that happened during the day, we're forced to recognize that there's no substitute for being there constantly; or rather, there are only substitutes for it.

But then there's hope. Dressed in clean jeans and sport shirts, we platoon up at Jetways on Friday evenings, waiting for the stewardesses to lead our mob of children—some wearing name tags like D.P.s—out of the tunnels to where we stand hoping they haven't seen *Gremlins* yet. Upchuck Cheeze Pizza is the last place we would ordinarily choose to dine, but the martyrdom of an awful meal is oddly comforting.

We yearn for things to go well. We're anxious. We fear our children's anger because it hurts us; we fear their love because we know it means they hurt. But we're also elated to have forty-eight hours to wedge slivers of ourselves into chinks of their armor.

During the divorce negotiations I tried for joint custody but met stiff resistance. My greatest fear was that Gay might whisk them off to another city; the saddest men I knew were those whose children were literally out of reach, and I have one friend who arrived at his children's home one day to find the house empty and no forwarding address left. So I asked my lawyer if I could legally prevent this. He chuckled.

They stayed put, though, and I took furnished digs ten minutes away in an old, Mediterranean-style building said to have been the residence of the man who penned "Home on the Range" in the 1930s, the decade from which the dusty wooden blinds, the furniture, and the smelly mattresses doubtless dated. I was not supposed to have children here, my downstairs neighbors constantly reminded me. On overnights, Keith and Nicole slept in a sagging Murphy bed and fought over the covers. Looking out my bedroom window, they had a view onto an alley where the wan, androgynous denizens of a unisex hair boutique met during break-time to compare rainbow-colored hair and to pass a joint, and sometimes each other's tongues, among them; I was cursed with the terror that my folly had led my own pink-cheeked babies out of innocence much too soon. My best hope was that years later they could tell their more sheltered peers about their lives with voices dripping with blasé sophistication; maybe they could wear all this like a badge.

In cold weather we stayed inside to play Monopoly on a rug so old, cross-hatched twine showed through the burgundy fuzz. If the weather was nice, I would walk them down to a nearby park to play Horse with a spongy basketball, or take them to the zoo, where I would see other Uncle Dads doing weekend duty. We could distinguish each other from the regular, full-time dads because they were allowed to look bored.

Once a week I drove Nicole to a town twenty miles away for gymnastics lessons; two afternoons a week I took my son to soccer practice or games. I took them to the movies and their pediatrician, showed up for PTA meetings, and talked to their teachers. I wanted to believe I was a good father, even from across town.

One evening when Gay was working late, Keith climbed onto the roof to rescue a mewling kitten and fell off, striking the air-conditioning unit. While he lay screaming on the driveway, Nicole ran up and down the block trying to find an adult who could help before she phoned for an ambulance. I discovered this twenty-four hours later. "I'm sure glad you weren't seriously hurt," I told Keith over the phone, as if I were a cousin across the continent. "You should be more careful." My words were altogether empty, coming so late and from one so remote that his name did not automatically spring to mind in an emergency.

I didn't worry about Nicole. She was gliding through her days on autopilot, so stunned I read her shock as acceptance. To make up for her broken home I got her an intact Barbie Townhouse where Ken and Barbie could all live happily with Francie; they had a working toilet and a pink-and-yellow van to take lots of fun family trips in. Barbie had a wedding dress and they could stay married as long as Nicole wanted them to.

Meanwhile, Keith was erupting in purple rages. Where before the divorce he had been a model child, he now roamed his neighborhood saying ugly things to adults and pelting people's houses with eggs. In family therapy I'd watch him braid his arms across his chest, clamp his jaws, and pretend he had nothing to say. His grades tumbled; he told his teachers that when he tried to concentrate, all he could think about was the divorce.

Occasionally my ex would call to ask me "to do something with Keith"; he'd be ordered to the phone, and if I reproached him, he'd simply hang up on me. Sometimes she would tell him that if he didn't behave she would call me to come over to spank him. She never did, for which in retrospect I'm thankful: to have barged into my children's home for that reason would have been a terrible compounding of insult with injury.

He said he wanted to live with me. I was having the time of my midlife living with my lover in an apartment over an elderly landlady, and I balked at dealing daily with my belligerent son, and that's the sorry truth. So I bought him a model airplane with a gasoline engine, something I had always wanted as a kid, and I thought it was good to give him what I had wanted (since I couldn't give him what *he* wanted), and I wanted to grab a little chunk of my own childhood back this way. Gee, Dad! the Beaver (Keith) would gush to Ward (me). Golly. It flies and it's got a real engine! He and I and Nicole went to the park, assembled the plane, got it started. I turned over the control lines to him, and he got dizzy turning on the plane's pivot after a few revolutions. Nicole took a turn, and the plane took a vertical swoop that arced into a loop that took it nose-down into the turf, where it exploded into pieces.

I bought Keith a BB gun to replace the airplane. He and a new friend, who had spiked hair and whose parents were also breaking up, chipped a garage window with a shot from the Daisy. The owner called the police and Keith's name probably went into a computer somewhere. I gave him a feeble lecture, but I knew that I shouldn't have bought the gun for him. "Keith says you're just trying to buy his love," Gay reported, obviously agreeing.

They were wrong. I knew I already had his love. I was trying to buy his forgiveness.

Three years after the separation, Gay announced that she was taking a job in Galveston, three hundred miles away. I panicked. I didn't have room to keep both of them, but I invited Keith to live with me. He turned me down, whether from resentment or loyalty to his sister and his mother, I don't know.

For the three weeks that preceded their moving they both stayed in my apartment while their mother looked for a house in Galveston. I remember wanting to give them such a booster shot of myself that they'd never be able to get me out of their systems. I doled out allowances and lunch money just like a real dad, and labored over Sunday dinner so that when we all—my two children and my new wife—would sit down to eat, there'd be some faint reminder that family life was still possible. The Sunday before they left, when they balked at eating at the table (it seemed it was no longer required at home), I complained, hearing my mother's voice coming out of my mouth, that I had slaved in the kitchen for hours so that we could enjoy a Sunday family dinner. Keith retorted, "This isn't our family."

I signed up for Sprint and wrote to people I knew in Houston, fifty miles from Galveston, about jobs. On Tuesday, November 16, 1982, I helped them pack; then their mother came and took them.

When they were settled, I called them nightly. I kept saying to myself, *It won't be so bad*, but it was. I was tormented by not knowing what the house just off the beach there looked like, how the kids' rooms were decorated. I didn't know anything about their school, and none of their teachers had faces. Their teachers did not know me, either, and so my children were, to them, fatherless. They rode a school bus; on the phone I coaxed from my daughter a yard-by-yard description of the route, picturing how the bus passed over a bridge, with the water below "kind of glittery, you know, when it's early and sun is shining on it," she said.

I thought of Chappaquiddick. Frolicking in the surf, they were swept out to sea by riptides, undertow. Sharks cleaved their limbs from their bodies, leaving bloody joints and stumps. Alone after school, they singed their palms on the stove burners and electrocuted themselves by turning on their hair dryers while standing in the tub.

But when I called, Keith was always "fine." Nicole was always "fine," too, even though, unknown to me, a great dark pterodactyl of depression was making a slow bank before gliding in to land on her rib cage. These telephone interrogations were, I suppose, typically fruitless. What did they do in school today? ("Nothing.") Who were their friends? ("Just some kids.") Where did these kids live? ("*Aw*, you know, everywhere.") What did they all do together? ("Just stuff.")

The phone was a crucial link. Sometimes I worked to hear in their voices all the minute aspects of their lives, the way I replay small night sounds in my inner ear to judge them malign or benign; while we talked I would ask them where they were sitting, what they had eaten that day, what they were wearing. (They had clothes I had never seen.)

To them these interrogations were a rip-roaring bore. I called some five times a week, and invariably they were about to watch *CHiPs*, to eat, to get a call from a friend, or had just gotten out of the shower, and answering my survey was as appealing as having a chat with a magazine-subscription peddler.

If there had been trouble at school, then I would not know about it, unless, say, Nicole happened to mention that Keith had been beaten up by some members of a gang *last week* or that he had called his band director an asshole, which Keith would instantly deny, then call Nicole a troublemaker and a liar, leaving me helpless to sort out the facts, let alone impose discipline.

Many times when I talked to them I felt I was hearing the kind of bland, remote, and superficial phrases about their lives I was accustomed to giving my grandparents over the telephone on holidays at my house when I was a child, and this perspective on how little I counted would leave me sad and angry, especially when it was obvious they did not want to talk. "You're not letting them have any choice about when to talk to you," counseled my new wife. "Ease up and give them a chance to call you."

Once I waited for days, and finally broke down, convinced then that if I walked altogether out of their lives they would never miss me. "Why didn't you call me?" I whined. "Golly, Dad," they said, "I was going to."

Gradually I learned telephone technique. I'd check the TV schedule to avoid pulling them away from their "favorite" shows, though these appeared to be almost anything on prime time. Instead of grilling them I would talk about my day or my work or my car or my wife or my friends. Sometimes I would ask about movies they had seen. This worked especially well with Keith because all twelve-year-old boys have a gene that compels them to describe every frame of a movie orally. I would let the content of his speech wash over me; I would listen instead to his inflection, the structure of his sentences, and to his mood. My ear was a stethoscope pressed to his voice, listening to his heartbeat.

These telephone tricks didn't improve the quality of the information I got, but they did keep my frustration at a minimum and let me think that at least my calls were serving their main purpose—to let my children know I still loved them, still missed them, still thought about them. But my anxiety disappeared only when they were present during their monthly weekend visits to Dallas. High anticipation would make me step lightly, whistling, as I made my way down the halls of Love Field to where I would eagerly await their flight from Houston. How wonderful this will be! I would have made a few plans for "family" fun, but, invariably, no sooner would we hug and start to discuss them than things would begin to unravel. Keith would want to see one movie, Nicole another; Nicole would go roller-skating, but Keith wanted to go to a party. Now they were twelve, going on thirteen; they did not mind using my house as a base of operations (although Keith was usually quick to let me know what offers he had turned down in Galveston), but they weren't enthusiastic about doing anything with Dad.

These are the normal aggravations of parenting made more difficult by abnormal circumstances. Playing chauffeur for forty-eight hours, opening my billfold, keeping as effaced as the most well-trained butler, I felt used. By Saturday night I would be soaking in self-pity; by Sunday morning I would be complaining about being mistreated (to which they might once again remind me of what they had given up to be there); by Sunday afternoon I would feel a wave of relief that they would be leaving, but by the time I would see them off, I could imagine how much they really needed me even if they didn't know it, and even some pale, innocuous heat lightning flickering through my windshield in the southern sky would be all I'd need to feel convinced I'd never see them alive again.

Most of their visits that spring left me feeling depressed—I had frequent colds and viruses, my blood pressure rose. On Mondays I would struggle to start anew, over the phone, the way you might hope to convince the hostess of Saturday night's party that some insult had been meant to be taken as a joke.

In the late spring disturbing hints seeped in like a slow water leak: What was that? Somebody found a partly smoked joint on the living-room carpet? When? And whose? "Not mine!" all the kids said. The neighborhood was a little wild. Then Nicole was said to have drunk a large glass of vodka once when she was alone in the house. *I just wanted to know what it was like.*

When Gay had to go out of town on business, I offered to stay in their house to take care of the kids. The house stood on stilts in a subdivision about a mile back from the beach; it had a high sun deck overlooking a canal laced with palms, and the location looked like every kid's dream—a short walk to the ocean, quiet streets for bike riding. Keith, I was happy to see, appeared to be doing well here. His friends had been teaching him to fish and to surf, and you could see him speeding off to a sandlot baseball game with his glove hooked over the handlebars of his bike. His friends wore run-down sneakers and T-shirts, and when you saw Keith and them with fishing poles over their shoulders they were a living Norman Rockwell *Post* cover. He seemed happy to see me and to introduce me to his friends. I was proud to be introduced, glad that we could claim kinship before people who mattered to him.

I found Nicole's new Schwinn ten-speed—this year's Christmas present—in the garage with two flat tires, the cables and spokes and gears corroded by salt spray and gummed with sand. Her room was papered with posters of heavy-metal rock groups on which sets of angry young men clad in black leather and spikes leered and postured. Clothes and papers and used tissue littered the floor; notes from friends were wadded or left lying about where even the most casual eye (and mine was not the most casual) could spot the horrific phrasing of minds just discovering how to relish the vulgar. Drawings she had done of hollow-eyed, screaming Medusas filled a sketch pad. Behind the shut and locked door she played Pink Floyd at top volume ("*We don't need no ed-you-kay-shun.* . . ."), and I had to pound on the door and scream to get her attention.

"Why don't you take better care of your bicycle?"

Shrug. Close door. She would shuffle out to fix herself a plate of food, then, moments later, disappear into the yard, and the odor of cigarette smoke would drift into the windows. On Friday night I took her to a dance program given by some of her classmates, where I met her friends; they all seemed older than her thirteen and were dressed in tight jeans and tight T-shirts, dangling earrings, and heavy blue eye shadow—the sort of girls a twenty-one-year-old red-neck cruising in his pickup would imagine to be an easy lay.

Sunday, I worked in a stranger's kitchen preparing a send-on dinner for myself and for them. Gay arrived two hours earlier than expected and I invited her to eat with us. This was the first time in almost two years that we had all sat at a table together. You could hear chewing, forks clinking on plates. Now and then she or I would say something polite the way you small-talk with a stranger seated beside you on a plane.

Nicole picked at her food, then abruptly got up and left the table; just a few seconds later Keith asked to be excused, as though the discomfort of the occasion had caused him to recall his formal manners. I had the feeling they both hated me for the adult pretense that nothing was different, nothing was wrong. *What right do you have to remind us that you aren't really here?* I ate far beyond hunger, and when I was finished with my own plate, I ate what was left on theirs.

I'm luckier than most divorced men. . . . Four months after this upsetting trip, my children moved back to Dallas and began their eighth grade. Whatever happened now, I would be nearby; I could chauffeur them to malls for shopping, skating, or a movie. They could spend parts of weekends at my apartment without feeling I had stolen all of their leisure time, or I could have them over nights during the week.

But they were not the same children. They had contracted adolescence. They ran with a pack at shopping malls on Friday nights. They attended a tough urban school where a custom van with an ear-shattering stereo system showed up promptly at lunchtime to dispense the drug du jour to kids, and where small white boys like Keith were regularly threatened with an ass-kicking from gangs of low-riders. Half the time he was afraid to go to school, but he learned the art of diplomacy by befriending very large black people.

Nicole's friend Alicia lived with her mother except when her mother was on a bender, when she'd go live with her father, a bricklayer, in a trailer park. She was dumb but friendly (rumor had it that she let college boys abuse her sexually). Nicole's friend Angie and her friend Denise dropped acid, stole some credit cards, and took off in a "borrowed" car with some eighteen-year-old boys and were caught two states away, for which Angie spent a month in juvenile detention. Nicole's friend Melissa was always so stoned that her friends had to prop her up in class and walk her down the halls, and she eventually spent several weeks in a drug rehabilitation program. They stole from their mothers' purses; they sniffed paint; they watched X-rated movies on cable. They all had a variety of parents but very little parenting.

They had no innocence of any kind, but they were ignorant. They could recite all the lyrics to any Van Halen album, but they didn't know if El Paso was a city or a state. Three of her teachers were very concerned about Nicole, but she was failing all of her classes.

And where was I? Largely in the dark. I saw her alarming report cards; I talked to her teachers, but mostly I was bewildered by her sullenness and her distance.

I was depressed, too. Having them back in town was not turning out as I had hoped.

When I wasn't bathing in self-pity, I could see we had to get Nicole into counseling. She agreed to it, partly out of curiosity and partly because she was a little worried about herself.

It was called "adolescent reactive adjustment syndrome," which means skipping school, flunking out, mouthing off, screwing up, getting drunk, taking drugs. Her psychologist was a pleasant and intelligent middle-aged woman who approached life with a perpetual Happy Face. She gave Nicole a battery of tests about preferences, aptitudes, and attitudes toward parents, self, and peers.

After several sessions, the counselor reported that Nicole suffered from low self-esteem, and we were advised to accentuate the positive. But when you gave Nicole a compliment, she would counter with, "You're just saying that because *she* told you to make me feel good."

She continued to sneak out at night to join her friends; trapped at home, she'd closet herself in her room amid the hurricane winds of the stereo and draw that black-and-white Fury I first saw in Galveston. The figure had wild, electrified hair, a square jaw, a Frankensteinian forehead, large hollow eyes without pupils, and a howling mouth.

What the counselor didn't know was that Nicole was stoned all the time. Her mother and I didn't know it, either. (Keith kept trying to tell us, but he had been caught at so many lies his credibility was low.) Arriving at school each day, she would load up with whatever drugs were available— speed, grass, Valium—and go blotto through her classes; she'd even attend her sessions with her psychologist three quarters under the influence of some chemical moon.

Then in April she took a horse tranquilizer (PCP) with the street name of "angel dust." It scrambled her brains. Voices in her head told her to hurt herself; she insisted the voices belonged to real people, characters to whom she gave fablelike names such as Bendikak. They looked like trolls when they popped into the frame of her vision. Some told her to do "good things," and some "bad things."

Her counselor advised hospitalization. While we looked for the right place, she was "sentenced" to stay at my house, out of reach of her friends and where my wife and I could keep close watch over her. She was furious and deadly silent. She kept drawing that face and broke off only to construct an odd tableau. Acting obsessed, she found an old Frisbee in the alley, washed it, and turned it rim up; she cut out a page from a magazine depicting a winter woods scene and attached it along one side of the Frisbee's rim like a backdrop; she glued silver glitter to the floor of the disk. I asked what it was. "Snow," she grunted. She next fashioned a small skirted figure out of tinfoil, a girl whose arms were spread in a cruciform position, and mounted it on the glitter-covered "stage." She then dug a clear plastic glass out of the trash and glued it in place mouthdown over the figure. She scissored an arm about the size of her little finger out of white paper and glued the shoulder joint to the top of the glass so that the arm waved slightly with air currents. It was as if the girl inside the glass had an extra, detached limb which had somehow managed to penetrate to the outside of this otherwise unyielding surface.

It was an eerie little sculpture; it would easily have served to illustrate an edition of Sylvia Plath.

Going into the hospital was scary for her. A part of her welcomed it because she needed help and knew it might be an interesting experience, but when she realized that she would be kept behind locked doors, she balked. She could not eat or drink when or what she wanted to! She would not be allowed to take so much as a measly aspirin on her own! We were putting her in jail!

That night I slept soundly for the first time in two months. I was not only relieved that she was safe. The anxiety I had experienced over the last several weeks had finally equalized my guilt for having been responsible somehow for her condition, and having put her in the hospital gave me a sense of accomplishment. I had earned the right to sleep; I could tell my conscience that I had, for the moment, made payment in full.

Her mother, her teachers, her brother, her case workers, and I visited constantly, and we had to learn to deal with the personality that had been buried under that avalanche of chemistry. She was being treated for depression by nonchemical therapies; she had been numb for so long that when her feelings were finally allowed to flow, the wildly oscillating emotional upheaval alarmed her. She deeply resented our "help." Nobody knew her mind except her! Only she could solve her own problems! She didn't *have* any problems!

With each visit there were new, recent renderings of the Medusa taped to her wall.

But as the weeks went by, she grew more sunny, witty; she had a kooky sense of humor that endeared her to the staff. She made close friends with other girls who had similar problems. Some days she was more like the person I had known—and had all but forgotten—before she moved away to Galveston. She grew hospital-wise and expressed a desire to someday be a psychologist. ("I acted out in group today, didn't handle things well.")

I went to the parents' group, where I discovered the obvious, that such groups are composed of people who share the same problems and that you feel better the instant you realize that. We were a motley crew; we had nothing in common but our troubled children.

. . .

Seeing them agonize, it dawned on me that not everyone in the room was divorced, that such things happened to "nice" folks, too.

Perhaps I was not altogether to blame!

We who have left our children live with the burden of guilt that makes judgment more difficult. When something goes wrong, we immediately go for our own jugular. What I learned in group was that nobody knows for sure why kids go haywire; the causes could be emotional, chemical, spiritual, psychological, genetic, or social. (Or, as it was in Nicole's case, because of depression.) And yet it is obvious that wholesale rejection by a father of his children will most likely leave a lifelong emotional scar, something my old college buddy whose ex-children "don't count" may someday have to face. "Leaving" my children was not a necessary or even a sufficient cause for it, but it certainly was a contributory one. My job was to minimize the damage. Whether I was in their home or not, I had better pay as close attention as I possibly could to how they were doing.

Nicole got out of stir with walking papers that pronounced her sound again, for which I am immensely grateful to the staff of that hospital. We kept her and her brother in constant motion over the summer—to camp, to Yosemite, to San Francisco, to Los Angeles, to Disneyland (she loved it!)—and she started ninth grade at a high school for the arts. Her first report card showed a string of B's interrupted only by a C in science.

Keith recently announced he was tired of living with women, so I invited him to live with me and my wife. He said that he would as soon as I moved into a house where he could have friends over and keep his dog. For a while Nicole kept drawing renditions of that Medusa, though each successive version seemed to represent something like stages of evolution out of the slime. One of the last she did she colored with pastel pencils: the woman has blond hair, high cheekbones with a slight peach flush. Her mouth is closed, and she has feminine lips; she isn't smiling, but the curve of her lips suggests repose. Her jaw has softened, and she has large, pale blue eyes with curving lashes. One brow goes up, the other down, in some faint intimation of melancholy. The old gal seems human now.

She gave that one to me. The inscription reads, "To Dad, a very special person who helped me through a lot of hard times. I love you."

As proud as I am for having earned those words, and as much as I'd like to end on that upbeat note, the truth is that no trauma is altogether erasable. The other night Nicole and I were talking about her future as an adult; she couldn't decide between being an artist or a psychologist. Well, there's your love life to consider, too," I said. "Oh, I think I'll just live with somebody," she said. "I don't think I'll get married." Why not? "Because then I might have kids and just get divorced."

C. W. Smith's most recent novel is *The Vestal Virgin Room*, published by Atheneum.

Just Visiting

Kip Eastman

It is the little things
that hurt the most:
The vacant place across the table,
the dolls aligned along the shelf,
one sock left there on the floor.
Melancholy thorns adorn the rose
that blooms on visitation days.

Visitation weekend number 104 is over. My daughter, Chelsea, is again "home" with her mother. I sit alone in the garden we have planted, weeded, watered— a ritual we perform when we are together. I watch the young plants struggle to reach the sun.

Eventually, one or another tendril will make the essential contact with the trellis, and the plant will thrive. But some shoots will remain in limbo, not quite useless, not quite needed. It is this feeling that washes over me after nearly every visitation. (I hate the word—like being in prison or a psychiatric institution.)

Am I still Chelsea's father when she is not here? In my heart and my gut the answer seems to be no. My mind knows better. We share the pattern of freckles across the nose, although in most other ways she resembles her mother. She calls me when she is hurt, cuddles with me in the quiet times, judges my women and my cooking. We finish sentences for each other, laugh and cry in synchrony. When we are together, none can mistake the relationship.

But we are together so little. Every two weeks we make the transition from estranged correspondents to father and daughter. There is a brittleness about the first few hours; there is a melancholy about the last few. It leaves a painfully sweet day or two in between, a time that makes the repeated assault on both our sensibilities worthwhile.

Longer visits are even more difficult for us. The parting leaves us feeling betrayed, yet each of us misses the patterns of our separate lives. I miss the woman-comfort, creative grumbling, and independent time of my single adult world. Chelsea misses friends and mother and baby brother. Besides, the pain is more than parting—we are made aware that our lives cannot run in the same channel even while the times we share show us how good it could have been.

Seven years ago I cursed the fact of my daughter's coming, in fear of losing my mate to a difficult pregnancy. I can remember standing at the window of the intensive care nursery, and feeling bubbled to the surface. At that moment I vowed that all my life, all my health, all my power, was that child's, if she would be okay.

Chelsea lived, her mother lived. I had made the transition from non-parent to parent, with a vengeance.

I blundered into and through the father/spouse/provider/protector role. I read the books, had the best of intentions, and failed. That failure cost me the dream of domestic bliss I had nurtured from age thirteen. I was thrust into a schismatic existence, the life of a divorced father without custody.

I was not so deeply hurt by my wife's leaving me as by her taking my daughter. I knew that for years to come I would be making the transition over and over from the single existence (which I had every intention of taking full advantage of) to that of either a committed single parent or a Disneyland Dad.

It was not in me to absolve myself of all but financial responsibility for my daughter's growth. I fought for, and won, joint legal custody. I refused to become a vendor of weekend holidays. The financial and emotional costs of that battle were significant, but the rewards were worth it.

Chelsea and I wash dishes, cook, clean (after a fashion), and commit ourselves to taking care of whatever business needs attention, in spite of our limited time. There are occasions, however, when I cannot interrupt my concentration on a project to join in an activity with her. Since age four, she has been able to work contentedly on her own for longer periods than I usually can.

In the four years since our schism, I've read over six hundred children's books, many of them repeatedly, reintroducing myself to that amazing fantasy world. I've arranged to volunteer at Chelsea's school, to increase the time spent with her, but I get so much more than just "time." I've come to accept shared love—I bear the title "Daddy" jointly with the man who married Chelsea's mother. While I once thought of him as "that SOB," now, through Chelsea's love, he has become co-father.

I have grown to care about women in ways my own relationship with my mother, and my adolescent exploitation, had never allowed. Participating in Chelsea's effort to grow up female has contributed immeasurably to my effort to grow up male.

But, of course, the waves of change have not come without great cost. A few episodes are typical of the catalytic forces of my intermittent parenting.

My wife and I had been separated but a few days. I'd honored her request for total isolation while she settled into her new apartment. One afternoon she came to the house unexpectedly, carrying Chelsea who was not yet three. I greeted them as calmly as I could and bent down to kiss Chelsea. She turned her face away and began to cry. Nothing, nothing before, not even the demise of my first love, nothing since, hurt me more, cut me deeper. That was the bulldozer that took my relationship with my daughter back to bedrock.

On a week-long trip, after a tiring day, hassling over sleeping arrangements for four adults and four children, Chelsea began to wail, "I want my Mommy." I overreacted, yelling at her, threatening never again to take her anywhere, never to see her again if that's how she felt. The impact was staggering—for both of us. Awash in guilt, I tried to hold her close, but, hurt and angry, she would have no part of it. Only after much talking and crying was an accommodation reached. I still blush over my frailty.

Finally, another time of tears, but for a much different reason. Chelsea and I sat in a nearly empty theater moments after the show was over, holding each other close and trying to staunch the flow of tears. We had sniffled our way through the last part of the movie, but when the alien assured the little boy that he would always be there for him, inside his head, we both lost control. Like fools we sat there crying. Then we looked each other in the eye and burst into laughter. We knew. We knew!

Crying seems to come easily to us. It is often the finale of our weekends together, although we both try to keep it in check. Most of our time together is just too damn good to have to end. Assurances that our love remains inside do not make it easier. I rarely leave Chelsea without the sense that something important has gone unsaid, and I always depart awkwardly.

The chronic state of transition brings some concrete hardships as well. I drive a fair distance to pick up and return Chelsea. There are all the usual difficulties with school, parties, lessons. I sometimes find it hard to adapt to the demands of being a father-in-fact after two weeks of furlough, particularly when I'm in the midst of a complex project. Then there are the schedules, revised schedules, and revised, revised schedules. They provide security, probably for all of us, and sometimes inconvenience that requires delicate negotiation.

From this alternating current I derive tremendous power. I live in the present; I've become unashamedly physical and affectionate; I fight and apologize unabashedly; I savor the moment. I treasure the past and try to communicate it more intimately. I have a concern for the future that goes far beyond the ecological abstractions of my education. There is a subtle force generated by Chelsea's unconditional love and trust that lingers when she is gone. It has transformed my life for the better.

A teacher and tour manager, Kip Eastman lives in Watsonville, California, with his wife, Kit. He has a daughter, Chelsea, and two stepsons, Michael and Pat. "I am well into my apprenticeship as a human being. Only my role as a world citizen is more important than my fatherhood."

A Single Parent, in Three Acts and One Scene

Robert Wexelblatt

Separate Tables

She is having macaroni and cheese casserole, peas, and milk in the living room with sit-com reruns on TV—the flickering ghosts of ten-year-old jokes, the clothing and crises of another generation, programming planned especially for the dining pleasure of the latchkey child. I am preparing round steak, a baked potato, and a green salad to be eaten in the kitchen with "All Things Considered" on the radio and the residue of last Sunday's paper. This is the shocking truth: my daughter and I eat dinner apart. I have betrayed that institution so dear to my father, my culture, and my class: the bourgeois dinner table. And why?

As a child, I hated the family dinner table. It was hateful. According to my mother I didn't eat anything during my first dozen years. I established fasting as a family spectator sport, in fact. Everyone watched me not eating my liver, trying futilely to bury the mashed potatoes under a little green cairn of beans. They commented on it, told me I'd have to stay put until it was all gone—and when I asked for the names and addresses of any two of the starving children on the other side of the planet who would be mysteriously comforted if I gained two or three pounds, I was punished for my freshness. And the conversations! the silences! Why dwell on it at all?

Perhaps I was secretly delighted when my daughter decided to follow in my footsteps. I recalled my mother's ultimate curse: some day I should have a child who wouldn't eat—then I'd *know*. Now the day had come, and yet it was no *dies irae*. Because I had quite suddenly become a single parent, I lost my model with tradition and was free to think the problem through. I could repeat with my daughter the scenes of my childhood, the daily dread of the long table and the long stare, or I could strike out on my own. I was a child of the sixties; I chose the latter. For example, why should eating and talking be indissolubly joined—as if the mouth can't get enough exercise doing only one or the other?

And so I instituted my first single-parental reform: we would eat apart and, if we felt like it, different food and at different times too. Why pretend? If the American family was going to be fragmented, why cling to customs forged before the detonation? If she doesn't like eating, why make it worse?

The tray is returned to the kitchen. The macaroni and cheese is almost gone; there are no more peas left than there were burghers of Calais; the milk is a chalky memory on the sides of the glass. My steak is sizzling on the Teflon.

Preface to Immerson

Nature abhors vacuums and doesn't leap, so new rituals evolve to fill up the space left by discarded ones. At seven o'clock every night began the joyous Hour of the Bath. Actually, I had been bathing my daughter each evening since her infancy—I have the embarrassing snapshots to prove it. But the procedure expanded by accretion once we were left alone. This bathing was a special business, too good to be vulgarized with that hopeful phrase of self-serving sophistry—"quality time."

It began simply enough as a direct and utilitarian procedure. We would go upstairs; I would fill the tub, undress the kid, scrub her, dry her off, put her to bed, and we'd talk a bit through it all. Little by little, however, each of these movements became more baroque, playful, dancelike, virtuosic. For example, going upstairs was transformed from a simple march up the risers into a game of hide-and-seek ending in the hilarious, inevitable capture of the daughter, a slinging of the little body over the right shoulder like a twenty-pound bag of spuds accompanied by a recital of an ancient street cry ("Any old rags, any old bones"), and a perilous rush up the stairs. The taps were turned on to run slowly (a necessity, given our petulant hot-water system) while games were made of undressing: strip-tag, one-armed wrestling, blindman's buff, continuous tickling. Later still, the games became numerous ends-in-themselves: Beat-the-Clock, rolled-sock basketball, daffy quizzes, self-evident riddles ("In what state is the University of South Carolina located?"), cycles of stories about the notorious Bad Peter.

We were determinedly silly and this frivolity made a bond, or bounced high upon an elastic bond already there. The both of us let loose like a couple of dada theoreticians. There were no rules except those private ones we improvised out of a devout lack of earnestness. In retrospect, I suppose there must have been a good deal of seriousness underlying all our fooling. It was a ritual, after all—not empty or inherited, but one of our own devising. My daughter and I were fearfully faithful to it, too. Once, for instance, I invited a dignified middle-aged couple to dinner. As we were sipping coffee in the living room and discussing something like the national debt, my daughter quietly informed us all that it was seven o'clock. We excused ourselves at once and left the guests alone for about forty-five minutes. It never occurred to me to do otherwise. Two weeks later, my friend (whose children were grown and gone) remarked that my behavior represented a level of rudeness quite unexampled in his wide experience. Flushing at the truth of his accusation, I agreed and apologized—more playmate than adult, more father than host. I was shaken. I was amused.

Aquatic Anarchy

Water is a magical substance, the proof being that it expands when it freezes. Water is equally magical in its tepid liquid state, the proof being the liberated and unpredictable behavior of people surrounded by it. My daughter's actual bath was an occasion that supported a wide variety of activities: reflection on the day's absurdities and tribulations, Platonic dialogue, shrieking, power-dousing (fill bucket, take to top of closed shower curtain, pour down on unsuspecting child), shooting water pistols and rubber bands, storytelling. The proceedings took a quantum leap the day we acquired a portable tape recorder, our most advanced bath toy of all. We still have some tapes dating from my daughter's seventh and eighth years. They are busy with the traces and spores of our ancient fun.

But all this is memoir, partial truth, nostalgia. I have not mentioned that there were many times when I resented such routines, felt my daughter to be jailer as much as joy, suffered guilt for spending insufficient time with her, for emptying uneaten food into the garbage, for escaping to my desk in the basement, for cutting short bedside readings from *The Wind in the Willows* or *The House at Pooh Corner*, for (and this was a terror) leaving her alone when she had a cold or the flu. Nor have I examined the chronic stomach problems which I helplessly knew to be the outward manifestation of her inward turmoil over her mother's departure, nor my worries over the very adhesiveness of our intimacy. As I say, the models were gone or of small applicability. My fatherhood was, in a sense, as improvised as our bath-time hi-jinks. My college course in child psychology had convinced me that whatever one did was—according to one theory or another—bound to create trauma or neurosis. Reflecting on the mutual exclusion of the experts, I ignored their books, reasoning that my daughter was at least entitled to the neurosis fate had provided for her. What father can guess how he might appear on a psychiatrist's couch thirty years down the line? The only parent of an only child—what is there except to muddle through?

An example: One afternoon in late March I came in to find my daughter on the living room rug drawing furiously with marking pens. She was a swell abstract expressionist up till the age of three, whereupon she was made into a fifth-rate realist. She was pretty clearly in something less than high spirits. We kissed a low-key hello: "Lo, sweetheart." "Hi, Daddy."

I dropped my briefcase on the club chair and headed for the cellarway to hang up my coat.

"I got a B on my report for Alcohol Ed," she said bitterly as I was on the way out of the living room.

"Congratulations," I shouted distractedly, trying to recall what sort of potential supper I had taken out of the freezer that morning.

" 'Congratulations?' For a lousy crummy B?" she cried, outraged by my low academic standards.

I came back as far as the doorway. "Gee, who wants a kid whose best subject is Alcohol Education? Are you planning to become a bartender or a wino or something?"

"Jenny *Bron*stein got an A," she mumbled loudly.

I joined her on the floor. "So what?"

My daughter gave me one of her you-just-don't-understand looks. "Jenny Bronstein *always* gets an A."

There was dinner to make, work to do; I tried to concentrate. "Well, it *could* be that Jenny deserved it."

She raised her head from her design—a crude thing of hexagons and triangles, closely worked; she had discovered cubism, it seemed. She started to answer, but I pressed on pompously, with a professorially raised finger. " 'The easiest and noblest way is not to be disabling others, but to be improving yourself.' That's how Socrates put it." I had told my daughter all about Socrates by then, but she was less than enthralled.

"Jenny Bronstein *al*ways gets A's because she cuts out so many *dumb* pictures and she writes in these *enorm*ous letters. All her reports are twice as long as everyone else's—in *pages*," said my sweet daughter with surprising contemptuousness and acerbity. "Her parents are so rich they bought her a computer for Christmas, and they've got *three* encyclopedias." She was actually commencing to whine.

"And Mrs. Block doesn't *read* all these reports, I take it? She only looks at the pictures and counts the pages?" It occurred to me that I was on perilous turf: it might well be true of Mrs. Block. But that was scarcely the point.

"Mrs. Block's Not Fair," she announced apodictically. There was no doubt this was intended as a final judgment. "*Also* I got hit in the head with a volleyball in gym. Pat just *whipped* it at me. I've still got a headache. And Paula called me skinny."

Ah ha, I thought, the heart of the matter at last.

"Paula's fat," I ventured, getting up to provide myself with the Scotch I felt I was earning.

"Paula wears these Jordache jeans every day. She has seven pairs of them. She told me, the show-off. Besides, she isn't *that* fat. It's just the way those jeans fit."

"What do you care? It's a wonder that girl can even walk," I shouted in from the sink and over the gracious sound of the tap water dribbling into the whiskey. "Why, I've heard that Paula can only play hide-and-seek in the Himalayas."

"Oh, Daddy, stop it, will you! You always make a joke. I *am* skinny!"

"Skinny? Skinny? By no means." I was on the way back in now, Scotch in hand. "Come here." I sat in the club chair by the window and pulled her

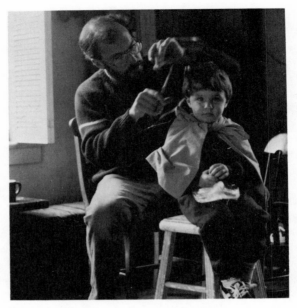

© *Claudia Majetich*

underweight, reluctant self onto my lap. I looked her up and down. "You are *not* skinny."

"Then what am I—*emaciated?*" The kid always had a good vocabulary.

"On the contrary, darling. You're just right. You are," I hesitated dramatically, considering: "you are . . . imperially slim!"

"Imperially slim?" she repeated the phrase, as theatrically unconvinced by E. A. Robinson as she had been by Socrates. That a depressed child is proof against all the blandishments of Western civilization is obvious, but I saw no harm in trying. It was all muddling anyway.

"Look, sweetheart, I know that fifth grade is sheer hell, but we've all got to go through it. There's just no other path to sixth grade."

Fifth grade, fatherhood.

"Oh, Daddy!" she cried and punched me affably in the stomach.

> Robert Wexelblatt, a professor of humanities at Boston University, is the father of a fifteen-year-old daughter, Ann, whom he has been responsible for raising "on his own" for the past eight years.

Chapter Twelve
Stepfathers

Stepping In

Jacques Leslie

The culture offers no models. From the Brothers Grimm to "Fanny and Alexander," we stepfathers are presented as pernicious, competing with our stepchildren for their mother's attention or preoccupied with our natural children at the expense of our acquired ones. In the popular imagination, we're considered something between fathers and uncles, deprived of the right presumably consigned only by genetics to command and instruct, yet looked on with hope for at least a measure of emotional and financial support. Our stepchildren fear we're usurping the role of their original fathers; our wives worry that, instead of spending time with us, they should be with their children. And even if we protest that we didn't seek the role of stepfather—after all, we formed stepfamilies presumably because we fell in love with our wives, not their children—we are inevitably recipients of what my wife called, when we first began discussing marriage, a "package deal."

In my package came not only Leslie, my wife (that's right, she's Leslie Leslie), but Tristan, 9 years old when I met him, and Karin, known familiarly to us as Kadie, then 6. When I met Leslie, she was six months removed from a trauma-filled marriage and still shellshocked. So, more subtly, were Tristan and Kadie. At first, I was the intruder who threatened the frightened clench the three of them forged in the wake of their separation from husband and father. Sometimes I resented the power the three of them had over one another. Except when the children were visiting their father (periods for which I was grateful but which seemed far too short), I was unable to spend as much time alone with Leslie as I wished. I tried exacting promises from her about how much time we'd have alone. But while Leslie was willing to make such promises, keeping them was another matter: Inevitably she had to attend to Tristan's bloody nose or Kadie's nightmare, or take them to school or a friend's house or the dentist or shopping.

And so, after a while, did I. Despite myself, I became an occasional car-pool driver and general errand runner. To be a part of Leslie's life, I gradually came to accept, was to be a part of her children's. It's a testament to the attraction I felt toward her, in fact, that Tristan and Kadie's presence did not deter me from wooing her. The fact that Leslie eventually acknowledged that she valued *our* relationship as much as her relationship with Tristan and Kadie was a crucial mitigating factor.

Yet it would be misleading to imply that for me the children were simply a negative, an impediment to intimacy with Leslie. For one thing, I believe it was partially *through* Tristan and Kadie that I endeared myself to Leslie. For if Leslie had a defect as a mother, it was in the application of discipline: She was not consistent. What I offered, what all stepfathers potentially can offer, was a measure of detachment: Unburdened by the panoply of emotions that children typically inspire in their parents, I could step in when, for one example, I felt Leslie's perceptions of her children were distorted by the anger she still felt toward her ex-husband or when, for another example, she was contradicting an earlier edict she'd issued to them. Often I found myself trying to explain her own children, particularly Tristan, to her. I drew upon the knowledge I'd gained growing up as *my* mother's son. I'd never planned on playing such a role, and still do not understand why it came easily to me. I believe, however, that my suggestions had a calming influence on all three of them. I think they appreciated me for that.

Furthermore, for all of my resentment toward Tristan and Kadie, I was both charmed by them and intrigued by the notion of having a family, an instant family at that. It seemed to me that I'd grown up almost without a family: Nearly six years younger than my only sibling, I was virtually an only child, and my parents kept their distance from our relatives. In my 20's, I was a journalist stationed overseas, so preoccupied with public issues that I hardly noticed I lacked a private life. My liaison with Leslie began soon after I realized the value of the sort of family life I'd never had. To accept my "package deal" meant taking a halting step toward what to me was the fearful but exciting prospect of a family union. When Leslie and I exchanged marriage vows, Tristan and Kadie stood beside us, the four of us in a row holding hands.

Since that moment almost four years ago, we've unquestionably grown closer. I've hugged the kids and yelled at them, sometimes in response to their need, sometimes in response to my own. I've helped them with their homework and I've even shown them my old stomping ground, Asia, where the four of us went trekking in Nepal a year ago. Slowly I came to understand that Tristan, Kadie and I hadn't quite been thrown together by accident: I cared for these children and had willfully involved myself in their fates. I believe that's a definition of love.

Yet even after marriage, our path was anything but smooth. Newlyweds typically enjoy a tranquil period that lasts until the arrival of their first child, but whatever extended time Leslie and I had together required deciding delicate logistical and financial questions involving the children's generally uncommunicative father, who lived 3,000 miles away. If, for example, we wanted a vacation during the last two weeks of June, would the children's father take them then? Did the children want to see *him* then? Did he expect to meet them at an airport a six-hour drive from his house, or would he pay part of the expense for an additional flight to the small airport near his home? Solving these dilemmas often led to angry exchanges over the phone between Leslie and her ex-husband: The emotions these confrontations evoked in Leslie inevitably touched Tristan, Kadie and me, and, I believe, in a mysterious way drew the four of us together.

As time went on, Tristan and Kadie's desire to make these visits decreased, and my role consequently grew. Sometimes I chafed against the parental responsibilities I'd taken on. Even terminology struck me as treacherous: Long after Tristan and Kadie began introducing me to their friends as "Dad," I hesitated to call them my "son" and "daughter." Could I be misrepresenting them? It's indicative of my confusion that at one point I informed Tristan that he shouldn't think of me as a father, but as a "friend." "Fine," said Tristan, angry and hurt. "I won't kiss you good-night anymore." In fact, a friend wasn't all I wanted to be: I wanted, for example, to give Tristan and Kadie guidance, and so took seriously my role as authority figure. Yet I worried that Tristan or Kadie could devastate me by saying one sentence: "I don't have to do what you want—you're not my father." They've been angry with me often enough, but they've never said that. Only gradually have I understood that a father is what they want me to be. A father is what I've become.

Jacques Leslie is writing a book about his experiences as a war correspondent in Vietnam.

Reconstituted Family: An Interview

Sam Rosenfarb

FATHERS' BOOK: How long have you been separated and divorced?

SAM ROSENFARB: My first wife and I separated in February of 1979, and we were divorced in November 1980 after almost ten years of marriage. We had three sons—one adopted, two natural born—ranging in age from five to nine years old.

FB: How would you describe your relationship with your sons before you were divorced?

SR: We were very close. I used to spend a lot of time with them on the weekends, but during the week I hardly saw them at all; I was always working late. By the time I got home, they were ready for bed. And in the morning, they left for school before I left for work.

FB: Was there a big change in your relationship with them once you were separated?

SR: I wasn't separated for that long a time before I met Marilyn, who would become my second wife. Once I met her, my life became more structured. I would see Marilyn almost every day; I would see my kids every weekend. I experimented with seeing them every other weekend, for two days, for some period of time, and then both days every weekend for some period of time. During the week I would see one of the children.

FB: Which one?

SR: I would alternate so that every week I would see a different child.

FB: Is seeing them that way very different from full-time fathering?

SR: Oh, yes. It's all fun and games when I see them. They don't come to me when they're sick; they don't have to do their homework; they don't have to make their beds; they don't have to mow the lawn. They don't have the responsibilities with me that they do at their home, or that they had before I was separated.

My relationship with my stepson, Mark, is similar to the relationship I had with my kids before I was separated. He lives with Marilyn and me, so he has daily chores that are his responsibility. With the three noncustodial children, there is no reason for me to impose responsibilities: their mother has to do that. She makes sure that they do well in school, and that they eat, sleep, and dress correctly. When I see my kids on the weekends, all my effort goes into planning how we are going to have fun. Of course, there's a negative aspect to all this fun and games: I do not get to take nearly as much a part in their growing up, in molding their values. I don't help with their schoolwork as I would if I were a custodial parent, so I don't work with them on learning the things in life that must be learned.

FB: Do you miss that?

SR: Well, it wasn't much fun, and taking a part in their play activities really is. I miss——I don't know that I miss——I feel guilty that I don't, but I don't miss living with them. Living with only one child, my stepson, is a lot easier than it was with three kids. And Mark is almost nine. When I was living with Sharon, we had a two-year-old and two six-year-olds. Imagine how demanding that was. It really is more fun now. The kids are very anxious to see me on the weekends. It builds up my ego. I'm thrilled. I love it!

FB: Do you have any regrets about your new relationship with your children?

SR: When I first separated from Sharon, my greatest loss was that of a family. And my greatest fear was that being divorced meant no longer having a family. Now that I'm remarried, I see that it is not true: I have my family. In fact, I have my old family and I have a new family. I lost a wife, but I had chosen to do that. I felt like I had lost my family, until I remarried.

FB: Can you picture your life if you had not remarried?

SR: I wasn't comfortable with being a single parent. I didn't like making plans to see the kids by myself. In fact, when I used to see them—before I met Marilyn—I would ask friends to be with me and my kids.

FB: Why was that?

SR: I felt "artificial." It was unreal, make-believe. I had a wife and three children, so why was I spending so much time, suddenly, with the three children alone? It didn't seem right. From the time I was separated until the time I remarried, I did not feel a sense of permanence. I knew I would remarry even before I met Marilyn, because I liked that life-style. I didn't like being alone—being a single parent or being a single person. I didn't like not sharing my life with someone.

FB: How old were you when you first married?

SR: I was twenty years old, so I've been married my whole adult life. When I was single, I felt it was temporary. I never even bought any furniture.

FB: What happened when the kids came to stay over on weekends, without furniture?

SR: I bought a king-sized bed, and they slept with me. All four of us slept together. It wasn't until I met Marilyn that they had to go from my bed to another one.

FB: What happened the first time they had to change beds?

SR: It was interesting. Marilyn and I didn't like the idea of sleeping together while the children were there. So the first time all of us spent the night together, I slept with my kids and she slept with Mark. But the children didn't like it at all! They wanted to sleep with Mark, and they wanted me to sleep with Marilyn. Their frame of reference seemed to be: "This is your girlfriend, and you should sleep with her. You always used to sleep with mommy. You never slept with us before, and now that you have a new girlfriend, you should sleep with her." It took us about two months before we decided that they were, of course, right!

FB: Do you find that having the kids around takes a toll on your new marriage?

SR: Yes, it takes away from our "alone" time, but so does going to work and eating.

FB: So you don't resent the children in that way?

FB: No, not at all: children are part of my life. Before I met Marilyn, I was taking care of three kids on the weekends, and she had to understand that I meant to continue to do so. She had to make time available for us to see my three boys.

I think that it was harder for Marilyn, especially when we were first married, to adjust to the planning involved in seeing three children. She didn't want that responsibility. Prior to getting remarried, it was all my responsibility; since we've been married, it has become a joint responsibility. Well, I *forced* it to become a joint responsibility. I didn't like that Mark was her responsibility, and my kids were my responsibility. I wasn't comfortable with that, with our lives having such separate components. So now all of our responsibilities are joint ones, and it's a lot easier.

FB: How did you work that out?

SR: I believe in forcing shared responsibilities. And I do mean force. It's a conscious and difficult decision to share that responsibility. And it doesn't come naturally. It's natural *not* to share it. It was natural for me to leave Mark's upbringing to Marilyn. It was a careful decision that Marilyn and I made to share the full responsibilities of each other's children.

FB: Have there been any problems about sharing that kind of awesome responsibility?

SR: A few months before I remarried, it suddenly became clear to us why we were having a difficult time, why there was friction, why hostility was developing among my children, Marilyn, her son, and myself. The basis of the tension was the nonsharing of responsibility. And once we figured out what the problem was, then we found the solution: to be responsible for each other and for each other's children. For example, Marilyn often calls Sharon to make arrangements about taking the children for the weekend. She even picks them up and delivers them back to Sharon's house if it's easier for her to do so than it is for me. So it's now *our* responsibility to pick up my children, to make sure that they have a good time, and then to drop them off back home.

FB: How have the children responded to this change?

SR: Before all this, they considered Marilyn to be my wife. They respected and liked her. But now Marilyn is as much a noncustodial parent as I am. They'll ask her if they can have another piece of candy, whereas before they always asked *me* if they could have another piece of candy. Before, they would ask me where they were going on any given weekend. Now they ask Marilyn. And that change made a big difference in my new marriage and in the kids' relationships with me and with Marilyn.

FB: Were your children angry at you when you divorced?

SR: I didn't feel that they were angry with me or with Sharon. They were confused, unhappy, and didn't like the fact that we were divorced. But I don't think they were angry with us. Luckily, we had a very amicable divorce and separation.

FB: Did they have problems in school?

SR: They weren't more difficult in school or at home. However, it was more difficult for my ex-wife to manage them without my help.

FB: Did you ever talk to them about your feelings toward Sharon?

SR: I don't believe that parents should force children to take sides. My ex-wife and I discussed the situation and decided—before I left—that we wouldn't do that. It is all right for the children to like both of us, even though we do not like each other. I wouldn't have left the house until this kind of issue was resolved.

FB: How did your children and Marilyn's son get along in the beginning?

SR: They didn't. And I didn't expect them to get along. Oh, of course when they first met they got on beautifully: they were new friends, and children like new kids their own age. But after a while they didn't like each other. My children didn't want me to pay attention to Mark or to his mother. They didn't want to give up any of their time with me.

FB: What did they say about your relationship with Marilyn?

SR: My children would ask, "Why do you want to see Marilyn instead of us?"

FB: How would you respond?

SR: Marilyn and I had anticipated just such a question and had discussed it before they brought it up! I sat them down, and said, "Marilyn is my lover, and you are my children. I'll *always* love you as my children, but you have to accept my relationship with a woman." And I explained to them that I want to be with Marilyn all the time, and that I don't want to be with them all of the time. They're my kids, and although I love them as children, I don't want to spend all my time with them. I want to be with adults and do adult things. And one of those adult things is to spend time with my lover!

They accepted that. Once I made it clear to them—that I wasn't moving from that stand—they liked the idea that I love Marilyn and that I want to be with her and that I want to spend time with her. Of course, they tested me and my position. Once they saw that my position was definitely not going to change, they were fine.

FB: What about you? Did you ever doubt your position and feel guilty?

SR: No. Well, I felt guilty until I was clear in my own mind that I was doing the right thing. Marilyn helped me see that I was not neglecting my children, that I wanted to see her rather than my kids, and that it had to be right for me since I really wanted it. And once *I* felt that it was right, it was easy for me to convince the kids that it was right. In the same way, I was able to convince the kids that they had to get along with each other. We forced them to get along.

FB: How?

SR: By telling them that they had no choice. I explained that they were going to spend a great deal of time with each other from now on so that they had just better get along. And they do.

FB: What kinds of problems did the boys have before you convinced them to get along?

SR: What my sons wanted from Mark was for him to be like them, from day one. And, of course, he wasn't. For openers, he never had siblings and he didn't know how to share. He resented having to share toys, his room, his space. He felt invaded.

FB: His mother, his stability, all were taken away.

SR: Yes, it was very hard for Mark; it was tough for my kids, too, but it was worse for Mark. I would talk to him about tattling, sharing, and rivalry. Now my boys can't wait until it's their turn to be alone with us so that they can spend time with Mark!

FB: So in what other ways did your relationship with Marilyn affect them?

SR: They used to ask me whether I loved Marilyn more than I loved them. I told them that I loved them differently. Not more or less, but differently. I talked to them about the different loves and how we only have one word but each is a different feeling. It's wrong that we only have one word. They understood.

FB: Did any of them ever seem jealous of your love for the other kids?

SR: They often asked me who of the three I loved the most. I would reply that I loved each one differently. But alone I would tell each one that I loved him the most. I explained it by saying, "My love for you is different than my love for your brothers, and my love for you is the most love I have."

FB: Do you also tell Mark that you love him as much as you love your own sons?

SR: I tell him that my love for him is different, but I love him the most. I don't think that he perceives my loving my children more than my loving him.

FB: Do you all feel like a family now?

SR: Yes. Before I remarried, on the weekends, I was a Sunday Father and we always went somewhere—a museum, a zoo, somewhere. Now, most of the time we just hang around. I make breakfast for everyone; it's nice. I have Mark living with us, and I like that. I'm happy that my new wife has a son. I'm happy having kids in the house again.

FB: You seem content.

SR: I like having a family again. I feel like I have what I used to have, only now it's much better because I'm happy: happy with my new wife, and happy with all my children. I have more of a family life, too. What more can you ask for?

> Sam Rosenfarb and his wife, Marilyn, live in Livingston, New Jersey. His stepson, Mark, lives with them, while his three sons live with his first wife. "I care about my responsibilities as a father, and I'm willing to, and do, share my life and myself with my children."

On Being a Stepfather

Gerry Clow

The stereotyped image of a stepfather is that of a cold, remote disciplinarian, untempered by the love and understanding of the natural father.

I have two natural children, ages three and five, and a stepson, who is thirteen. I have known him since he was five. In fact, my introduction to him was baking a cake for his fifth birthday. I had never baked a cake before and it turned out terribly—overbeaten—yet it had a decent frosting. Maybe the cake was an omen, a metaphor for the mixed feelings to follow.

Parenting comes naturally to me, as I'm the type of guy who enjoys playing a domestic role. I like to cook, and when I lived with a group of other men, I tended to start up the kitchen details. Later, I lived with an older couple and took care of their children. I've also been a teacher, sports instructor, Big Brother, and camp counselor. But the challenge of dealing with a stepson, in comparison to dealing with natural children, has been a very difficult one for me.

Matthew's father and mother divorced when he was four. He's a tow-headed boy, who in those early years wore thick glasses for his farsightedness, which magnified his eyes and made him look vulnerable and irresistible.

His father left the area we were living in shortly after I moved in with Matthew and his mother. The father went to live far away, and eventually Matthew's older brother went to live with his father permanently.

For the first five years, my relationship with Matthew was one of a "big brother," someone who clearly loved his mother and was generally fun to have around. There was no particular pressure on either of us to be something that we were not.

Things became more complicated when my wife and I had our first child. Matthew was then eight and at first enjoyed having another kid around the house. Matthew had gone through the sadness of losing his brother to his natural father, and having another young person in the house made us more of a family.

Then it dawned on me that my new son would have my last name, but Matthew would retain his natural father's name. For all ostensible purposes, I was Matthew's real father: I provided for him, tucked him into bed at night, nurtured him, and was considered his father by his friends. What would happen when my new son realized Matthew had a different last name, a different father? It would be easier if his natural father played a role—supported him, saw him frequently—but he did not.

The other lurking anxiety was losing Matthew to his natural father. We had lost his older brother; would the same thing happen with Matthew?

I asked his natural father for his permission to adopt Matthew. He agreed, on the condition that he be able to see Matthew for at least one month each year. The courts went to work, and one day before Matt's eleventh birthday, a kindly judge looked down at us from a bench and announced, "Family unity is a beautiful thing." The adoption was completed. Matthew was now my son.

But I never was able to achieve the bonding that occurs between natural parents and their child. I was able to be with my wife at the births of both of our children, and those memories are still clear to me today. I was proud of having a son and a daughter, and that pride was later reinforced by all the snuggling and smooching that continues today with my two young children. They are my "bunnies," and nothing thrills me more than passing by their rooms and seeing them asleep in their beds. Those feelings, however, are missing in my relationship with Matt.

Another issue as a stepfather is my age. I'm thirty-three and just beginning to get into my work. I try to get Matthew involved with me in my work on our house and summer cabin, but he's interested only to a point. I try consciously to take a trip now and then with him alone, and the few times we have attempted this, we have had fun together. But a trip requires planning and discipline and taking time off from other things. For me, this does not come easily. The love for Matt is there, but my life-style is out of sync with my ability to act on that love. In comparison, it is easy to work on our house and cabin with the little ones around; they take afternoon naps and seeing me work is natural to them. By the time they are older, these home improvements will be completed; and we'll have more free time together. I wish for Matt's sake that I had this work behind me. But I don't.

My father-in-law pointed out an important parenting lesson when he explained that with his most difficult child, he ended up making his peace this way: "She gave in one-quarter; I gave in three-quarters." I think the same maxim may apply between myself and my stepson. If I'm to continue to regain the early closeness we once felt, I'll have to adjust more to him than him to me. I get cross with him at times because I'm expecting him to adapt to my habits and pace, but I remember being thirteen, and you don't give up any part of yourself at that age.

I realize that at the deepest level Matthew will always be a stepson, but in all other ways and at all other levels, he will be my son. He will always have the comfort of knowing that he is a full member of our family, and at the same time he'll have the opportunity to know his natural father and his grandparents on that side of the extended family.

Matthew has provided me with some valuable lessons in life. I hope to continue to make the time to be with him, for as long as he lives with us.

> Gerry Clow is a publisher in Santa Fe, New Mexico. He and his wife, Barbara, have two children. His wife also has two sons from a previous marriage, one of whom Gerry adopted.

POSITIVE IMAGES, © *Jerry Howard*

Chapter Thirteen
Adolescent Fathers/ Fathers of Adolescents

Teenage Fathers

"People would say to me, when you're in your twenties you'll have graduated from high school and will marry and have children. So, I'm seventeen now and am going to have a child and get married. Maybe I have a chance to experience some of the joys of what I've helped to create a few years earlier than I expected."

Seventeen-year-old father.

"You know, it's interesting the way people talk about teenage fathers as irresponsible; you get funny looks sometimes. It's strange, a lot of people treat you like a kid, that is, except the bill collectors."

Eighteen-year-old father

Personal Perspectives
An Interview with Two Teenage Fathers

James S. Kahn

James S. Kahn: *Describe your relationships with the teen mothers prior to their pregnancies and tell how this changed after finding out that you and your girlfriends were pregnant.*

Elwood Chick Crowell: My relationship with my partner was very strong. We had been dating for over a year before finding out she was pregnant and were more like best friends rather than boyfriend-girlfriend. While I thought my partner might get pregnant, I also thought it only happened to *other* guys and didn't realize the responsibility I would be forced to accept if it did.

When we found out my girlfriend was pregnant I was emotionally very scared and upset. At first I wanted to run but was scared and couldn't leave my new family behind. I loved them very much. I wasn't sure what my parents would say and how they would react. I found myself always looking for a fight. I was depressed because I realized that I would have to grow up and take responsibility for my actions. Although I wanted to party with my friends and wanted to be free, I realized that I desired a good life for my upcoming family and would be forced to make many sacrifices.

Behaviorally, I took responsibility by getting a full-time job and graduating from high school. I refinished the basement of my parents' house so we could live down there after the baby was born.

Darren Holt: We also had a close relationship, but we had our share of problems. Although my partner and I had both wanted to have a child eventually, we weren't sure if this was the right time or not. When we found out she was pregnant we had mixed emotions. We talked about running away so we could be together but realized this would be one of the stupidest things we could do.

JSK: *How did your family and friends react to the news of the pregnancy?*

Darren: After getting over the initial shock, my parents were understanding. Maybe because they had been through this before with an older sister. My wife's parents were more shocked but gradually accepted the pregnancy. I did lose a few friends, and some of my teachers reacted negatively.

Chick: Well, telling my parents about the pregnancy was probably the hardest thing I'll ever do. I knew they would be disappointed in me, and they were. But after the initial shock wore off, my parents realized that I was going to take fatherhood seriously and they started to treat me like an adult.

Friends at school avoided me in the halls and would have nothing to do with me. But a few teachers were concerned and, after recognizing that I was settling down, treated me as an adult. I appreciated that. Of course, I still had to work for my grades.

JSK: *What sort of relationship and pregnancy-related decisions did you make?*

Chick: One of the first things we did was contact the Teen Mother and Child Program. If we had a question or needed help, the program was there for us. We talked about getting married but decided to wait until we graduated or were in college.

Darren: We decided to get married and raise our child together. I tried continuing high school but it didn't work out, so I dropped out and tried to find a job. There was nothing that paid decently. I decided to settle for a job paying minimum wage and to finish my education through an alternative high school program. After I graduate, I hope to go to college. In fact, someday I'd like to become a high school counselor to help teens who get pregnant.

JSK: *Please describe what the pregnancy and childbirth experiences have been like for you.*

Darren: The pregnancy and birth were hard for me. A lot of decisions had to be made. I was also jealous of all the attention my partner was getting and felt a little left out. Seeing my son born, however, was one of the most memorable experiences of my life.

Chick: The pregnancy was a great experience for me. Labor lasted thirty-two hours and the baby had to be delivered cesarean. I got to watch it all while holding my girlfriend's hand. I just about cried when I finally saw that I had a son. I was the third person to hold my son. That morning was the greatest day of my life. I was the proudest person in the world. I went back to high school that morning with my head up high and never looked down again. I had a beautiful son and a wonderful family.

JSK: *What are some of the joys and sorrows that you've experienced as adolescent fathers?*

Chick: The best thing that has happened to me is seeing that my son looks like me. I have created a son out of love and you can tell he's mine. I love to watch him laugh and play. I have enjoyed watching my son change from a screaming newborn into a playful, beautiful little boy. People say that teenage marriages don't last. We have a chance to prove them wrong, and I hope we will.

The greatest sorrow I've experienced was the realization that my desire to pursue college football would not be fulfilled. I've had to settle down and concentrate on a family and not on sports. I've had to alter my career plans because my son comes first.

Darren: One of the greatest joys for me was realizing that here I was, more or less just a kid, and I had a kid myself! I had accomplished one of the most fulfilling aspects of life; I had created a family. What makes me sad right now is that since my wife and I have separated, I'm unable to live with and spend as much time as I'd like with my son.

JSK: *Finally, is there a message you would like to relate to your family, friends, and society as a whole about being an adolescent father?*

Darren: I think society as a whole should not be so quick to judge people like myself. Whether or not people believe it, there are a lot of teen fathers in this country—married and unmarried—who are dedicated to their children and want to be good fathers. Adolescent fathers are people, too.

Chick: I would like to tell other adolescent males to be careful and take responsibility for contraception. I probably wouldn't have become a father at this age if I had a chance to do it all over again. If you do find yourself in this situation, remember that there is help available. And think about your wife or girlfriend; they are going through a lot and deserve to be treated with love and respect. I think it's important to be an active partner in the pregnancy and in raising your child.

One final message: Teenagers like us need help and should not be treated as outcasts. As Darren said, we may be young fathers, but we're people, too.

> James S. Kahn is a psychologist who interviewed Chick Crowell and Darren Holt, two adolescent fathers with whom he worked in the Teen Mother and Child Program, sponsored by the University of Utah Health Sciences Center. Both of the fathers were eighteen years old at the time of the interview. One is married and the other is separated from his wife.

Population Exchanges

Richard J. Israel

Irma Bombeck has written about her six children, the three terrible ones who live with her and the three gracious, helpful, and pleasant ones who visit her friends and family. The message is simple: good children are somebody else's children or your children at someone else's home. My corollary is that once children are about six years old, good parents are someone else's parents. But is there any way to deliberately take advantage of these rules in ways that might provide relief for both parents and children?

Three families we know went on a cross-country vacation trip in vans and swapped all their teenage children. The necessary discipline and support were provided by the "adoptive" parents. Parents were good friends to their own children, but refrained from saying anything that might be suspected of being good for their character. No "Don't swallow your food whole" or "Wash your hands and face" or "How can you go out dressed like that?" They all reported that it was a wonderful, tension-free vacation. My wife and I have just lived through a similar population exchange, with equally wonderful results.

We think Jonah has wonderful parents, but Jonah couldn't endure staying with them for another moment. When his grandmother gave him a hundred-dollar bill for a high school graduation present, he took off the next day. Adventure and self-discovery were his goals, whether it was being a lobster fisherman in Maine or a farmhand in the Midwest. But he ended up at our house, 125 miles from his home.

We had not seen Jonah for a number of years. Though he drove his parents crazy, we found him interesting and pleasant. He stayed with us about a week. During that time we tried to get him the names of some potential job leads, outfit him for the road, and persuade him that a pencil and a raincoat might be useful pieces of equipment for a summer's adventure. Then we pointed him off in what we hoped would be the right direction.

I had stayed in touch with our friends, his parents, correctly assuming that Jonah would never consider letting them know what had happened to him or where he was. In the course of one of our phone conversations with his father, I mused out loud about what splendid people we were from his son's point of view, while his peer, our own son and youngest child, had just announced that he saw no reason to have dinner with us anymore. This was because he had nothing to say to us and found it very difficult to spend time in our presence. Half in jest, half in earnest, I asked Jonah's father if he might have a summer job for our terrible teenager. He did. Our kid shipped out eagerly the next morning, no questions asked.

Soon the reports began coming back to us about our charming, polite son, who helped with the dinner and who trimmed the bushes without being asked. (He had given no prior indication that he could even identify a bush, let alone a bush trimmer.) Our kid, the clam, regaled them each evening with stories of his adventures of the day. It was hard to imagine that this was our surly son and that such a miraculous transformation could take place so quickly.

The summer is over now and both boys have returned home older and wiser than when they went away. Now that a little time has passed, we have begun to think about the significance of what happened.

Real parents have an impossible and contradictory set of tasks: to provide steady, unconditional love and, at the same time, to convey standards and expectations. It is not easy to provide both when children are small, but it can be done. You may be annoyed at your little kid who just spilled lemonade on the rug but can probably manage a squeeze and a hug three minutes later.

But when they are our size or bigger, and they challenge and test us at every moment, when they always know where we are most vulnerable, then the system simply gets overloaded and doesn't work. It is very hard to give a hug to a kid who has just totaled the family car, come home at dawn when you thought he'd be back at nine the previous night, or who has been on the telephone for the last three years—except for the times she was sitting in front of the television set. As parents of adolescents, we find it amazing, not that there is so much child abuse in the world, but that there is so little.

Though it took a different form every time it happened, each of our four children moved in with a different family at some critical and particularly difficult point in adolescence. The time they spent with the other families was brief, but very significant.

Our older daughter spent most of one summer taking care of a dying neighbor, a professor of anthropology. Several years after the woman died, our daughter elected to get her B.A. in anthropology and wrote her senior thesis on her friend's anthropological work. Our second child was close to a family that is in the art business. He never spent any prolonged time there, but there were a lot of overnights. He is now majoring in art history at college. Our third, another girl, moved in with a family a few miles away and worked as a nanny to their children for half a year. She came back to tell us that we had indeed done some things right in raising her and her siblings. If I had to guess,

I would predict that she will probably end up in some field connected with the education of children. Since his return from the summer, our youngest has been musing about whether he might like to be a doctor, like Jonah's father, and now he talks to us at the dinner table, sometimes.

In every case, the adults in the families selected were people we knew of our age and with values very much like our own. The element of escape, of running away from us, was very strong, but the places they chose to run to were not radically different environments from their own.

When our first child left home, we were distressed and ashamed. Were we really so terrible that she had to run away? Couldn't she have stayed with a favorite aunt or uncle for a week or so, the way we did? After all, that was family. And then we realized that we didn't have any aunts and uncles who lived nearby. They had found and used an appropriate substitute in a situation in which an extended family or a formalized *wanderyahr* was not available.

In order for a child to work out one of the essential tasks of adolescence, becoming his or her own person, or what is called in the language of the trade, differentiation, an adult who is not that child's parent can be a big help. Parents are responsible for providing a child with love and support, but also discipline. Healthy adolescents may know at some level that their parent's rules and standards are necessary; still they find them intolerable. Having to pay attention to rules that feel arbitrary seems a large part of what is keeping them in the world of children. In the other houses, our children did not experience discipline the way they did at home. The adults they selected were able to be nurturing and wise, without the children feeling that they were being too close or fully responsible for them. Though these people treated their own children pretty much the way we did ours, they didn't treat our children the same way.

Our children had the privileges and responsibilities of welcome guests. The structure and rules were those necessary for the comfort of all the members of the household, not standards designed to mold them at a time when they were trying to find a personal identity. They were not intended to make them neater, more reliable, or harder working. Once they were able to see rules and standards as functional rather than infantilizing, they could come back home and talk to us again. In turn, recognizing that they already were decent people and that they would be able to fare in the world pretty much the way they were, we eased up on the character building and the household became more peaceful.

In retrospect, we probably should have loosened up on character building earlier than we did. By the time they have hit fifteen, our parental failures and successes are pretty much built in. Our big surprise, one that took us three children to discover, is that as they grow up, they keep their rooms clean and wash their faces even, or rather especially, when we are not around to check up on them.

Our children had to do it for themselves. That our most recent "outplacement" worked even though it emerged from our initiative was either dumb luck or a measure of our own and our child's desperation at that moment. But if you can't make it happen, if the opportunity is right, you can let it happen. What may look like the ultimate rejection, leaving home and adopting someone else as parents for a while, may turn out to be an adolescent's way of being able to accept parental values and standards without feeling like someone who has sold out to power.

A psychiatrist friend of ours assures us that adolescence is a form of psychosis. We believe it. The trick, of course, is to keep that craziness as carefully encapsulated as possible so that it does not spill over into later phases of life. If a little child swapping can take some of the burden out of that extraordinarily difficult age, it is a resolution well worth considering.

> Richard J. Israel is director of Central Services and Judaica in the Boston area. He and his wife, Sherry, have two daughters and two sons. "I have discovered how much more confusing, exhausting, and sometimes even desperate a task parenting is than I imagined. I certainly no longer believe that if you are sincere, everything works out nicely. But though we have had moments together that have been painful, I can honestly say I do not regret any of them. I have come to view even those hard times as part of what it is all about."

The Teenage Years: Trial and Error

George Vecsey

As I sit down to write this article, my mind is distracted by events of last night and this morning. Why was my son so sweet and huggy last night after I yelled at him? Why was he so casual and friendly this morning as he got ready for school? Does this mean we are doing something *right*?

This is a pivotal time for me to be writing about a father-son relationship. My own father died six months ago, and I am just beginning to realize how much I miss him. I am also beginning to realize that it is not enough that I consider my son my best male friend. I am also his father and must begin to act more like an authority and less like a peer. I must be tougher with a fifteen-year-old who does not always do his homework.

Our daughters have both been encouraged to seek careers, to plan to support themselves, to make independent life choices. Our son sees his older sisters becoming writers like their father. Do people perhaps expect him to be equal to them? To be equal to me? Perhaps that is a burden he rebels against.

Growing up with four verbal, creative older people in the house, David has never lacked for stimulation or entertainment. Only now, in the belated wisdom of my old age (which forty-five seems to be at times), do I realize that this kind of environment is not necessarily positive. He fits right in; he is the least judgmental person in the family, and sometimes he is even the most mature. But has the family—and in particular, his father—given him the space, the distance, the silence, in which to grow?

I think I have been selfish. I think I love him too much. I would rather watch a ball game or a movie with him than with any of my friends because, frankly, he is more fun. He lends me his Duran Duran tapes, he gives me good lines for my articles, and he tells me when I'm acting like a jerk. If I rave intemperately about somebody or something in my work, he rolls his eyes. Sometimes he acts twenty-five, other times five.

Because I work at home a lot, I am usually around the kitchen when he comes home from school or back from his job at the fast-food store. I enjoy telling him about James Joyce or Loretta Lynn or Casey Stengel or the Dalai Lama. I enjoy the role of teacher and mentor. But lately I have begun to realize that these roles are not quite the same as that of father.

He knows about my spiritual values and my politics and my love of work, but our strongest bond is baseball, and that's all right. Since he was tiny, there have been games on the radio or television; there was an afternoon in Shea Stadium when he was three; and since he was five we have practiced together. He will take grounders at second base with far more diligence than he will study his German verb endings, and part of that is because it is our ritual together: I slap grounders and call out the names of all the second basemen the New York Mets have ever had.

This is not Clarence Day hitting grounders and it is not Robert Young hitting grounders. When practice is over, we laugh on the walk back to the house, and I might put my arm around his neck and remind him, "Your father can always clean your clock." We can share the same space and not be uncomfortable, the way I see so many fathers and sons. Our home is our clubhouse.

When infield practice is over, I go back to my word processor and the telephone. My wife, who is an artist, is probably working at her desk or her easel, and perhaps our daughters are visiting between work assignments. A lot of creating is done in this house. If osmosis really worked, David in turn would come back from infield practice and do his homework. It doesn't always work that way.

"There's always something else I'd rather do," he said last night, in between my yelling. "Listen to the radio, read the paper, sleep, or hang out with whoever's home."

It is beginning to dawn on me that life is too comfortable for him. It is not that we don't talk about the major things in life. David knows how I feel about cruelty and chemical abuse, about promiscuity and the political swing of the eighties. We talk a lot about relationships within the family and relationships with society. But I have come to think I have enjoyed his company too much, have terrorized him too little, and have trusted osmosis too much.

In a Johnny Cash song a father named his son "Sue" to toughen him up, because the father knew he wouldn't stick around to raise him. In my old age, righteous anger will have to be a substitute for naming my son "Sue."

I grew up with a suspicion, or perhaps a fear, of anger. I did not like people to be mad at me, and I did not like to be mad at other people, at least overtly. Emotions were to be suppressed, not expressed. A father should not have to yell at a son, unless things got bad and he lost his temper. There should always be a moderate way to work things out. Let's talk.

I began to appreciate the value of emotion when I was forty and visiting an addiction treatment center while working on a book about alcoholism. The center would let me visit only if I participated in the group encounter sessions, involving families whose existence was threatened by addiction. Not only did people prod at me and draw me closer into the circle; but I began to feel the need to express some things when I got home. Since then I have occasionally expressed anger at my wife and at both my daughters. They all know me a little better now; the air is a little clearer. But it is the last of the dynasty, the last child still at home, who may gain the most from it.

David is fifteen now. I won't say "all boys are . . ." I will just say "this boy is" alternately energetic, lethargic, private, verbal, mature, stubborn, perceptive, and lazy. The faculty members at his school are good people with a common purpose. I can count on them to let us know when work is not being done, and they have done so, often. (David seems to forget, each time, that they will most surely send notes home if he is not living up to his potential.)

And yet. I can remember being fifteen and being so tangled up, so distant, that I couldn't get my homework done or my room cleaned, couldn't find time for the three children in the middle, but enjoyed helping to raise my baby brother. I could do what was important to me: get to work on time, organize a softball game, hide out and read a book, but I could not and would not do everything that was expected of me.

"Boys are different," I sometimes tell my wife. "They grow up slower. They shrug things off. They don't know how to help themselves. They rebel. Besides, David has good friends, he's respected at work, they want him back as a camp junior counselor. He's like Tom Sawyer. He'll be president some-day—if they don't hang him first."

I've taken my father's underlying sentimentality and my mother's dedication and tried to be as good a parent as they were. I'm still learning how to be a father, and my son just happens to be the last child home, so he gets my on-the-job training.

Last night he got my anger. He had been silently defying his German teacher, a fine instructor and one of the major reasons my son chose his school. A C+ paper that should have been signed by me was not, and when I found out about it, I yelled. I yelled at my son for half an hour, face to face, like a Marine instructor, and called him some names, and then my wife and I talked to him, and we saw a few tears that told us that we were getting somewhere. When we were alone later, I told my wife I felt better for yelling, and she said, "I've been trying to tell you that."

This morning, while my son and I had breakfast together, he gave me a big hug and said, "Did you see Carter hit a grand-slam last night?" I'm still a little mad at him, and he knows it, but my judgment is we both feel better for the yelling. I also think he did his homework last night.

George Vecsey is married to Marianne Graham Vecsey, an artist. They have two daughters and a son and live in Port Washington, New York. He is coauthor of *Martina*, the autobiography of Martina Navratilova, published in June 1985 by Alfred A. Knopf. He has also covered Appalachia and religion for the *New York Times*, where he is currently a sports columnist.

Of fatherhood, George says, "Being a father has been enjoyable, something I wanted to be, not happened to be. I enjoy my children's company more than I enjoy work, play, recreation, hobbies."

Teenage Daughters and an Old Fogey

P. E. Judge

My experience in fathering began in tragedy and ended in jubilation. One spring in the mid-sixties, my two southern nieces, Pearl and Ruby Stone, lost both of their parents. Their father was killed in an automobile crash and their mother, my sister Opal, committed suicide a few months later, leaving me the guardian of her two teenage daughters.

As I think back on the period during which I was a pseudofather of teenagers, I wonder what I learned from it. It certainly was a learning experience. I learned that I didn't like to learn from experience like that. For instance, I learned for the first time what I appeared to be. "Oh, don't be an old fogey!" Ruby once yelled at me shortly after we had set up the apartment and I had asked her to turn down her stereo over which Bob Dylan howled. I was astonished at the time and quite hurt. I was not really old yet; I was a popular and enthusiastic teacher of young people, and prided myself on being a liberal and progressive thinker. An old fogey? But now in looking back I think she was right: without realizing it, I had become in private something of an old fogey. Fatherhood had only exposed my sad condition.

Like so many well-intentioned fathers, I insisted that the girls eat a balanced diet, including plenty of milk, fresh fruit, meat, and vegetables instead of permitting them (as I finally did) to have just what they craved: plenty of cashew nuts, Twinkies, anchovy pizza, chocolate kisses, fried chicken, and double whoppers. I set strict hours for TV watching until Ruby zapped me one night by screaming: "Don't you know that nothing really good comes on before midnight? Your idea of the Late Late Show is 9 P.M.!"

Even when I tried to make them feel I was "with it" by resorting to their jargon and said once, "That's positively groovy!" they mocked me. In those days I thought a year's membership to a museum was a better Christmas gift for them than a single ticket to a rock concert. Typical old fogey that I was, I never grasped the difference between being broad-minded and thick-headed. Assuming I had the perfect right to be critical of their conduct, I threw up their past mistakes like a Roto Rooter. Often, I suppose, I seemed about as tactful as a bulldozer. I used to wait up for them when they went out on dates until I realized this was resented rather than appreciated. One night Pearl, all dolled up in a blonde wig and long eyelashes, called out to me as she was going out the door with a sailor, "You only have a right to worry about me when I don't show up for breakfast, and then it'll be too late!" Her tone of voice delivered the deadly message: "You're just an old fogey!"

When we went sightseeing, I always insisted they should rest when I got tired. It wasn't my age; it was my attitude, which stank. I urged them always to be sane, sensible, and safe. Instead they were usually silly, sassy, and sorry. Fortunately, I changed before it was too late. One day, in one of naturalist John Burroughs's books, I came across a passage that struck home. He pointed out that the two greatest dangers facing a man as he grows older are petrifaction and putrefaction—turning to stone or rotting. He might have put it more briefly as one deadly danger—that of becoming an old fogey. When I realized that nothing could be more restrictive of child or parent development than old fogeyism, I was determined to change, to be looser, less like a stone or a stinker. Fortunately, the experiences of bachelor fatherhood that my nieces brought me aerated the roots of my thinking and revitalized my emotions. Now I'm a born-again old fogey.

P. E. Judge is a pseudonym.

© Carol Palmer

Chapter Fourteen
Gay Fathers

Is Daddy Different?

P. Gregory Springer

Ten years ago, I was a confirmed gay man writing with pride and self-assurance for gay liberation newspapers, and marriage was simply not on my agenda. Children were an even more remote possibility.

Today, I still write for those newspapers, sometimes with my son Henry—soon to be three years old—sitting on my lap in front of the computer screen.

When Lee and I decided to marry, we both knew the situation could not be easily labeled. Neither of us believed I would ever change or that I would need to.

For the first years of marriage, Lee insisted upon only one rule. If I were to be sexually active outside the marriage, I must agree to take the battery of cultures necessary to test for sexually transmitted diseases before we could resume relations. This was sometimes bothersome, but it was an arrangement she insisted we work out between us.

There were slip-ups, arguments, flare-ups, doubts. But unlike many gay men, I never actively sought a permanent gay lover. I could be drawn physically to a man, but family has supplied me with most of my important emotional needs. Even before the unwelcome arrival of AIDS into the gay community, I had virtually ceased sexual activity outside our marriage. But it was not always easy.

There are hundreds of gay fathers in this country. Many of them keep their sexual feelings secret, whereas others are—to my way of thinking—more fortunate in being able to share the truth with friends and family. One particular difficulty in living a "disclosed" life is in finding a way to explain yourself to your children when they inevitably ask: Is daddy different?

In the early seventies, my female friend Lee and I lived together, sharing rent and space and occasionally the bed. When I confronted my true sexual feelings—with some difficulty—I left Lee for Richard, someone I needed for a while, in order to discover and open up the feelings I had repressed for years. Lee, also with some difficulty, accepted this, and we lived apart.

I began to get writing assignments from gay periodicals. Several years later, on a tour of Iowa for *Blueboy*, I invited Lee along for the ride. Between interviews in Des Moines gay bars and a tour of hot spots at the Iowa State Fair, we discussed the possibility of merging our friendship into a permanent relationship.

Soon after marrying Lee, I wrote an article for the *Advocate* about such mixed-orientation marriages. We discovered there were hundreds of other couples in this same situation, unhappily typed by media-drenched labels, floundering in a state of being both happily married and sexually specialized. For a brief moment, it appeared that such marriages would constitute "a trend," the topic appearing on book shelves and the "Phil Donahue Show." In retrospect, the serious studies conducted by Dr. David Matteson and Michael W. Ross (*The Married Homosexual Man*, Routledge & Kegan Paul) have revealed that the problems faced by gay married men are not very different from the ordinary difficulties in any marriage.

The gay organizations and magazines I was affiliated with did not always respond favorably to my marriage. On some staffs, I'm the token straight. Others simply rejected me. A prominent gay bookstore in New York still refuses to stock publications related to gay married men.

Parenthood follows patterns. Gay men learn to change diapers with the same trepidation and fumbling as nongay fathers.

When Henry was born, new worlds of identification opened up before me. Suddenly, those movies about children and fathers brought tears welling inside me. (They still do, even something so remote as a well-edited telephone commercial can reach out and touch me into blubbering.) My feelings for and understanding of my own father shifted from one of tenured indifference to genuine appreciation. Watching him play grandfather also unleashed a new feeling of sameness. I see myself in him, and him in Henry. At first, I experienced these psychological connections to some age-old, mainstream masculine habits and attitudes. Nervousness, pride, cuddling, roughhousing, and protectiveness were there for me to accept. Mostly, fatherhood turned my world on its head with joy.

As with all new fathers, pains of responsibility must follow in the wake of delight. Discipline and nurturing aren't the exclusive rights of heterosexuality. By the ordinary means of procreation, one is granted the status of father. But true fathering entails many more years of follow-up.

Even now, as I attempt to explain the importance of naptime to a three-year-old, hints of a future communication gap surface. How could I ever be able to explain my voyeuristic visits to a gay bathhouse to someone who can't comprehend simple sharing of a toy truck?

I'm not particularly worried about it. I have no grand plan or expectations as to how to handle the question that inevitably will arise. Henry plays with "guns" now, shooting people and beasts and bad guys in imitation of television. Some of this playacting is unavoidable, and without owning any guns myself, I avoid flustering and overemphasizing his behavior. Someday, he will be able to reason for himself. I must wait, with as much patience as possible. He may follow the lead of my behavior, or he may not. We can teach only so much.

Henry's first word was *ball*. Before he was two, he could recognize and name every sport played in northern America. He insisted on owning a football, baseball, soccer ball, tennis ball, and various others. Suddenly, I found myself thrust into a world of competitive sports, which I had managed to elude all my life.

It's confusing, how different we can be already, yet how closely bound we are. Observing the differences doesn't clarify a thing. It only raises more questions about environment, heredity, learning, models, and influence.

Children are, as Freud claimed, highly sexualized beings. Changing diapers, shared bathtime, slobbery kisses good night, and the minimum requirement of daily hugs enrich any parent's life. How tragic when those moments are curtailed or completely denied because of a parent's sexual insecurity. On only one occasion have I felt some strange vibrations from friends, concerned about my gayness and my willingness to hug their children. Although the overwhelming majority of sexual abuse of children is committed by heterosexuals, the explicit sexual component of homosexual rhetoric may cause the question to surface more quickly.

I would sooner deny a child water than a daily dose of affection. We starve and whither without touch. I suffer, too, knowing that so many gay men are denied or deny themselves a child's kisses by too closely associating their lives with their sexuality.

Loving children can fill many gaps in life in profoundly satisfying ways. Many gay fathers have married in order to experience fatherhood. In a few of these successful marriages—Freud notwithstanding—it would seem the drive to raise children has outweighed the sexual drive itself.

How will Henry and my new baby, Ernie, respond when they learn daddy is gay? It is something we must wait to face. Homosexuality in our house is discussed with the same lack of passion given to the mention of potato salad. It is not an issue—not yet. Any concern that possibly the children would reject me for having a minority sexual identity seems—at this point in an exciting ongoing relationship of learning and growing—impossible. And if one of my sons should be gay, I probably will have to relive much of the difficult self-examination that I went through for myself. But in that case, the boy will have a supportive, loving father who can at least offer some advice on the subject. He need never fear my rejection of his feelings.

For myself, most of all, being a gay father has altered my conception of what it means for me to be gay. I speak for myself when I say it has been neither an immutable curse nor admission into a social club of outsiders.

In many ways, I expect that the extended self-acceptance period in my life will help me watchfully groom my children to adulthood. Tolerance, pain, rejection, individuality, confusion—these are some of the less subtle traumas of growing up, traumas that gay people sometimes are forced to face again and again in their lives.

Since becoming a father, I have come to know two things more deeply than ever before: my homosexual feelings are an undeniable presence, but the ways in which human feelings can be explored are manifold. The fact of being gay doesn't have to mean giving in to a stifled or stereotyped life. The fact of being a father is a creative challenge that draws from the very depths of being.

My gayness, like my fatherhood, has an undeniable biological component. But there is so much more. The other aspects are the important ones: growing, learning, seeing, sharing, knowing, loving. Until we deny these, there are no constrictions on the conditions of life.

> P. Gregory Springer and his wife, Lee Petrie-Springer, live in Urbana, Illinois, with their three-year-old son, Henry, and their three-month-old son, Ernie. P. Gregory Springer is editor of *Men and Wife Newsletter* for gay men and their wives.

Should Kate Call Me Dad?

Keith Mann

Kate is my daughter. We don't live together. We see each other a few times a month. A friend of mine, Stephanie, is Kate's mother. Stephanie is a lesbian. She and her lover, Pam, had wanted a child for a long time. Stephanie wanted to be the biological mother, and two concerns were important for them about the father of their child. One was that the father be identifiable. They wanted their son or daughter to have some contact with the father. The second concern was that the father be gay. Because the politics of being lesbian mothers were complicated, it made sense that a gay man would be more sensitive.

So that's where I entered the picture. I was in my early thirties, the same as Stephanie and Pam. I had established Boston as my home and I had been out as a gay man for ten years.

I suppose that if I were to take an in-depth look at my reasons for choosing to become a father, some interesting information would surface. Perhaps I was seeking attention or wanted a biological offspring out of some nihilistic need. Maybe my choice was a giant "fuck you" to a society that had too often and too long backed me up against the wall. Maybe it was a way of getting at my family. Or maybe it was a way to heterosexualize myself and become accepted. Perhaps it was an action of choosing a responsibility that would finally qualify me as a traditional adult. Or maybe it was purely a choice to be a part of an exciting revolutionary alternative.

The truth lies somewhere in all of this, and more. On turning thirty, I came to realize that no single event or man or bundle of money was going to descend on me and miraculously make my life work out. I was the only one who would create fulfillment in my life, and it was only through my choices that my life would have meaning. When Stephanie and Pam approached me, I felt the time was almost right. After a year of deliberation, I agreed to become a father.

Since Kate is only a year old, there wouldn't be much substance to a discussion about what it means to be her father. When I see Kate each week, I usually baby-sit so Stephanie can go to an exercise class. For those few hours, Kate smiles and sleeps and plays and cries and eats. I react to each one of those spells with a calmness that I usually don't feel during the rest of my rushed day.

I remember one of the first times I held Kate for any length of time. Stephanie, Kate, and I had gone to City Hall to arrange for my name to be included on the birth certificate. The wait was interminable. At one point, Stephanie handed the baby over to me. Kate was in one of those carrying sacks with straps all around like a parachute. When Kate's small body pressed up against me, her warmth floated through my stomach and touched all the extremities. At one point she lifted her head back, opened her eyes briefly as if to say "Oh, it's you," and dropped back into sleep as her head bounced a little on my chest.

I don't feel as tied in emotionally with Kate as I imagine many fathers feel about their daughters. I see her as Stephanie and Pam's child, for they are clearly her parents. I see myself more in the uncle or grandfather role, with little or no parenting responsibilities.

Pam, Stephanie, and I sat down together and negotiated points of agreement both before and after the conception. The purpose was not so much that we have a legal document, although this was a goal, as that our common ground of expectations be concrete. From the very start, I wanted an understanding that I would have no more than once a month visitation responsibility while I lived in Boston. Pam and Stephanie, on the other hand, felt that five times a month as a maximum number of visits was a good boundary. So for the first year and a half my visits and baby-sitting would fall between one and five times per month. I have no financial obligations for Kate's upbringing. And in the event of Stephanie's and Pam's deaths, I am to have the opportunity to raise Kate if closer friends choose not to. In a court, however, the rights of a child, as interpreted by a judge, far outweigh any document we might have. These agreements are most useful outside the courts.

One of the first difficult things about having Kate that I had to face was the realization that I had really wanted a son. When we were discussing the artificial insemination process long before Kate was conceived, I had come across a piece of information that said there was a higher incidence of boys among births of artificial inseminations as compared to general birth sex percentages. I was very pleased about this. I saw us bike riding and jogging and going out for something to eat. Dad and son, together.

Well, Kate was born prematurely. At first my only concern was that she be healthy; little else mattered. She turned out to be fine and went home before it dawned on me: Kate was a girl.

For the past ten years, I had identified with men on all levels. I worked with and lived with women and had some women friends, but basically I was committed to men, how they thought, what they did, where they were going. Still, here I was, involved not in a relationship with a man, but in a committed, long-term relationship with three women. Who were they? It took some time and awkwardness, but with Stephanie and Pam's patience and support, I was able to look closely at the situation. It has only been recently that I've realized that, indeed, Kate and I will be able to bike and jog together, as well as walk down Boston's fashionable Newbury Street. I look forward to and am optimistic about the future with Kate. I feel lucky to have had the opportunity to have a daughter. Her parents are wonderful. Kate is clearly loved not only by them but also by a large circle of men and women. She will be well raised and well cared for.

Sometimes I do worry about her and wonder about what it will be like for her to grow up. My imagination can create all sorts of future conflictive possibilities. I worry about our relationship. Will she hold a lot of anger toward me for this unusual parenting situation?

I recently visited a psychic. Without being familiar with any of my past, the psychic nevertheless knew that I was gay, and she also told me I have a child whom my parents don't know about. I posed a question about the future to her, about Kate and my relationship. I asked her if she could foresee any major difficulties. The psychic looked off for a few seconds and said no, she didn't see any. Then looking into my eyes sympathetically, she told me the only major problem we would have would be when Kate decides to get married. Probably to some loud heterosexual jock from Missouri, I quipped.

Keith Mann is a pseudonym.

Joys and Pains of Gay Fatherhood

Frank S. Gallagher, Jr.

How can you not enjoy being a gay father when two finches belonging to a friend of one of your children are named after you and your lover "because they are always rearranging the 'furniture' in their birdcage—just like someone we know"? At this time in life (I am fifty-seven) being a father *and* being gay are both so natural that it is hard to remember clearly the evolution to this stage. Actually, it is not hard to remember. Sometimes I wish it were. It is just hard to remember *clearly*.

There is no typical gay father's story any more than there is a typical father's story or a typical gay man's story, but mine certainly had some common components. I remember being called a sissy and a little girl in elementary school because of my quietness and mannerisms at that time. The worst offenders—distressingly enough—were not other kids but certain adults, such as the school bus driver in our small town.

I vaguely recall my first significant sexual experience as an encounter with a boy my own age, about ten, when I was visiting my grandfather in Vermont. There were times when I was aware that I fitted uncommonly well in the social milieu of the girls. There were more times when I was painfully aware that I did not fit in easily with the general social milieu of the "guys." However, there were some boys with whom there were easy, friendly, nonerotic relationships. I just don't make it as a stereotype even in retrospect.

I necked with girls on dates. I also engaged in several episodes of active homosexual sex. It felt good, was always initiated by the other person (except for perhaps a little seductive behavior on my part), and did not seem to be something about which I had a terribly strong taboo. Social and work relationships were both generally easy during my hitch in the army. I became an essentially asexual being for those two years of my late teens. Don't ask me how.

My twenties were something else. Sex, specifically gay sex, became wanted and needed as a major part of my life. Although my social life began to conflict with my postgraduate training, with the help of a therapist and good friends, I opted to continue studying for my chosen psychiatric career. I also decided to marry and have a family. What happened to the homosexuality at that point is still not clear to me.

My first child was born nine days after our first wedding anniversary. She was (and still is) such a miracle. Since I was the light sleeper in the family, I got the honor of a lot of the night work. The baby was so responsive to silly noises and singsong chatter at that age that I could keep her happy and express my irritation over interrupted sleep by saying the most outrageous things in a chirpy, lilting voice. My daughter and I thrived.

My first four children alternated—girl, boy, girl, boy—two years, one year, and four years apart. Each was healthy, beautiful, active, and unique. By now, my medical training was finally finished, and my practice established and going well. The long years of training, however, had left us with a serious debt load, and a family the size of a Norman Rockwell picture is an expensive proposition. There were also problems with the underpainting. The positive bonds between my wife and myself were not strong enough to withstand various difficulties that were accumulating. The kids meant the world to each of us, but we did not mean the world to each other. Life was complicated enough that it needed that direct link of love to withstand the external pressures.

During my twelfth year of marriage, our fifth child, another boy, came along. He was born severely multiply handicapped. This added serious emotional, physical, and financial burdens to our already strained lives and marital relationship. Soon before this, I had become involved in a homosexual relationship with a young man who has remained a close friend, without any continuing sexual involvement. My wife knew about the relationship and tolerated it. Her apparent reason was maintenance of the family unit plus social and financial security for the children and herself. She could not tolerate the idea of the handicapped youngster being the youngest and had another child a year later.

Even though all gay activities stopped again, or maybe partly because they stopped, the marital relationship continued to be very difficult but was not dissolved. For my part, I sufficiently disliked the possibility of being separated from the children that this factor overrode all other considerations. It is important to note that this was not the situation of "staying together for the sake of the children." Rather, I was staying together for my own sake in relation to the children. But eventually, as they grew older, the time seemed right to separate.

My wife and I will always have one dependent child. Fortunately, we have a good enough relationship and understanding that we communicate and even cooperate a good deal about him and the other children as well. We remain friends even though we are incompatible as spouses. It does not seem to be absolutely necessary to be great spouses to be happy and successful in the role of parents. The kids have been and are doing generally very well.

There have been ups and downs to be sure. But overall, they seem to be faring at least as well as the children in most families I know, including many that are seemingly thoroughly conventional.

When the decision was made to separate and I decided to come out again, I also decided to tell all the children, individually, that I was gay. At the time, they ranged in age from twelve to twenty-five. It was very important to me that they hear about my homosexuality from me first rather than from anyone else. Their reactions ranged from noncommittal to thanking me for telling explicitly what had already been suspected. One of my teenage sons was understandably concerned about what implications this had for his own sexuality and seemed relieved when reassured that it had none. Sometime later, one of the straight children let me know that a major concern had been that I might like the one gay child better than the others.

Lest this make it sound too easy, I hasten to say it has not been without strain for either me or them. I suspect there are things they say to one another, to their mother, or to friends, that they do not say to me directly. One of my children and, at another time, one of my lover's children have lived with us during school vacation. This has not appeared particularly strained. Each has had friends over during their stays. However, I am quite sure they have been selective in whom they invite. Also, I've noticed that they have kept themselves either isolated in their rooms or out of the apartment when we have had gay gatherings. There is not the same feeling of family that there was even in our previous stormy household. But it does not seem as different from the situation that would pertain in a step-parented family as I had expected. Having had a stepfather, I believe I have some sense of that.

The most hostile reactions I have experienced came from a source I did not anticipate, certain other gay men, generally those who "have always been gay." Some of them frankly do not like children. Few have ever been explicit, although a couple have said that it seems as if I have had "the best of both worlds," and that they are envious. Others act as if it has been a traitorous act to marry and "breed." Such negativism has not been frequent, but it was unnerving to me to experience such a reaction from such a source. Most of my gay friends do not act like that and many of them have met one or more of my children. What I had anticipated was derision from straight acquaintances, but most of them have been remarkably accepting.

A recent event made me feel that I have arrived as a gay father. One of my straight sons called me up to ask if I could come over to his house to talk with a couple of his school friends who were moving back to our city after some years away. They are gay and wanted information about good areas to live in as a couple of gay young men. He had told them that he had no good information about that but knew someone who probably would. Needless to say, they were startled when I arrived and he introduced me as his father.

Somehow I do not think my situation is so different from fathers in other nontraditional situations. Sometimes I feel I have been selfish and unfair. At other times, I feel that I have more to offer my children because I am true to myself and therefore more relaxed and content than ever before. Having faith and being grateful that things have worked out as well as they have makes coping with problems possible.

The fact that relations and communications are as good as they are with the children, their mother, and my lover is so wonderful that all I can ask is continued growth in all those relationships and a lot more years of life to share with all of them.

.   Frank S. Gallagher, Jr., is a psychiatrist specializing in work with people who are both mentally retarded and emotionally disturbed. "I am blessed with family and lover who love me and are tolerant of the complications of my life and the complications I bring to theirs. A situation that could be dreadful is wonderful, thanks to them. Added to this is the peace that comes from self-awareness and honesty to self."

POSITIVE IMAGES, © *Jerry Howard*

Chapter Fifteen
Infertility/Adoption/ Vasectomy

Becoming a Father—
The Hard Way

Tom Holman

In early 1985, my wife Shireen and I fulfilled a dream and ended a nightmare by going to India to adopt our daughter Sumati. It seems like such a short time ago that we were mired in infertility testing and treatment, and hope for the future was in very short supply. Now, only a few months later, I am getting well acquainted with fatherhood, staying home with Sumi half-time, watching her grow, and enjoying having a family. But I remember clearly the terrible times.

Infertility told me I didn't have what it takes to make a baby. I became all too familiar with the many ways one can be deficient in what should be one of the most intimate, protected areas of life. I masturbated into little plastic cups and gave them to a technician. The report came back: not enough sperm, and the ones I have didn't swim well enough to do their job. The urologist seemed happy even to find a diagnosis; the reasons for male infertility are barely understood relative to female infertility. I had varicoceles, and they would need surgical repair, so the "incompetent" veins in my scrotum wouldn't make the temperature too hot for healthy sperm. Quite minor surgery, only a day in the hospital. But the impact was major. I had grown up, like most men, thinking that becoming a father was natural and easy. I was afraid of becoming a father too early, but never of not being able to become one at all. How could anyone tell me my sperm wasn't good enough? I was even invited to take a look in the microscope and see the anemic little things struggling slowly along.

The surgery was a "success"; I became "borderline" instead of "low" in my sperm statistics. Afterwards there were some sessions of AIH—artificial insemination with husband's sperm. Procreation seemed especially bizarre at that point. My part of the process involved leaving depressing mechanical orgasms into plastic cups, and watching while a nurse tried to help my sperm along by inserting it into my wife.

Meanwhile, Shireen's infertility problem was severe—incapacitating endometriosis. Over the years, and in spite of drug treatment and both minor and major surgery, her illness progressed. With it came the extraordinary pain that prevented her from living a normal life, or at times from even getting out of bed. Ultimately, a hysterectomy was required to return her to health and normal functioning. During our five-year struggle, we had gradually been saying good-bye to our chances of having a biological child. Then came the final good-bye, and the need to acknowledge and mourn the loss of the child who had lived in our minds, but would never live in reality. A terribly sad ending, it was also a beginning. Finally Shireen was healthy enough to become a mother, even if not a biological one.

As we picked up the pieces after Shireen's hysterectomy, we realized that our urge to be parents was just as strong as ever. Long ago, Shireen's gynecologist had advised us to look into adoption. We had done this rather haphazardly because we were still battling infertility and remained hopeful. As we let go of the energy we had put into having a biological child, we found energy to begin in earnest the adoption process. This path involved great expense, in time, money, and work. But we found ourselves growing stronger and determined to meet and master the obstacles on the way to parenthood.

The adoption process started slowly. Submitting to the expense and intrusiveness of the agency home study process was, in some ways, similar to the infertility process. Had we been fertile, we would never have paid an agency to scrutinize us and make sure we would be good parents. Although we ended up with an excellent social worker and agency, the process inevitably contains many reminders of the unfairness of infertility. We also discovered how strange the "adoption industry" can be. The agency we initially went to closed because of scandals involving Latin American babies and lawyers. Setbacks such as this brought back the old feelings of bitterness and depression, and the fears of not having what it takes to be parents.

Gradually, however, other things began to fall into place for us. Since Shireen is from India, it was logical that we adopt an Indian baby. A trip to India began to take shape and, with much help, became possible. The network of people on whom we relied for help was indispensable, for no couple can handle adoption of this type alone. An American volunteer with the Indian orphanage, the support of Resolve (the national infertility self-help organization), friends, and family were all important to us during this time. We secured three-month leaves from our jobs, completed the home study, and collected documents for the American and Indian legal processes. Finally, and fearfully after the disappointments we had experienced, we bought baby furniture and prepared our second bedroom to receive an infant whom we had not met or seen, but who by that time had undoubtedly been born. We felt the sacrifices of parenthood beginning with our plans for the trip. We could allow ourselves only ten days for sightseeing, and then the rest of the trip would be devoted to the adoption. This would include getting the baby, going through the Indian court to become legal guardians, and obtaining an Indian passport and an American immigration visa for a baby who would come to this country as a resident alien.

Other unforeseen anxieties also had to be endured. As our date of departure approached, the prime minister of India was murdered, and there were rumors in India of CIA involvement. For a short time the State Department advised Americans not to travel to India. Soon after, India was struck by the Bhopal industrial disaster, involving an American corporation. This also generated anti-American feelings. Like so many couples doing international adoptions, we had to wait through these political crises, even though what we were doing seemed to us so completely personal and apolitical.

Finally, when we left for India, I had the sense that I was leaving a large part of myself and our life together behind forever. I would return to an irrevocably different life. The discomfort and claustrophobia of the long plane trip gave way to a few days of busy sightseeing. But even while seeing the Taj Mahal, anticipation, anxiety, and hope were in the backs of our minds. We were about to meet a baby, a person who would become our child forever. Would it go all right? Would we like each other? Had we allowed enough time for everything?

The orphanage was in Pune, a city of about 2 million in the Deccan Plateau near Bombay. We arrived and spent a brief time getting to know Shireen's family. Then we were immersed in adoption work. The short time it took to get Sumi is a marvel that I will never be able to explain logically. There were many babies, but Sumi was for us. Was it like love at first sight? We certainly seemed to choose each other. How could it have seemed so effortless? Then we were a family, though at first we were only foster parents.

The effortless part was now over. Sumi, taken from the foster family where she had been for four months since the day after her birth, was frightened at first. When Shireen's family gave us a *Barsa*, a Hindu naming ceremony for the new baby, Sumi clung to Shireen. She must have wondered where she could be and who all these people were. I thought later that she must have felt kidnapped (even if by people she loved at first sight). She didn't sleep unless carried for hours; she looked away when we smiled at her. She made me jealous with her preference for people with brown skins who spoke Indian languages. Slowly she taught us about becoming a family. She taught us that bonding and attachment aren't magical things that just happen to parents and children. They have to be built by what we do every day, and adoption makes this especially clear. After several days of upset, we were all exhausted. Things began to change, though, as we discovered the little secrets of calming down *our* baby, helping her to sleep, understanding her signals, and anticipating her needs. She began to get used to our strange looks, sounds, and habits. She began to trust us.

We had been away from home long enough to be relieved to come back. Would Sumi like it here, too? It was cold and snowing the night we got back, weather she would never have experienced in India. She clearly didn't enjoy her first stroll around the neighborhood, bundled up so that she could hardly move. But we saw that we really had become a family, that she was with us wherever we were. After a few difficult days of jet lag, we began to create our normal life as a family at home. Perhaps Sumi sensed our joy at being in our own home with her, for she adapted without difficulty. We settled into our new lives with a tremendous feeling of joy and success, a sense of growth and purpose and love. Becoming a family was difficult, to say the least, but certainly the most rewarding thing we have ever done.

> Tom Holman is a clinical psychologist who works with children and families and, in recent years, with adults struggling with infertility issues. He and his wife and daughter live in Arlington, Massachusetts.

The Call: Reflections on the Arrival of My Firstborn

Donald W. Glazer

It was a Sunday afternoon. Ellen and I were in my study. I was telephoning my Sunday tennis group, confirming the time and place of our weekly game. Between calls we were rehashing—yet again—what to do next about our childlessness. Ellen had read about another possible cure for infertility. I was skeptical. It sounded crazy to me even to suggest that the solution after all the miracle drugs had failed was a baking soda douche.

The telephone rang.

"Don, this is Pam. I have a baby for you. A girl."

"No shit." Not an exclamation of joy. More a question. What had we gotten ourselves into? We'd been married thirteen years. I was thirty-seven, settled in, just back from a business trip to Paris. In fact, Pam, our adoption social worker, had held off calling until my return.

"Ellen, it's Pam. She'll be dropping off a baby tomorrow morning."

Ellen flew off in a hundred directions. We hadn't expected Pam to call for many months. We had to empty the small bedroom of accumulated junk. We needed a crib. We needed diapers. We needed baby clothes. But what we needed most was help.

The first call went to my parents in Florida. "Mom, I can't believe it. They are dropping off a baby tomorrow. How soon can you fly in?"

"Donny, I'm so excited for you. I'd give anything to come. But Kelly and Scott arrived last night. We leave for Disneyland tomorrow morning. I don't see how I can disappoint them."

My younger brother Neil's two children were visiting from New Jersey.

Well, how about Neil's wife, Sandy? No, she had just taken a full-time job. And Neil? Well, he was awfully busy at work, but he had a few extra vacation days and volunteered to come—to help set up the new room and to teach me to change diapers.

Time was racing by. I called a few friends to borrow baby things. That was easy. They'd all been through this long ago, and had neatly washed, folded, and set aside outgrown clothes, blankets—even cloth diapers—just in case, or maybe for a friend some day. I was glad to oblige. While Ellen left with a friend to pick up all we had arranged to borrow, I grabbed my racket and headed for the tennis courts.

Later, when Ellen and I had our first quiet moment together, the reality of what was happening began to sink in. First off, we needed a name. We had previously agreed to name our firstborn, at least by using the first initial, after my maternal grandparents, both now deceased. Meyer, the opera singer, my boyhood hero, a fervent, long-suffering Cleveland Indians' fan. And an E for Edith, who had eyes only for her children and grandchildren.

Emily Meyer.

A child conceived without my knowledge, born while I was on a business trip, was to join a lineage that would connect her with a small town in Poland that my grandparents and my mother, then herself a child, had fled fifty years ago.

Next day I left early for work. I had scheduled a breakfast meeting to brief Barney Raymond on my trip. Barney, about sixty, was the head of our law firm. He had hired me. He had passed many of his clients on to me. He had been my special friend. Barney had been married many years and was childless. In a few hours the parallel lines of our careers were to diverge. I told Barney the news. He was pleased for me. He never mentioned the decision he'd made (or that was made for him) many years ago. We discussed our client's problem, and Barney said he'd attend to the details for me during the next few days.

I then quickly made the rounds of my partners, gathering up their hand-me-downs, and hurried home.

Emily arrived in Pam's arms a few minutes later. It was less than twenty-four hours since Pam had called us with the news.

Almost four years have passed since Pam's call. Ellen says men don't know how to express their feelings. That may be so. But while I sit here early in the morning, before work, tears come to my eyes as I write about my family. I'm in the small bedroom, now my study. Emily is asleep across the hall in my former study, the blue walls now painted pink. Asleep in a crib catercorner to Emily's bed is her one-year-old sister, Cathy (yes, the baking soda worked). During the last four years, after thirteen years as a twosome, we have become a family of four. I am madly in love with my daughters, both of them. But that's not to say that my feelings for them—one adopted, one not—are the same.

Emily thrust herself into our lives. The stork dropped her on our door-step. For me she was and is a little miracle. Strangers have commented that in Emily they can see her father. Little do they know the irony of that. In loving Emily I have no misgivings, not even a tinge of guilt, that I am in fact loving a reflection of myself. I can admire her good looks, her determination, her grace, her athletic skill, her singing ability, for what they are. They belong to Emily. She deserves all the credit. A beautiful woman came into my life, unexpected. It was love at first sight. First love. She knocked me off my feet. And I'm still head over heels.

But, of course, life is never that simple. In real life babies don't drop from the sky. Emily is not and never will be mine alone. During her first weeks, she was in the arms of someone else. And that's something Emily and I will have to deal with all our lives. In the back of my mind, I can see a couple. The woman, blond like Emily, beautiful, strong-willed, determined to see the pregnancy through. He, handsome and athletic, romantic, and ready to be a father. But they are both still in school, and she's more practical.

Pam says I'd like them. I have no doubt. These two people I've never met, whom I can see in my mind's eye, are part of Emily's and my life. Emily doesn't know yet. One day, a few years down the road, she will.

When Cathy arrived, our friends commented that a second child would make a big difference, that we would all have to learn to share. I am afraid they missed the point. With Emily, we have never had any choice but to share. Each year around the time of Emily's birthday we send Pam an unsigned letter describing Emily's progress. Pam passes the letter on and relays to us a little information she thinks we should have. The exchange is an annual reminder that we can't lay sole claim to Emily's birthday, that March 4 isn't our date (our date didn't come until two weeks later), but a date commemorating an event in which we had no part. Firstborn of the firstborn of my grandparents' eldest child, heir to Meyer's silver kiddush cup, Emily—like her namesakes— came from a place I've never been. Like them she may never return. But knowing Emily's curiosity, I wouldn't be surprised if someday she chose to revisit her past. I accept that and, in a curious way, look forward to it. I'm curious, too.

With Cathy it's not so complicated. We had plenty of warning, and plenty of time to plan. We watched her progress. And when she arrived, I cut the cord. Biologically Cathy may be my first. But as a day-to-day proposition, she's Emily's little sister. She looks like me, but her middle name belongs to Ellen's side of the family. I'm crazy in love with Cathy, but when I speak of her, I do so with restraint. I don't feel the same license to praise the product of my own genes.

Each morning Cathy wakes me and watches me do my exercises. Emily comes in just in time to be sure that Cathy and I don't have breakfast without her. In the evening, I put Cathy and Emily to bed. I sit on the floor and sing fifties' rock-and-roll songs while strumming my guitar. Emily knows the words to all my old favorites and sings along. Cathy will soon, too. We usually end up with a song I wrote for Emily (I've added Cathy's name where appropriate). The tune sounds something like "Earth Angel":

> Emily (and Cathy)
> I love you so-o

> I'll never leave you
> And I'll never let you go-o
> Emily (and Cathy)
> You're the ones for me.

Meyer wouldn't like the music. But I'm sure he'd sing along.

Donald W. Glazer is an attorney. He and his wife, Ellen, have two daughters. "What's most important for me in terms of fatherhood—at least for now—is all the fun we have, all the adventure, all the new things to do and explore. One difference between men and women is that men tend to emphasize doing, and feelings flow from that rather than from heart-felt conversations. Raising children is as doing a thing as I can imagine, and for me it is pure joy."

Reversing My Vasectomy

Gordon Hayward

Six weeks after my vasectomy, I had a semen analysis. The results showed that all the sperm were cut off; I was sterile. I was pleased with my decision to have a vasectomy. I was making a serious statement of responsibility to our marriage. I had also freed my wife from having to take the pill as she had been doing for seven years; I did not want her to bear the consequences of its uncertain short- and long-term effects any longer.

I'm sure she was pleased that I was making what I then saw as a gesture in the name of our relationship and its future. We could both continue with our careers with complete assurance that they would not be disrupted by having children. We would be free to travel. We could design our lives exactly as we chose.

Six months later, for a myriad of reasons, I was divorced. I took a leave of absence from a teaching job and traveled in Europe for several months. During that time, I began to regret my decision to have a vasectomy. Perhaps the distance in space and time helped me to understand what I had done more clearly. Tradition, family life as lived for hundreds of years in Europe, threw my tendency to reject such timeless ways into high relief. I felt that my vasectomy prevented me from moving wholly and naturally into a future that was consonant with my new feelings toward family and fatherhood.

The vasectomy, I began to realize, did not allow me to choose. I was held in check by an earlier and drastic act. I knew that I had to do what I could to reverse the results of that decision.

When I returned from my travels, I spoke with a urologist about the reversal operation. He was discouraging, telling me that only a third of such operations were successful even in reestablishing an unobstructed passage for the cells through the vas deferens tubes. Another told me the chances were fifty-fifty, but that since less than one thousand operations of this kind had been performed worldwide to date, the statistics were scant and unreliable.

I found a doctor whose success rate was clearly above the average, and two and a half years after having the vasectomy, I spent a long night pondering the series of events that had led me to the operating room. It was during that night that I gave up feelings of regret. I accepted the fact that I had done what I needed to do at the time of the vasectomy, and now I was doing all in my power to right what had been wrong about that past decision.

It wasn't until about two months after the operation that I was able to walk or sit without being conscious of some pain. The operation cost about $2,500, only part of which was covered by insurance.

But I felt deeply relieved at the sense of being whole and intact again. Although there was a distinct possibility that I would not be able to become a father, I felt assured of my ability to face confidently the results of the year's tests. I had done all that I could as well as I could. When I went for my third and final test, the result was negative. The tubes were intact and healthy, but the sperm were not. The doctor held out little hope for improvement. I struggled with the implications of my apparently permanent sterility, but I never gave up hope.

One year later I was happily remarried. My wife acknowledged the fact that, in all probability, we would not be able to have our own children, but even though the medical information offered little hope, she simply refused to accept that I was permanently sterile. Her optimism was encouraging, it never lapsed, and it may have engendered its own reward. Two and a half years after the reversal operation, we learned that Mary was pregnant. Because we could not take our ability to have children for granted, we were especially aware of how miraculous and wonderful it is to anticipate the birth of one's own child.

Now, six and a half years after the birth of our son, I still see my vasectomy as an unnecessarily drastic act, but I do not regret having had it. By facing and accepting the painful feelings that resulted from my self-imposed sterility, I overcame a deep sense of impotence and loneliness. In so doing, I believe I now bring a richer and deeper love to my wife and our child, who was not supposed to be. His birth has meant, in many ways, my rebirth.

> Gordon Hayward is a teacher and free-lance writer in Vermont, where he lives with his wife and son. "I have organized my life so that I am assured of time, lots of time, with my son."

© *Harry Stuart Cahill*

Chapter Sixteen
When Things Go Wrong

Portrait of a Child

George Ellenbogen

Alone she danced and called to mind
the aloneness of the candle's dance
negotiating with the dark.

The pelican's tender step
before the flight that balances
wind and wings
measures her whirl and tip-toed song.

She became all
and all were her
as gyrations
long and taut
funneled down the pressing air
made her soft
and nestling land
into fantasies of chosen fur.

What of other children trading
scorn, shoves, and chalk—
savages in little savage games?
She danced wind to their motion;
not lonely, but alone,
rehearsing for those drifting steps
in the long concrete corridor .
beyond mile and measurement
when we all dance
alone.

George Ellenbogen is chairman of the Department of English at Bentley College. He is divorced and has two children—Sara who is twenty-one and Adam who is seventeen.

Alike but Not the Same: Father to a Child Who Is Different

Stephen D. Grubman

Ironic, isn't it? I am a speech-language pathologist. My professional education and training is in the field of communicative disorders. I teach others how to identify, assess, and treat people with communicative disabilities. And then, my own daughter is born with a communicative disability: a language-learning handicap. Something in the way her brain functions prevents her from using language to learn more language and to think and solve problems more easily. She is intelligent, yet it takes her longer to learn people's names, complex directions, and new words. She does not yet know how to use her eyes and ears and sense of touch to learn more easily. It is still difficult for her to use language and speech to her full potential. Ironic, yes.

Over time, I have learned to accept my child the way she is. And I am learning to recognize and to respect her first as a child—my child!—and then as a special child, unique, adding to the rich diversity of humankind. I am once again (as I was during her infancy, for example) awed by her changes, her improvements, her growth. Now I am awed by the "simple" things: her increasingly complex drawings, her questions, and her chatter that once had not been present in her language. Now, too, I take much less for granted. "When I pick a flower, does it hurt?": the poetry of language as it emerges from her teaches me lessons in creativity and language I did not appreciate before she came to us. I learn with her; I learn from her. And I am learning to share, to admit my vulnerabilities and fears and concerns.

What had it been like? A private hell during the period I suspected a problem, denied it, minimized it, internalized it, took responsibility for it.

I can recall that period when I held in so much, when I held back, when I seemingly held up, till all my tensed muscles ached and my eyes burned, and I hated myself for expecting more—too much—and then, one day, alone in our home, I yelled out my anger; I screamed in pain; I shouted out my disappointments and my fears. And finally, I wept. I sobbed and then

I began to grieve for what I thought I had lost: the perfect child. The package in which I had so neatly wrapped myself came undone, and the questions, the fears, the suspicions all gained voice, and my guilt for not knowing fast enough, for not being able to control circumstances, for having denied the problems, for the shame I felt, the sadness, the myopia. And always the question, why me?

"A child like that." That's how someone once referred to her, when noting with some degree of "professional objectivity" her insecurities, her delays, and her confusions. I have faced too many "clinical" professionals whose evaluation comes across as criticism. I needed warmth and understanding and sensitivity then; I still do. I can still recall how my face burned with embarrassment and then turned to gray stone, and how I could taste the lump that began to rise in my throat; I gulped—and gulped again—and said very little, and I moved away very quickly. A *child like that?* What does that mean? Then, of course, I asked myself: A father like that? What did I do wrong? What do I still do wrong? What can I do now to correct the wrongs and make everything better?

I have been impatient with her, and angry, and then remorseful and self-critical. I have made demands of her so she would "fit in," and when she did not, I felt at first annoyed, then disappointed, and then depressed. Why couldn't she walk up the steps without holding on to me? And why did I try to loosen her grip on me? How terrifying the lack of support must have felt to her. What possessed me? I didn't know. I had to learn; she and I had to learn, as part of a team.

But today, I rejoice in small changes. I am awed by how much she learns and does and tries. It is the world, if we allow it, that creates the barriers to her learning, that accompanies messages with confusions. I have developed an assertiveness that I did not know I would need, or that I could create, as a parent. At times, I remind myself of a bird flying over the nest, trying not to hover, giving her space and nurturance, allowing her opportunities to fly, and ready to pounce on anyone or anything that would hurt her. I know I appear overprotective, but what does that mean? How does anyone define what is too much? I am learning to let her be who she is. I work to reach a balance: I know her difficulties, yet I recognize her need for self-expression, growth, and independence. As I understand and accept her difficulties, I am less impatient. As I accept the explanations for her difficulties, I am more accepting of the responsibility for her therapy programs.

She has a language-learning disability. She has a number of difficulties with understanding, processing, and expressing some of the more subtle aspects of language. She has trouble sometimes remembering certain things, such as names. She sometimes strays from a topic. She has some trouble with sensory integration, so heights frighten her, and she has some trouble with balance; loud noises and drum rolls have disturbed her. Although she learns a lot of things very quickly, there are some things that are difficult for her. One such item was her learning the task, "alike but not the same." The selection of this task was to help her concentrate more on details, to perceive gradations, in order to help her with judgments, with learning new information, and with perception. As we all struggled with ways of helping her with this task, I became more aware of how we need to allow her to be aware of these similarities and differences, and I also saw that *she* is not the same, that she need not be different, but that she, like everyone else, is alike but not the same. So her struggles with the concept helped me through my struggles of accepting not just where she is but who she is, especially in my life.

Being the father of a child who has handicaps has come to mean that I produce a balance sheet of sorts, listing deficits and credits. And doing that makes me angry. Why do I need to go through this process? Do you? Why do I feel the need to explain her to anyone? Why do I feel the need to explain me to anyone? And of course, I have a partner who has shared a lot of these experiences with me. Each of us reacted to our guilt, our sadness, and our denial separately. We began to drift apart, frightened by our pain and by our blame. We hurt each other with words of blame and anger. I started to grow impatient, wanting everything to go away: the grieving, the aching, and most of all, our child's problems. These were painful times for us. As a couple, we struggled. Never in our relationship (almost twenty years) had we suffered such a strain, such pressure. We were feeling so sorry for ourselves that we were beginning to forget to feel anything for each other. We allowed our child's difficulties to block our visions; we concentrated too much and too hard on her difficulties and differences. Our conversations and our disagreements centered around her problems. Only later did we concentrate on our reactions, then on movement, and finally, on ourselves and each other, first as a family and then once again as a couple.

How easy it is sometimes to be handicapped by the handicap, to be disabled by the disabilities.

At various times I have felt: resentment, helplessness, anger, withdrawal, loss, ignorance, powerlessness, possessiveness, hope, pride, and a strong desire—a need—for her to accomplish, to be correct, to do well, even to excel. I have been ambivalent toward her therapists. I want to shout: Hey, I know that. I can do that. And I also feel at a loss because I don't know something and I can't do something. And sometimes, I feel stupid, a terrible feeling. I do not like not being in charge.

And I wonder sometimes if our child has similar feelings of frustration and of lack of control over her schedule. Perhaps she occasionally wants to stop the process of therapy and say: You move too fast. Slow down. I can't always keep up with you. I don't always understand what it is that you want me to do, to be, to say, I'm only human.

I need to resolve my fear of asking for help, of admitting failure, to resist my knee-jerk reaction to run away and find a place for the three of us where we will be safe, away from the pressures of life, away from the tests that label her, away from the therapeutic sessions that show what she cannot do.

And sometimes, I just want to cry. And sometimes I do, and it's now a more positive expression, an affirmation that I am human. Period.

I have moved away from the self-centeredness of denial and withdrawal. I do not look for pity or even sympathy. I do seek understanding and compassion and patience, for her as well as for myself. Those changes have been gradual, but they have come. It was very difficult at first talking about our daughter's "problems." I am reminded of how superstitious I was; if I did not mention it, no one would notice it. IT. And, if I do not use her name, then you will not know who has the difficulty that makes her different, and that's that! I shudder that I tried to deny the problem. I am angry with myself that I tried to separate the problem from the child because I think, in a sense, I was trying to separate the hurt and rage and shame from myself. There is no "it." But there is this wonderful, loving, friendly, bright, and terrific kid who lives with us by the name of Davi Black Grubman.

And sometimes, she is a first-class pain-in-the-neck kid, who dawdles as we scurry to get us all out of the house, dressed and carrying our respective parcels for school and work. And sometimes, she appears to know how far to push me—how close to the edge—as I demand a hand in clean-up. And sometimes, she looks and becomes so vulnerable and lost and confused and frightened when too much is happening, too fast, by too many people, and I have learned (through trial and error) when to offer her a hug and when to offer her a chance to leave (but not escape), and when to allow her the choice to retreat, observe, stay, or move away. It's tough.

Davi. From the moment I knew she would join our lives, when I referred to her as "little D" (we knew this child would be named in honor of the memory of my father-in-law), I was overwhelmed by a strong sense of wanting everything to be fine, perfect, just right. I worked hard at attaining a level of perfection I mislabeled as peacefulness. I worked my schedule so that I could have consistent flex-time for caring for her. It seems now that I took so much responsibility—as if orchestrating a major entertainment event, in which everyone would be pleased by the food (vegetarians, kosher, meat-and-potatoes, low-sodium, hypoglycemic, and diabetic), the music, even the weather and the moon—that I certainly had set myself up for one big surprise: Hey, buddy, your kid's got a problem. What are you going to do about it? The dare, the challenge, ultimately, the confrontations with reality, brought me to a new level of understanding. I used to prefer the ideal; now I like the reality. I have become more comfortable with myself, so I am more comfortable with Davi. I am proud of her accomplishments. But more than all of her achievements it is her self that I love the most. And I can write (and mean it) that, because with support and help I, too, am learning her lesson: Alike but not the same.

> "Overall, parenting has humbled, awed, surprised, pleased, scared and satisfied me," writes Stephen D. Grubman. "So, fatherhood has helped me remain in touch with myself. It is important,

too, because through my daughter I have learned unconditional love—a beautiful and spiritual awakening in me." The Grubmans live in North Kingstown, Rhode Island, and have a daughter and a son.

Parenting a Premature Infant

Jay Scott Schinfeld

I guess that I will always be more concerned about Seth than about his older brother. Eric was over eight pounds, a few days late, and strong as a bull. He always seemed to stay two chapters ahead in the baby books, never really giving us much to worry about as first-time parents.

Seth came six weeks early, after a pregnancy marked by bleeding and premature rupture of the membranes. Because he weighed only half as much at birth as his brother had, we feared for his survival and his normality.

The pregnancy started easily enough, with conception the first month we tried when Sandy turned thirty. We were planning to have our kids three years apart, and for an infertility doctor, an easy conception was a blessing in itself.

Early in her fourth month, however, Sandy spotted and then bled several times. Many of our friends had spotted during their successful pregnancies. All my fellow physicians gave me the same reassuring statistics that I had quoted for years, but somehow I was not calmed by them. It became a source of tension between us, as Sandy, who was also knowledgeable and worried about the bleeding, wanted to concentrate on the ultrasound showing fetus and placenta healthy and normal. We went on with our life, and vacationed and visited friends.

We ignored the fact that Sandy was not as large this time as during her first pregnancy. She seemed perfectly healthy and ate everything she saw, but still gained no weight. I kept the worry inside, as her obstetrician reassured us that all was well. Then suddenly a trickle of clear fluid in the vagina. Sandy had ruptured her membranes two months early.

Nothing was ready. I had just started a new job, and we had moved into our first house in a new neighborhood. We had not prepared Eric or ourselves. All couples question whether they can love their second child as much as their first, or whether there would be enough energy and affection left over for each other. Why have another child just when our first was trained and getting easy? Sandy could have gone back to work or spent more time for herself. Tears, anger, and anxiety. The fear of the unknown combined with the fact that all my secret worries had come to pass.

In fact, it was a relatively easy labor, with a safe vaginal delivery of our four-pound, two-ounce little boy, who looked like a shrunken old man. He was rushed to the arms of the special care unit nurses, and we fearfully questioned whether the baby was harmed by Sandy's half-destroyed placenta.

The first few days Seth did well for a premature baby. He had some minor breathing problems, would not nurse, and turned yellow for a few hours on the third day. He was a grower, requiring relatively little care. But in contrast to our rooming-in experience with Eric, Seth was in the bright and huge intensive care unit, hidden behind a plastic dome and tied down with tubes and monitors. Sandy went home quickly to care for Eric, while I visited to touch and feed Seth day and night, often in between delivering someone else's baby. Leaving the hospital without the baby was a horror. Despite the warmth and reassurance from the nurses, we wondered if he would ever leave the nursery.

On his tenth day of life, we did bring him home, too early perhaps, but necessary for our own bonding and our need to be with him. He barely could eat the tiny amount of breast milk fed from a bottle in my arms while Sandy struggled with the electric breast pump to keep her milk supply. Every two to three hours, day and night, we fought to nourish Seth. It was a time of closeness for us, especially as he started to gain weight. Clearly he was going to survive, but, we agonized, would he be normal?

His progress was slow but steady. When people asked us his age, we found ourselves apologizing, "But he is really six weeks younger because he was premature." We watched him like a hawk to see if he could lift his head or roll over. The tension returned as we compared him to Eric, which was hard to avoid. Slowly, we learned the delicate balance, dividing love between our children.

Just when we were relaxing, having moved Seth from a carriage in our bedroom to his own crib and room, a well-meaning woman burst our bubble. She told us, without being asked, about her own premature child. She said that prematures never catch up and that her own son could not write at age fourteen. She suggested that we arrange for special schooling and teaching of fine motor skills. Was our son going to be retarded or handicapped, we wondered.

My first reaction to the woman was anger, while Sandy began to prepare herself for a "special child." Fortunately, our pediatrician took over. Although he was in the middle of moving to New York, he came over and talked with us. He explained that it was too early for testing, but that he could arrange it if we wanted. And he went over in detail why he felt Seth was making normal progress, but six weeks' delayed as expected. He said we should stop worrying about his prematurity and realize that Seth was Seth. He would simply progress at his own speed. We were indeed lucky to have someone so wonderful and competent to counsel us at that point.

Seth must have heard all the commotion downstairs, because he immediately started turning over, rocking, and rolling, and, in a few weeks, crawling and standing. Always a happy child with a big smile on his round face, he took special pleasure in showing his parents that all the fuss was for nothing.

Today Seth is progressing normally. He will be one, and his brother four, and we have two birthday parties this year to celebrate. I now take pride in the fact that I can give special attention to my patients who have bleeding during pregnancy or premature births. I can relate to them as only another human being who has lived through the same trauma can do.

Yet sometimes at night I wake up and listen for Seth's breathing. When I'm sure that he is okay, I wonder how things might have been if he had been born at term. I can never forget the helplessness I felt or the look on my wife's face during that time. I guess I'll always worry about him just that much more.

> Jay Scott Schinfeld is chief of reproductive endocrinology and infertility at the University of Tennessee's College of Medicine. Living in Memphis with his wife Sandy and their two sons, Dr. Schinfeld says: "I think that I've learned that it's possible to maintain a balance between career and family. At work, you get instant recognition and satisfaction. At home you build for the long-lasting satisfaction of helping your children grow. The latter is what counts, but both jobs are important for both parents to perform."

One Day at a Time

Kenneth H. Wolff

We finally were parents—Jackie, a mother, and me, a father. I felt happiness, elation, and relief all at the same time. As any father who has witnessed the birth of his child knows, words are very hard to come by to describe the experience and feelings. Of course, Tira was perfect: six pounds, seven ounces of perfection. Next I did what every father since Adam has done. I told anyone who would listen about the birth of our beautiful Tira. This was, indeed, a very special time.

A few days later we took Tira home to our happy house with its bright new yellow curtains. It was a very cold crisp day. I remember a feeling of wanting to get us all home so we could be safe and warm.

But we didn't remain safe and warm for long. About two weeks after Tira was born, I received a frantic message at work. There had been a freak accident involving Tira. Our dog bit her severely in the head and neck. It took only seconds to happen, and if ever I could have taken anything back in life, it would have been those few seconds.

I cannot begin to tell you what heartache Jackie and I went through. I felt overpowering rage toward the dog, who up to this point had showed no aggressiveness whatsoever. I believe I let this hatred become the outlet for other emotions, such as guilt, that I felt at the time. I remember the phrase, "that ------- dog," coming to my lips constantly as Jackie and I tried to cope with the unbearable.

Tira was in the hospital for the next nine weeks, six of them in the intensive care unit. She was very close to death. I remember when she was being wheeled on a stretcher down the corridors to have one of her many neurosurgical operations. I saw her little arm go straight up in the air, her hand clenched tightly into a fist, as if to say defiantly, "I am going to make it." I knew this little bit of a thing had a will to live, and that if it were within our power she would.

Our motto during those weeks, and in fact all the times things have gotten rough since, was to take one day at a time. No matter how good the medical care—and we couldn't have asked for better—we still have to live with the pain. And how it hurts. We've had to learn to let the bad things slip by and hope that tomorrow will be better. What else can we do? I believe the only way I got through the nightmare in the hospital was by subconsciously distancing myself from it. Not knowing if Tira was going to live or die was driving me crazy. Ultimately, denial seemed the only way I could cope.

As I look back now, I realize the experience had a great affect on my fathering. I think I was preparing for Tira's death. I felt I couldn't get close to her for fear of losing her. I was afraid the accident would turn me into a custodian and deprive me of being a father. In time I realized that I would be both. As a father I would provide what was necessary to make Tira as comfortable as possible.

While Tira was hospitalized, we spent as much time as we could with her, hoping that any bonding that took place would help us overcome at least some of this tragedy. As the days turned into weeks and it became evident that Tira was going to live, a whole new set of problems emerged.

Tira was definitely brain damaged, the severity and effects of which were not known at the time. The major damage was not from the dog bite itself but from a meningitis, or swelling of the brain. This was caused by a bug the dog carried that the antibiotics could not kill fast enough.

When we brought Tira home from the hospital for the second time, I was a nervous wreck. I don't think I slept soundly for the next year. I would listen for her breathing and be up in a flash if I couldn't hear it or if she coughed, all the while fearing she might have choked on some food and suffocated, or that some other problem may have developed. I was determined not to let anything more happen to her, ever.

As relieved as we were that Tira would live, it soon became evident that she had major problems. Her gross and fine motor skills were not developing normally, nor were her cognitive skills. The key word used to describe Tira was, and still is, "delayed."

It was very hard to watch Tira not walking and talking like other kids, who achieved these milestones at the normal times. It was even more difficult having to explain her problems to friends and relatives, who had good intentions but no idea how painful it was for us to talk about them.

Around the time of Tira's first birthday, she was diagnosed as having a seizure disorder, yet another in a series of setbacks that we were not sure we could get through. Sometimes it seemed as if the only thing to be thankful for was Tira's great will to live. It must be the good Irish and German stock she inherited. Every time we became depressed over these setbacks, the phrase "take one day at a time" would help us cope. Perhaps the fact that we survived the first year means we can survive anything.

Tira finally stabilized as much as we could expect. We were emotionally drained, but coping. At about eighteen months, she began a wonderful early intervention program. This state-run program assessed Tira's total needs and designed a specific program for her. For the first time I felt that we were not alone, that someone else was going to help. I felt, if nothing else, that she was moving in a positive direction. The pressure on us was eased a little and that was very important. It gave Jackie and me a little rest and gave Tira a lot of therapeutic attention.

I would be kidding myself if I said there is no depression attached to this nightmare. It creeps up on you when you are at your weakest. In my case the depression has come when there is a major crisis with Tira. Although I try to function as well as I can, I know my capacity to handle everyday problems is diminished. I put off simple chores, like taking out the trash or watering the plants. I found recently that if I do these things when they need doing, even though I don't want to, it makes me feel better. The lack of motivation, however small, is the tip-off, if you will, to the beginning of depression. So much for self-analysis.

Tira continued pretty much the same, although there was some progress. One problem, however, surpassed all the others: how could we communicate with her? We didn't know if she could understand us. This question was answered in a small way one day when we were riding in our car and she became very fussy. I began singing the nursery rhyme "Hickory Dickory Dock." Not only did the crankiness stop, but by the time the clock struck seven she was giggling and laughing. We had finally found a way to reach our Tira. It was through music. We purchased a set of recordings that brought Tira to life and gave us a way to communicate.

There have been times, however, when not even music helps, and these times are the blackest. They usually come about when the medication controlling Tira's seizures fails to do the job and she goes into a semicomatose state, unable to eat or drink; she requires hospitalization then until a new drug therapy takes control. These are always major setbacks for the three of us, but her ability to bounce back from these ordeals is truly heartwarming.

Tira finished the early intervention program, and at the age of three she went to preschool where she has been for the last three years. She has shown us her ability to pick and choose from different pictures she recognizes. She is making decisions. She understands! She can now understand us enough to nod yes or no in the correct context 75 percent of the time. This has come about through very arduous and patient work on the part of Jackie and Tira's preschool teachers. It is their inventiveness and persistence that has brought Tira into a world that is brighter than it might have been otherwise.

Today we look back at all we have been through and are better able to cope with the problems as they arise—not because they are any less acute than those of the first dark days, but because we have experienced so much we now know where to turn for help. Being the father of a handicapped child has taught me that fathering does not come easily. There is no right way or wrong way. You do what you think is best. I no longer feel that I am performing custodial care—I am being a father to my daughter.

> Kenneth H. Wolff and his wife, Jackie, have two daughters, Tira and Johanna. Currently a dormitory manager at Massachusetts Institute of Technology, Ken's approach to fatherhood is "to take one day at a time."

POSITIVE IMAGES, © *Jerry Howard*

Chapter Seventeen
Serious Illness in a Child

Errand of Mercy

Judson Esty-Kendall

I had been a father for only two and a half years when my son, Luke, was diagnosed with leukemia. Just as fatherhood itself had forced dramatic changes in the conditions of my life, changes that were generally desired but never fully anticipated, so my child's illness again altered my approach to time, to work, and to my view of myself as a father.

Luke was hospitalized for several weeks immediately after diagnosis and returned to the hospital twice more that winter for careful management of infections. The treatment initially consisted of intensive radiation therapy and chemotherapy. The radiation lasted about three weeks; the chemotherapy continued through a series of slowly tapering cycles over the next two years. Luke has now been in sustained remission for three years following the end of his treatment, but we have two years yet to go before "remission" becomes "cured."

My own emotional reactions to his illness were intense and varied. Far more emotional energy was created than could be easily released through ordinary social channels, so I found outlets both through writing down descriptions of various incidents and my reactions to them and in sharing my thoughts with a group of other parents of cancer patients who met regularly under the auspices of the Candlelighter's Foundation.

It is impossible to overstate the importance of communicating with other similarly situated parents "when things go wrong." Each parent, each family, lives with its own private fears and frustrations and comes to feel that its situation is unique. These fears, when contained solely within the individual parent or family, can assume gigantic proportions. Through contact with other parents who are as afraid as we ourselves, the experience can be generalized, and we come to understand that we are not alone, that we are not the only ones who sometimes feel unequal to the task before us. The five passages that follow are ones I shared with other parents in our group.

Double glass doors slid apart at the silent command of an electric eye. I hurried through, harried by this stop at the hospital on the way to a hearing. The note, carefully placed on my desk, had said only, "Cindy called. Drop by hospital before your eleven o'clock. They're admitting Luke for tests." I was running late already, couldn't keep the judge waiting, feeling irritation approach anger. Luke's tiredness and pale complexion, the signs that had led us to call the doctor, had suggested some form of simple anemia. I guessed that they would probably look at his blood and make him pee in a bottle and then send him home with no orders beyond bed rest and aspirin.

Hospitals always seem so gigantic and mechanical, almost menacing. The walls here are poured concrete; the architecture is massive and complex. As I strode past the bank of elevators in the enormous front lobby on my way to the information booth, a bell rang like a jackpot and a yellow arrow flashed, pointing up. The heavy steel doors slid open, and people began to move in many directions.

After some confusion and the waste of more of my precious time, I finally found Cindy and Luke in the young doctor's office at the family clinic. They had apparently been there for some time, the doctor attempting to make small talk until I arrived. Cindy's face was red and her eyes puffed. Luke stood beside her, as pale and slow as he had been all the previous week, but with those brown eyes still soaking in detail. I began to feel like a skater on thin ice—must keep moving, must not stop to think.

"Your son speaks well for his age," the doctor observed by way of greeting. "Just two and a half, I understand."

In my impatience I half resisted this obvious pitch to my parental pride. Doctors are seldom subtle. "He usually manages to mix up his words just enough to give us a chuckle. So what do you have to tell us?"

He responded with the serious look from his patient rapport repertoire and began his explanation in a solemn voice. "I don't want to alarm you. We don't know for certain and won't until we perform a bone marrow test, but the preliminary signs from the blood count we did indicate a 90 percent sure thing your son has leukemia. His blood counts are extremely low. If you or I had the same levels, we probably wouldn't be able to walk. He's being admitted for the bone marrow and for an immediate complete transfusion."

I felt as if I had just stood up hard under a low ceiling or had slammed my finger in a car door; there was a sudden shock and then a calm moment of indescribable clarity as the body braced for extreme pain. Cindy's tears began anew. Her lips were trembling as we reached out and intertwined fingers instinctively. Luke said, "Mommy's crying," informing us of an odd fact he seemed just to have noticed. She touched his cheek; he accepted the gesture by laying his head on her knee. I thought of his symptoms during the past week when I had tried to convince him to run again.

"Hey fella, why won't you run with Daddy?" I had asked as we strolled along the dirt road behind our house on a warm afternoon.

"Because I'm walking," he had said simply, as if that explained all.

Soon, after several oddly perfunctory questions and answers about treatment and causation and percentages, I carried him out of the doctor's office and back through the long corridor into the main hospital for admission, a two-year-old child facing two years of difficult treatment, perhaps inconclusive, perhaps ineffective. As I walked with him through the lobby and past the small crowd waiting by the elevator, thinking of the terrible journey he was about to undertake, I heard the bell again and saw the arrow flash. Luke turned in my arms, pointed toward the sound and the light and the people milling through the steel door, and said in a voice of soft regret, "I want to ride on the alligator."

I wrote the following poem on the occasion of Luke's first bone marrow test, a procedure involving the insertion of a thick, spike-like needle into the child's hipbone, which is repeated regularly in the course of treatment and is the source of much fear.

The white hot room
Silver and glare of
Unshadowed light.

Needles and knives,
Blood on the floor in
Droplets fresh and dried.

Screams of my own
Son held bruised by
Unrelenting hands in a
Belly-down spreadeagle.

Nightmares of Nazis who
Call themselves "Doctor"
Vanish
As our doctor smiles,

The sample is good
And soon we will
Know
Where to begin.

Lord but
An errand of mercy
Begins
At the gates of Hell.

He hadn't eaten anything since Tuesday morning a week ago, nothing. It was because of the Adriomycin they said and the Vincristine, those medicines with names like demons or warrior gods. Not to worry, they said, he would eat when he needed to, but we had become obsessed with the need to have him eat something, anything, in order to gain strength and fight back.

Now, suddenly, to our glorious surprise, he was demanding an ice-cream cone. The children's ward refrigerator always held plenty of ice cream in a wide variety of flavors, but somehow on this particular Sunday there was not a single cone in the entire hospital. Luke is a stubborn child, a stubborn person, and he made it clear that it was to be an ice-cream cone or nothing. We gathered like conspirators while he pouted in his bed, holding the metal railing like the bars of a jail. We decided to try the simplest solution first, and so brought him a large dish of dark chocolate ice cream and a spoon.

"No!" he wailed. "I don't want that. I want to lick an ice-cream cone!"

We were crushed. Then Cheryl, Cindy's friend, had a brilliant idea. She busily rolled and folded a paper towel into a perfect cone shape. Cindy quickly set a beautiful scoop of the chocolate ice cream right on top. We all leaned forward as she handed it to him, smiles forced onto our faces as we waited breathless for his response. It was not long in coming.

"No!" he cried, aggrieved. "I want the other ice-cream cone."

The nurse went to call the cafeteria one more time to double-check their failure to locate cones. Doctor Dina, the calm, friendly young woman who reads his charts and test results and gives us encouragement and advice, left the room suddenly and returned almost immediately with a Popsicle.

"Luke, would you like one of these, instead? It's just as good."

The doctor smiled and handed it to him. He pulled his arms away violently, looking at Cindy and me with an expression of horror. We were clearly letting him down. Cheryl put a scoop of ice cream between two graham crackers, but when she presented her creation, his eyes and mouth slowly folded into a cry of deep despair, and he began chanting beneath his sobs, "I want an ice-cream cone, an ice-cream cone, an ice-cream cone." Cheryl shrugged her shoulders and ate the cracker sandwich herself.

It was all too much. How could fate so conspire? The nurse returned to say there were definitely no cones in the cafeteria or kitchen. Cindy picked up her purse and car keys and stamped out to find a store, any store, that would sell us cones on the Sabbath.

Doctor Dina and I were left with him with orders to occupy his attention until real help arrived. She began slowly peeling the paper from her Popsicle, saying, "Luke, if you're not going to eat it, then I will." Her eyes twinkled, and she said to me, laughing, "I've eaten more of these since I've been working on this ward than I did in my entire childhood." She turned to Luke again. "Are you sure you don't want any of this? It's awfully good."

"No!" He gave his most defiant shout, but quickly stopped crying in favor of a more quiet, but very emphatic, sulk. Then I saw his eyes, just his eyes, turn to the sound of the paper tearing from ice. Dina began to take small tentative licks while we made small talk about children and Luke's condition. His eyes stayed straight on target, fixed by the fluorescent orange pop. I saw him lick his lips once, and I nodded encouragement to Dina.

"What about just a bite, Luke? Just one bite?" Her eyes flashed, and she smiled as if telling a joke.

"No! I want to lick an ice-cream cone!" He flared again in real anger, but calmed quickly and, touching his lips with his tongue again, swallowed hard.

She smiled again and took another delicate taste. We looked at each other and laughed, silently and inwardly, at his child's pride. I knew he couldn't hold out for long; no child has that sense of time. Any second now he would demand the remaining Popsicle. His brown eyes continued staring; he opened his mouth to speak.

"Eat the other side," he ordered suddenly. The doctor looked up, truly amused. I was astounded.

"Are you sure you don't want——" she began.

"No." He stated this as a simple fact, but after a pause he pointed and said, "Lick it there."

This couldn't be! Maybe a little more encouragement was necessary. "Look, fella, she took one of the sticks out. You'll have to eat it quick or it will fall." I felt like a member of a committee debating the proper mechanics of Popsicle consumption.

"Eat a bite," he ordered, pointing to the now melting remains. Finally she was down to the last taste. He licked his lips, he swallowed again, his eyes were wide, but he refused it quietly, almost sadly, with dignity. I wanted to both laugh and cry. He had not eaten; he had held out. If he was truly that stubborn, perhaps after all he had the strength to fight his cancer, to meet it head on and win.

Soon Cindy arrived with a package of sugar cones. He didn't lick his prize when it was finally placed in his hands; he ate it as if he were a carnivorous beast and it was raw meat. Then he complained of a tummy ache.

The night nurse seemed harried, almost pale. We could see her at his door as soon as we turned the corner from the main corridor onto the pediatric floor. Cindy asked immediately if he had had a hard night.

"That boy's awfully smart for a two-year-old," was all she said. The nurses often say things like this, the nurses and the social worker and the doctors and the play therapist. Sometimes it is because of a cute thing he says or an odd fact he remembers, and sometimes it is to touch the pride in our hurting hearts. But something was different this time. This nurse had not been laughing, was not trying to please us. She seemed touched by a dream or a ghost, glancing this way and that as if the night were closing in.

"I went in early to check on his IV. I didn't think he was awake, but he looked up at me with those cute little brown eyes and said in the smallest voice I've ever heard, 'don't kill me, don't kill me.' "

Cindy and I shifted eyes to each other and then back to the nurse, speechless, uncertain. She continued, needing to break the pounding silence.

"He's too young to say that. Don't you see? Don't you understand? He's just too young!" She was talking too loudly now and the light in her eyes pierced an imaginary darkness. We ran from her into Luke's room and held him in our arms, both of us beyond tears.

The first evening he was home from the hospital we sat around the dinner table, once again a family of three. He wasn't hungry, was still only eating on occasion, but seemed to be feeling all right. In the middle of the meal Cindy and I happened to look at him at the same time. He was playing with his knife and fork, unaware of us, lost in his child's game. His face was still pale, although not as white and translucent as it had been. His blonde hair was thinning rapidly because of the medication, and delicate golden strands decorated his blue jean shirt.

The same thoughts passed through our minds together—the knowledge of his difficult and uncertain future and our awareness of his complete inability to understand these things. His Eden had not yet presented the apple; the burden of knowledge was ours to carry, while the burden of the present, whatever that might be, was his alone. We could not explain these things to him or truly understand his struggle; we could only offer comfort when he needed it and hold his hand when he hurt. Our own hands touched and fingers intertwined; we each saw tears in the eyes of the other.

Sensing our silence, he glanced up from his play and stared at us for several seconds, at our love and despair. I expected him to cry as well, but instead, after a moment of obvious indecision, he smiled an exaggerated smile. He scrinched up his nose and ducked his head like a Hollywood child star. He began to say nonsense syllables, a child's way of making jokes, and then laughed out loud and made another face. Cindy and I began to chuckle with him; we simply couldn't help it. Our laughter grew, was infectious, broke out of control to the point of exhaustion where every word spoken, every gesture made, seemed completely and indescribably funny.

There we sat, a young family in a moment of private joy. A small child, sick near to death, clowning to cheer up his parents, and those parents, who have said a thousand times to each other and to themselves, "if only I could bear some of his pain," having their burdens lifted by the child, all on an errand of mercy.

Judson Esty-Kendall writes, "I was born in St. Louis, but escaped East as a young teenager, finishing my education in England and Boston. My current home is Portland, Maine, where I work as a legal writer, although I am most at home in Glenburn, Maine, where my family-raising activities began. Beyond fatherhood, the things most important to me are love, words, music, and the great outdoors."

My First Priority

Dave Van Manen

My experience as a father has led me down many roads. Most have been extremely joyful and rewarding, a few have been a bit difficult, and one was a nightmare. Two weeks after her first birthday, my daughter, Sierra, nearly died from spinal meningitis. Sierra is now almost three, but to this day just thinking of that horrible period and the pain it caused us can bring me to tears.

Sierra seemed to enjoy life right from the start. The smile on her third day in this world may have been gas, but I don't think so. She was always happy! By nine months, she was walking. She loved to nurse and was still nursing very often at one year. People would constantly comment on how healthy and happy she looked, and indeed she was never really sick that first year.

The evening of May 14, soon after her first birthday, was typical— Sierra was full of energy, shining as usual. But the next morning, she didn't awaken as she usually did. We checked her and she felt slightly feverish, so we figured she wasn't feeling well and needed the sleep. A couple of hours later, she still wasn't awake. I carried her from her room and sat her up on the couch, but she barely woke up—she seemed only to want to sleep. She had a fever, but it wasn't excessively high. At this point, we recalled Sierra colliding with a swinging door about four days earlier. Thinking she may have been suffering some delayed reaction to that collision, we called ahead to the clinic, got her dressed while she was still in a dream state, and raced over.

We live in a small mountain community twenty-five miles from the nearest city, and I still remember reassuring Helene while we drove to town that Sierra had only a slight concussion and they would simply tell us to go back home and watch her closely. But when we arrived at the clinic, they took us immediately—not making us wait the usual forty-five minutes. Still, I assumed that was normal policy with potential head injuries. Sierra had become, by this point, lethargic and totally nonreactive to our futile attempts at stimulating her. The pediatrician pointed out her short, rapid breathing and accelerated pulse. The doctor's obvious concern made me nervous. Then, without warning, she said simply, "This looks like spinal meningitis." At that moment, all I wanted to do was take my daughter in my arms and run away. But I bit my cheek and hung in there.

The doctor first wanted to do a chest X ray to eliminate the possibility of pneumonia. When I strapped Sierra into the brace for the X ray, she seemed so far away—as if the tremendous life force that was in her only the day before was quickly slipping away. She just sat there, staring into space. I can still hear the X-ray technician commenting on how he had never seen a little child so passively surrender to being strapped into that brace. I began to cry, but again I fought back the tears. The X rays showed up negative.

Back in the examination room, the doctor suggested we meet her at the hospital emergency room where she could do a spinal tap. I simply couldn't believe any of this; how could this be happening to *my* daughter? We followed a natural vegetarian diet, Sierra was breast-fed, we lived and played in a healthy, clean, mountain environment. This wasn't supposed to happen to people like us!

I kept my cool enough to request a second opinion. So off we went across town to another clinic. Again, the red carpet treatment, and we met the second pediatrician. He seemed calm, relaxed—he even seemed to respect us for our "natural" way of living. By this time, Sierra seemed to be almost in a coma, she was lifeless. I was, for the first time, becoming painfully aware of the fact that she just might be dying. Imagining life without Sierra horrified me—I was nearly sick to my stomach.

This doctor also suggested that we immediately meet him in the emergency room where he could do the spinal tap. Ten minutes later, we were at an examination table, watching a nurse set up the tap. The doctor asked us to leave while he performed the tap, promising to call us as soon as he was done. He said he would be nervous if we hung around and watched. My initial reaction to this was, "No way, Sierra is *my* daughter, and I am staying right here with her." My preparation for our home birth had taught me to be assertive and made me aware of my rights. I had no trouble letting him know this, but his honesty about how he would feel made sense. What I wanted was to make this as quick and easy as possible for Sierra. So, after one last kiss, I left the room.

While waiting, I suddenly felt no more inhibitions about crying. Who cares if men are not supposed to cry? I never believed that anyway. The wait, which seemed like an eternity, yet was only about five minutes, was a mixture of tears and prayers. I couldn't understand why God was letting this happen to Sierra. I would have traded places with her in a second.

Finally, we were called back into the emergency room. Sierra was awake now—crying, but awake. They wanted to take some blood, so I stayed with her while Helene spoke to the doctor. I hated holding her down while they poked for a vein. She looked searchingly into my eyes, asking "Why?" I knew she couldn't understand. All I could do was hold her and love her and assure her that she would be all right.

The spinal fluid came out cloudy, which was a sure sign of spinal meningitis. There was no time to lose. We had to get her upstairs and started on an antibiotic. I barely remember the next few hours. I do recall phoning my brother and completely falling apart as we talked. I managed to convey the fact that Sierra was very sick and asked him to bring some things to us at the hospital when he could.

It was now late afternoon and Sierra was asleep, the IV dripping the life-saving antibiotic into her. We finally got to spend a few minutes talking to the doctor. He painted a grim picture. Initial tests on the spinal fluid showed she had a severe case of bacterial meningitis. All that could be done was being done. Her chances of survival were fifty-fifty; should she survive, there was a very high chance of residual effects, such as retardation or deafness. He suggested we go home and try to get some rest; she'd be well cared for and we would be notified if anything came up.

Well, there was absolutely no way I could have left her. Sierra was my precious daughter, the child I received into this world only a year before. Leaving her there was an outrageous thought, a thought that even now, as I write this, makes me furious! I suppose they sensed my anger, because we were never asked to leave again. It was firmly set in my mind: Sierra was to have either Helene or me at her side at all times.

That night was spent praying, crying, and painfully trying to accept all that had occurred during the past twelve hours. Nurses were in and out constantly; the little sleep either of us got was on the floor next to Sierra's crib. I remember but a few details of the next few days. Sierra seemed somewhat improved to me, but the doctor was not very encouraging. The second spinal tap showed some improvement, but the white blood cell count was still much higher than it should have been. Finally, that Sunday, the doctor announced that he felt sure Sierra would make it. He added, however, that the chances were still very high that she would not be normal. At least we knew that she was going to live.

By this time, we had literally moved into Sierra's room. Most of the nurses, we knew, would have preferred that we leave so they could take charge. But I saw no reason why I couldn't take Sierra's temperature, why I couldn't bathe her, why I couldn't be there for her. They were paid nurses doing a job, but I was her father. So we stayed, bugged the staff, and witnessed Sierra's miraculous recovery.

I resumed going back to work the following Tuesday. I am a private guitar instructor and was teaching in the afternoon only a few days a week at that time. Being away was very difficult; my ability to concentrate was practically nonexistent. But, once I adjusted to the reality of my child's illness, I realized that we still had financial obligations. I was reluctant to leave Helene alone with Sierra, but she convinced me that she felt confident and could always call me should something arise. So my students had to put up with a very spaced-out guitar instructor for a while.

Mercifully, it was becoming obvious that Sierra was not going to suffer any major handicaps as a result of the meningitis. She still knew her parents, her relatives, and her friends. She knew all her animals and animal sounds, could hear a watch tick at both ears, and retained her incredible interest in books. In fact, she couldn't have been kept confined and hooked up to an IV *without* her books. She spent hours and hours looking through them, and I spent hours and hours reading to her. To the amazement of both the doctor and the nurses, Sierra proved that meningitis wasn't going to stop her; her love for life was as strong as my love for her.

The next week was spent playing with toys, reading countless books, relearning to walk, and longing to go home. Fifteen days after we entered the hospital with our lifeless daughter, we were ready to go home. Sierra literally ran out the front doors of the hospital! Driving home that beautiful spring evening, I was the most thankful father alive.

> Dave Van Manen and his wife, Helene, reside in Beulah, Colorado, where they are a performing duo—guitar and vocal harmony. They have two daughters, Sierra and Sequoia. "Through my music," writes Dave, who is a member of the Baha'i faith, "I seek to touch the hearts of my audience with feelings of peace, happiness and love. My involvement with childbirth education reflects my feeling that both the woman and the man are equally important in the preparation for and experience of childbirth, as well as parenthood."

Chapter Eighteen
Miscarriage and Death

Aftermath

A. Chris de Laurier

Aftermath
A word most appropriate
Old English for "after the cutting down"

Aftermath
It has been a long time since the cutting down
Of my son
By wayward, uncontrollable cells in his body

Before
During his illness
Model behavior was the rule
Was the expected
Model father
Model husband
Model parent
In the home
At the hospital
In the community
Yet my heart screamed out
In silence
To silence
  Something is terribly wrong!
  I am hurting
  What is happening to my world?
But the model remained
In place

In step
Insane!
Within that insanity, the appearance of sanity
Which was the most insane thing of all

And then the cutting down
The end
His death
The insanity continued
But the model remained in step
The hurting grew
And the anger, the rage
The rage always there
Began to flow

Rage at the universe and at all within it
It rose up quickly and spilled
Flooding my plains of existence
My son was dead
Someone would pay for that obscenity

But where to place this rage
God?
Futile
My wife?
No sense
Our doctors?
Easy but wrong targets
My friends?
Meaningless
Myself?
Yes
Yes, that was the solution
But there was still the model
And the model remained
Outside
But inside
The rage flowed and then washed back
Like the tides
Pains and guilts, uncovered, covered
By this sea of rage
And the self slowly drowned in it
Not for days
Not for weeks

Not for months
But for years
The aftermath

Withdrawal
Normal reaction to pain
But the withdrawal spread
To my wife
To my sons
To my friends
To everyone
Withdrawal
But the model remained

Then the surprise
Part miracle
Mostly miracle
Miracles often come as surprises
A miracle of love and friendship
She took my hand and held on
For my life
   The currents are strong and swift
   The waters treacherous
   Find the shallows
   Stand up and be free
She counseled
Standing
Impossible at first
I was used to the pain
I was used to the model
I was afraid of the uncertainty
I was afraid to believe
In myself
Finally, I struggled to stand
I fell back, battered by my hidden tides
But she held firmly
And I tried again
And again
Standing and falling
And standing
Each time the standing becomes more possible
More probable
More necessary

Sometime
In recent times
I let go
And let my son die
That death that he died over five years ago
He is not ever forgotten
And there is still pain
Most likely for always
But now I do sing
With tears
I do sing of his life

A. Chris de Laurier is a physician who lives in San Diego, California, with his wife and two sons. "To live my life so that my children (and others) respect me, all the while knowing that they could be loved no more or no better than they are loved by me—that is what is most important."

Life Miscarried

Tim Page

It was early one June morning when the doctor called and confirmed Vanessa's pregnancy. I had been listening to the Brahms F minor Piano Sonata—to the rapturous descent of melody that opens the second movement—and the soft, still sense of wonder I felt will follow me forever, with this tender andante a soundtrack for the memory.

The remaining four months of the pregnancy more closely resembled a Mahler scherzo: a grimacing series of phantasms that shattered hopes and balances. For it was obvious, almost from the beginning, that something was wrong. Days blurred together, a confused mixture of tears and blood, centered only by visits to the obstetrician. Any joy in the pregnancy was always tempered by fear; I cooled our loved ones' enthusiasm with mumbled admissions that there were problems along the way.

After Vanessa was confined to bed, we endured the New York summer as near prisoners in our apartment, the leaden heat relieved only by an occasional breeze off the Hudson. Finally, in late September, it was over. My wife, nearly four months ahead of schedule, entered the hospital for a 16-hour labor—the most excruciating pain, it is said, that a human being can bear—all to produce a half-formed visitor, a child that could not stay.

Every manual provides a different statistic: one out of four, five, seven or 10 pregnancies ends in miscarriage. By any standards, it is a common occurrence. Yet miscarriage is a subject that few men can easily discuss. One is tempted to pretend it didn't happen, to relegate the experience to the safety of nightmare. During an era when every intimate human phenomenon has been catalogued, dissected and analyzed in clinical detail, it is perhaps revealing that there should be such wide, expert disagreement about the prevalence of miscarriage.

It is not merely the numbing, animal sense of loss that causes us to flinch from the subject; it is the abstract quality of that pain. For an unborn child could be anything at all: it is ours, it is us, but we know little more. We can only imagine the color of its eyes, the chime of its laughter, the breadth of its dreams. There is nothing concrete to mourn, only a negation of infinite possibility.

Men are physically excluded from the birth process; no matter how many Lamaze classes we attend, no matter how much of the burden we wish to shoulder, our knowledge of motherhood is necessarily vicarious. Still, if I could not ease Vanessa's physical pain, I wanted to provide a base of love and support. So, assuming a well-meaning boosterism that I now fear may have seemed roseate and superficial, I found reassuring answers to all of my wife's complaints and relayed tale after tale of disastrous pregnancies with happy endings.

And, at times, I thought we had a chance. During those occasional days when everything seemed, however temporarily, to be progressing smoothly, we would talk for hours, meticulously planning our first 20 years of parenthood—discussing nutrition, religious training, sex education, even college tuition.

But the pains returned, with increased severity, and optimism ebbed. The doctor confessed his helplessness: There was probably a healthy baby inside Vanessa, he said, but we could only watch, wait and hope that she didn't go into premature labor. It became my duty to keep her comfortable—adjust the television, fetch some ice water, cook an amateur meal, and occasionally kiss her swollen abdomen and beg our baby to hold on for just a few more weeks.

It was not to be. The agonies of childbirth are usually assuaged by anticipation, but Vanessa entered into labor without hope, full knowing that her child could not yet live outside the safety of our womb, but unable to stop the impending expulsion.

What may I write of my firstborn son that will neither demean nor romanticize his brief life? Born after sunset, dead by daybreak, his 11-hour scrap of existence was little more than a shuttle down fluorescent hallways, a tour of wards and laboratories. He surely felt the violence of his birth, may have sensed a few flutterings of human consciousness when they placed him in the incubator, and then fell back into darkness.

For a man, the decision to become a father is, in some ways, a *memento mori*. It is an admission of our own mortality. We resign our supremacy in the vanguard, and take up the good fight for somebody even newer, even more helpless than ourselves. Yet it is also a supreme affirmation. I have heard it said that all young men believe in their primacy, but it sometimes seems that the members of my age group came to maturity believing—silently but profoundly—that these were the final days; that we were to have no sequel. Our fear of immediate extinction has caused many of us to pass through life as though it were an endless Sunday brunch, grasping out halfheartedly at trends and textures. I have spent my share of time mouthing the platitudes of nihilism, while secretly frightened of caring too deeply. If you hold on to nothing, little can be taken from you.

I will never again subscribe to this philosophy; a conscious decision has been made—not merely to survive, but to live. Vanessa and I fought—failed, to be sure, but fought hard all the same—and discovered a new selflessness, even a peculiar glory, in the struggle. We hope to become parents soon, with as little pain as possible. But, come what may, we are now caught up in life's intensity and gifted, for the first time, with an awareness of our fragile place in the continuum.

Tim Page writes about music for the *New York Times*. He is the editor of *The Glenn Gould Reader*, recently published by Knopf.

A Father's Miscarriage

Michael K. Robinson

Intellectually I have always believed that a miscarriage is Nature's/God's way of saying that something serious is wrong with a fetus and that it must not be allowed to continue growing. I have believed that it is far better to let it go than to have medical technology impose its will on us and upset the natural order of things.

I also know that the occurrence of a miscarriage is relatively common and have several friends and relatives who have experienced a miscarriage during one or more of their pregnancies. When this happened, I would express my sorrow to the woman in as few words as possible, and that was that. What else was there to do? After all, I have never known anyone—male or female—who seemed to do anything more. Armed with this perspective, I considered the possibility of our first pregnancy terminating early through a miscarriage as a throw of the dice; what would be would be.

Our first son, Matthew, was the result of a healthy, uncomplicated pregnancy. Two years later, with our biological clocks steadily ticking away—I was thirty-five and Kathy thirty-four—we began talking about having another child. But it was not to be. Eight weeks into our second pregnancy a miscarriage occurred. Kathy was ill for a while (nauseated, tired, weak from bleeding), and was hospitalized for a D&C—a routine procedure after a miscarriage (as I later learned). She experienced the range of emotions that most women who have had a miscarriage experience: loss, anger, self-doubt, and fear. Everyone seemed to sense that this was a difficult and emotional time for Kathy and responded accordingly by expressing their concern and offering her their support.

I was usually taken aside by female friends and coached as to how I should react to Kathy, what I could expect her to be feeling, how to comfort and reassure her.

Some time after the miscarriage, I began having flashbacks to when we were first pregnant with Matthew. Then, as now, the focus of everyone's concern was on Kathy. I was, then as now, merely the conduit through which messages were funneled and questions answered. I remembered feeling that everyone assumed that pregnancy is a "woman only" condition and that parenting is a "mothers only" activity. As a man and a father, I was expected neither to have much interest in "Kathy's" pregnancy nor much interest in or skill at parenting. And now, it was assumed that, as a man, I didn't have any feelings associated with the miscarriage. I was once again relegated to the status of observer of events that I wanted to be a part of, to understand, to feel, and to learn from.

Why were people so sincere and well meaning in responding to the sense of loss that Kathy experienced, while never once recognizing that I, too, had experienced a loss? I resented their attitude just as I did when we were pregnant. And I felt isolated again, just as I did when there was so little support from others for my decision to be a full-time, at-home father, while Kathy returned full time to work. People told me what to expect Kathy to feel, how to respond to her, how to comfort her. But what about me? Why didn't someone respond to me, comfort me, tell me what I might expect to feel? I was angry that the miscarriage had occurred. I wanted another baby. I felt a tremendous loss. I remember holding tightly to Matthew and being overwhelmingly grateful for his existence. And I was worried about Kathy, about her physical as well as her emotional well being. Would she in fact recover completely? Could there be complications? Would she be able to get pregnant again? I didn't know the answers, and I was frightened. Most of all, I was alone with feelings that I wasn't expected to have, allowed to have, or even aware of having at first.

We now have two sons and are out of the baby-making business. I haven't forgotten our miscarriage; neither have I fully put to rest the unsettledness it caused me. But if I have learned nothing else from our experiences of the last four and a half years, I have learned that feeling unsettled means being open to experience and thus open to growth. Our miscarriage reaffirmed for me that Kathy and I, different as we are as man and woman, are more similar than we think in regard to our reactions and feelings about pregnancy, birth, miscarriage, and parenting. If men and women can recognize their similar needs rather than assuming themselves to be biologically determined opposites, then we can all fully participate in life's joys and tragedies.

Michael K. Robinson describes himself as being an "at-home full-time father" for the past several years. Living in Bloomfield, New Jersey, with his wife and two sons, he is associate editor of *Nurturing News: A Quarterly Forum for Nurturing Men*. He also teaches part time at the college level.

Joshua's Death: A Parable

Mark Oberman

A wise man, often sought for counsel, loved his only child with all his soul. While he was away on a trip, the child died suddenly, and his wife had to think long and hard about how to break this devastating news to him.

When he returned, she told him of a dispute between two men. One was very wealthy, and before going away on what he knew would be a long journey, he entrusted a responsible man in the community to look after the most precious of his jewels. The second man was trustworthy and kept them under his protection. As the years passed, he grew proud and extremely attached to them. He derived much pleasure from them, and they enhanced his status in the community.

After several years the owner came to reclaim the jewels, but the responsible man was reluctant to part with them. The wife asked her wise husband how he thought the dispute should be settled, and he responded that painful as it was for their temporary caretaker, the jewels should be returned to their rightful owner. Then she told her husband of their child's death.

On a still, hot Indian summer morning in 1972, my only child—Joshua— died suddenly in an unexplained freak drowning. He was twenty-six months old and his younger sister was six months in the womb.

I was twenty-six years old and had given him perhaps the best, certainly the most spontaneous two years of my fathering life. As I remember it, once he was mobile in his last year, we were going everywhere together—getting groceries and lumber, picking blackberries in the fields surrounding our country house, working in the garden. Enthusiastically, I taught him to pick a red tomato and leave the green ones to ripen. With great pride and delight he learned and imitated. We were able joyfully to share the child in us with each other. I loved his curiosity, his innocence, his spontaneity, his freedom in being un-self-conscious. I loved being an important person to him.

Unlike most two-year-olds I'd seen, he demonstrated an uncanny ability to sense what other people were feeling. Many friends who had been sad in his presence had been comforted by him. He would look at them lovingly and stroke their hair or face gently. They were deeply grateful and held his friendship in high regard. He made people laugh, and he laughed infectiously with them. Somehow Joshua had gotten out of his crib (for the first time), toddled past our bedroom and downstairs, opened a massive wooden front door swollen tight in the jamb from humidity, and walked outside. Ignoring us. Ignoring the candy open for his inspection in the front foyer. The dogs were out. Surely they knew where he was, but they were of no help. When I awoke that morning and couldn't find my son anywhere in our house, I called our nearest neighbors, two hundred yards down the road, to help us look for him. Then I ran off, calling and searching, growing more and more frightened.

My wife's screams a quarter mile away brought me running. They coursed through my body as if I'd been electrocuted. I ran toward them in total panic, like my life (or his) depended upon it.

Our neighbor was holding my wife in a bear hug in the road. She was screaming and struggling, pointing to his backyard, to the unfenced ground-level pool way in the back. I ran straight to the water, no one blocking my path, and reached him where he lay by the pool. He looked like pale blue marble. Perfect, beautiful, and lifeless. He looked like a copy of Joshua, not Joshua. Joshua was gone. The difference is indescribable. I touched him. Cold. I lifted him and cradled him and rocked him and cried and went numb. And felt like a part of me had died.

And then commotion and people, some standing speechless and frozen, others running around trying to take charge. And hands pulling me away. I can't remember the details or sequence. Somehow I was with my wife. Then we were separated and I was with the priest saying prayers and offering last rites over this material form that resembled Joshua. Then he was gone. I didn't see who took him.

Suddenly I was caught up in the process of doing: calling immediate family, contacting a funeral home, deciding on a date, what kind of casket— open versus closed. Friends and family were trying to locate my father who was camping out somewhere in the dunes of North Carolina's beaches.

News spread incredibly fast. Within hours people were there: friends, family, neighbors in various emotional states—comforters, comfortees. In contrast to the glory of the magnificent fall day, people were mostly inconsolable. The house was charged with loss, shocked disbelief, and bitter anger.

I remember being very active that first day. I could not share my grief openly, publicly. As a young man, I had a difficult time accepting the role of one who needed comforting. I feared that if I started to cry I might never stop, and I didn't want to be seen that way. So I pushed the sharp grief down and comforted others—my wife, my neighbors, some friends. If I cried it was *with* others, but rarely alone, comforted by someone in more control than I.

My clearest memory of that nightmarish time is hearing my mother making animal-like sounds in the bathroom, horrible, disturbing, restrained. Her grief and bitterness were so intense that her face and body were distorted as if she were about to explode. When I began hugging her, she was stiff and full of rage, and her language became understandable as she cried in a raspy unhinged voice, "Damn you God! Damn you God! Why did you do this to me? How could you do this to me?" I slapped her across the face, furious, and told her that if I heard her say that again, I would tell her to leave. Then I turned my back and abandoned her. That is the only time I have ever struck her.

Joshua was buried in a simple closed pine box. The service was short, nonsectarian, and appropriate. There was no wake. The same priest who had performed last rites led the service. He told the parable I have written.

Intellectually, I embraced the philosophy of the parable. I had been the temporary caretaker of a jewel of inestimable value. My pain and sorrow were understandable. I had to accept that God had a purpose, that there was a reason, whether I understood it or not. The priest and a novice, also a friend, confided that during prayer that Sunday morning, at the time of Joshua's death, the novice's concentration had been broken by a vision of Joshua being carried up to Heaven in the arms of the Virgin Mary. This was unexplained until they returned home to receive my message of his death. This gave me great comfort and strengthened my belief that this wasn't the "end" for Joshua. He was in good company.

I grieved quietly, both inwardly and outwardly. I felt and expressed no anger except the one incident with my mother. I never shook my fists upward and asked, Why? Why Joshua? Why me? Why now? *How* was the constant haunting question. How had he slipped past our room? How had he opened the front door? What made him go to the neighbor's pool? (We had never been there and it was well hidden.) How had he fallen in? Had one of the dogs pushed him by mistake? The irony was he had always hated water—from baths to wading pools.

Shortly after the "accident" (the *apparent* accident—there was undoubtedly a cosmic explanation), I was quite passive. My wife and I were besieged by well-meaning people who all had the same refrain: "You must prepare for your new child. You must not stay in a grieving place. You must look ahead to the new life that is soon to arrive and will need your nurturing." All of Joshua's furniture, toys, and clothes were given away, and the room was repainted. New curtains were made. New furniture was bought. All new everything. There was hardly a trace of Joshua left behind. My wife's parents were the primary initiators. They did the work, they bought the new things, they gave away the old things. They were the energy, the encouragement, the support. I had no initial objections. At least my dim memory does not recall my having any.

I was a framing carpenter working for a small construction company in a rural community. The owner was a gentle, understanding man who showed my family much kindness. I was a new employee of three months and he told me to take as much time as I needed and not to worry about money or my job. I took a week off and then returned to work. I was dazed for many months, quiet and far away. Slow. Going through the motions. Yet work was important to me as a distraction. To a certain extent I had to be alert and in the present or I was likely to have an accident. The men stayed away from me, shy and uncomfortable. My presence restrained them. This was true everywhere, a phenomenon that in turn made me uncomfortable and shy with people who were awkward, obviously not knowing what to say to me. I felt unwanted there. I stifled the natural banter that usually went on. It wasn't anything I did—just my presence. Our neighbors were unable to look me in the face.

I started having fainting spells. I would become lightheaded and dizzy, and fall to the ground if I wasn't able to sit down quickly. It occurred once when I was two stories off the ground walking on a two-by-four partition, and I became frightened of serious injury.

I sought help from my doctor, who like everyone else had heard about the accident. When I told him about the fainting spells, he directed me to observe my breathing. Unknown to me, I was constantly sighing deeply, something I've learned many people do when they are depressed. "You are hyperventilating," he said, "and that's the cause of your problem. Watch your breathing. If you feel lightheaded, take nice, deep, easy breaths and you'll come around." I became conscious of my breathing, the constant weight and dull ache in my chest. Of my slowness. Of my diminished will and interest in things. The frequency of my sighs became the barometer of my depression. I never took any medication.

In three months Jennifer was born: full term, healthy. The dread of something going wrong had been following us like an enemy with a pistol cocked. Had the shock and grief done harm? Would the child carry any physical or emotional legacy? Here was a happy, active, aggressively nursing baby. We were grateful that the child was a girl; it discouraged comparisons. We told ourselves that we were relieved she had been on the way, because otherwise there would have been a sense of making a baby to replace Joshua.

Jennifer's coming displaced much of our grieving. The full daily routine of caring for a child, which we had desperately missed, returned with a welcomed busyness that answered many of our needs.

Joanne's family were still frequently with us, which made me feel increasingly stifled. It was difficult to be natural and fall into a comfortable routine surrounded by so much overly positive enthusiasm and help. I felt like I was always being watched. Before Jennifer's birth, there was usually someone around to help ward off unhappiness. I was constantly being distracted and "cheered up"—never left alone for long. This exaggerated gaiety had created an uncommunicated tension with its attempts to minimize sorrow and depression. Still it lingered. There was an overcompensation to protect this new and fragile life.

It took around six months for things to return to "normal." But "normal" as we knew it had changed considerably. We were unable to relax around the baby. There was a constant watchfulness while she was awake and frequent bed checks while she was asleep. Separation caused tremendous anxiety. We were afraid to leave her with sitters, and it was many months before we were able to take a night out together. When we finally took the chance, several calls home were necessary to make sure everything was all right. The worrying took the pleasure out of the evening (this continued to be true with our next born, Jesse, two years later). The sight of water—pools, the ocean, even baths—was almost unbearable at times. We even had anxiety about our obvious overprotectiveness.

Joanne's tension was greater than mine. Her need to control the environment, to guard against the possibility of any accidents, seemed excessive to me. And oppressive. Leaving Jennifer unattended for a matter of seconds (in a child-proofed room) to run into the next room to bring her back a rattle brought Joanne screaming at me like a banshee: "What if something should happen!" I felt trapped between satisfying her standards of vigilance, which made me nervous, or adhering to my own more relaxed standards, which often set her against me like a righteous mother protecting her young. At these moments I felt that *I* was the enemy, and I was drawn into my own guilt feelings, the omnipresent gnawing thought that there must have been at least *something* I could have done to prevent the accident. I had the uncomfortable sense that people were judging me as an irresponsible or negligent parent, but I was not sure if the observation was real or imagined. I still constantly relived the events of that September morning, trying to make sense of them.

Family life, which had always been foremost to Joanne, now became everything. I was made to feel guilty about any non-family-oriented personal interests and activities. Yet equal decision making and involvement in parenting, which Joanne had been reluctant to grant me before Joshua's death, became impossible. I slowly disengaged and allowed Joanne unchallenged authority in child-care decisions. Our relationship became increasingly strained. She was the full-time parent; I was the wage earner. I attempted to be totally committed to my family, but always felt that I fell short. I could never be a good enough father in Joanne's eyes and ultimately in my own as well. In the aftermath of Joshua's death, I was fragile and uncertain of myself.

I became more serious, more responsible, and strongly drawn toward medicine. I entered a training program for physicians' assistants, and maintained the discipline to work fourteen to sixteen hours a day, six days a week, for two years. The study of medicine strengthened my mind at a time when I needed to separate myself from my feelings of pain.

Four years after Joshua's death, my wife and I separated. The death had placed stress on an already poor marriage but at the same time made divorce more difficult. The marriage ended badly. I continued to see the children regularly.

A year later I renewed a very old relationship with a woman I had known and loved since adolescence. Upon completion of my training as a physician's assistant, we began living together. Susan was divorced and childless. After two years, both of us aged thirty-three, we had a daughter, Sara.

Our relationship is strikingly different from my marriage. I am encouraged and supported to maintain an active and involved life regarding my work and independent interests, as is she. I am both able and encouraged to have full and equal responsibility for child-care decision making. And we live in a stable collective family (six adults) rather than in a nuclear-family setting.

When Sara was one week old, she was admitted to the hospital with jaundice. Her bilirubin, a normal by-product of broken-down red blood cells, was so high that exchange blood transfusions were considered. Brain damage and even death were possible. Lethargic, she lay in a neonatal intensive care unit. Everyone was frightened, sick with worry. What separated me from everyone else was that their thinking and fearing the worst was an abstraction. My experience of it was concrete. Death in this context was already real to me. I was filled with a gnawing agony and feared not only for the infant but for myself. Could I withstand it again?

Sara did fine and was home in a week with no further problems. But I was badly shaken. My pain was grounded in an old reality that still lived inside me, much of it unresolved. It made me back off from Sara in certain ways and redirect those nurturing feelings toward Susan, her mother—supporting and encouraging her, helping out when she needed relief and offering experienced advice in areas new to her. I was a caring and responsible backup, but often didn't involve myself when others were handling things well. I was very involved in determining Sara's diet, shopping, and preparing special foods for her, making her wooden toys. But there was a subtle passivity when it came to relating to her directly.

As Sara grew out of infancy, I continued to be aware of a tension in myself that caused me greater and greater concern. Although I relaxed and became quite spontaneous with her when we played, all too often I still found myself watching her with warm loving feelings but with a reluctance to jump in.

I also had much to contend with in my relationship with my two children from my first marriage, which caused great pain for me—and for them. The coming together for short periods of time with great expectations of one another, and the separations that dashed any continuity, were difficult for all. I carried a sense of loss of them almost as tangible as the loss of Joshua. And they for me.

I decided to see a psychotherapist because I was becoming more frequently depressed and anxious and unable to connect it with anything. Almost from the start, I kept bringing up Joshua. When I talked of my own deep unidentified feelings of sadness, I kept alluding to him. It had been nine years since his death, and yet I began to realize that ever since that time, a part of me had held back from my children. It had nothing to do with loving them, but more with how vulnerable loving them made me. Together my therapist and I relived what happened. A torrent of grief exploded. It became clear that this was the major reason I was there.

I realized that I had not been allowed, both by myself and by others, to cry, to mourn, and to fully experience my grief following his death. A child's death is probably one of the worst external (not of your own body) things that can happen to you. Perfect strangers react with great emotion when they hear stories about the death of a child. Joshua's death had a powerful impact on people close to him, or not so close to him. Yet no one wanted to deal with it. It was too intense, too threatening. I have spoken with many parents in the course of my work who have painfully described how friends with children of their own have literally crossed to the other side of the street rather than talk to them following the death of their child. It's as if it is catching. They feel like they are carrying a disease.

It took me nine years to contact my rage. After one of my therapy sessions I drove off, suddenly started crying, and had to pull off the road. I heard myself almost timidly wailing, "Joshua, how could you leave me?" A fierce grieving surfaced as those words kept repeating themselves in my head. Then, as I transferred the responsibility to God, a violent hatred and rage spewed forth. I thought of my mother in the bathroom the first day, full of anger at the apparent senselessness of it all. And I understood that my fear of contacting those feelings and my need to give that horror meaning had caused me to hit her. All those years I had used my mind to explain things and had not dealt with my feelings about the unexplainable. The child in me that had been an integral part of my fathering experience with Joshua, that had contributed so much to my joy—the part that now raged like any other child who has something special taken away—had not been given a voice. And so, following the death of Joshua, the child in me died as well.

My father and I have been able to talk openly about Joshua recently. We had very little connection after the death. He had been camping and couldn't be found for three days after Joshua drowned. He was finally flagged down and told by a North Carolina state trooper, and then drove home, apparently crying continuously. He got back too late for the funeral. On arrival he was emotionally in Day One, and everyone else was at Day Four. No one wanted to go back emotionally to that day with him. He, who had loved Joshua tremendously, must have suffered intensely, alone.

I talked with him about writing this piece, and how I always broke down when I read the part about all of Joshua's things being given away. I told him how deeply I regretted having nothing of Joshua's. My father quietly admitted that he had "stolen" a pair of Joshua's sneakers and that he kept them along with his shoes on the floor of his clothes closet. He said that I could have one sneaker if I wanted it. Since we made that poignant exchange, I, too, keep that one little blue sneaker on the floor of my clothes closet along with my shoes. Somehow it gives me great comfort and makes it all seem more real. And it helps me, in a small way, to accept and enjoy the child in me and to live more fully in the present.

> "My children teach me how better to play and to be in the present," says Mark Oberman. "They contribute to an important balance between work and loving relationships." A physician's assistant, he lives in East Northport, New York, with his wife, Susan, and their two daughters, Sara and Nora. His two other children are Jennifer and Jesse.

© *Carol Palmer*

Chapter Nineteen
The Fruits of Fatherhood

Youth Not Wasted

Michael Kort

George Bernard Shaw wrote that youth is wasted on the young; but, then, Shaw never had children. If you do things with your kids, they can let you feel, albeit fleetingly, what it is like to be young. And that flash of youth, because it touches an adult presumably wise enough to appreciate it, is not wasted.

Witness, for example, the simple act of consuming ice-cream. Adults eat ice cream; it tastes good and that's about it. My kids savor it, adore it, cherish it. Getting to a favorite ice-cream parlor, it turns out, is half the fun. My two daughters don't walk. They bounce and bound. Nor do they talk. They giggle, laugh, sing, and shout. I may just be walking and talking, but I'm certainly having a good time. Once in the store, I like to watch them figit and squirm as they anxiously watch me wait in line. Of course, I'd enjoy all this even more were it not for the urgency of making sure that I get Oreo ice cream in a cup with Reese's Pieces (not m&m's, please) and chocolate in a sugar (not regular, please) cone. Usually I don't order my own portion, but not because I don't like ice cream. It's much more fun to get some from each of my kids, for that ice cream, laced with their passionate craving for the stuff, tastes so much better, especially if I can get a spoonful of Oreo with two Reeses Pieces or a bit of the chocolate just as my three-year-old is getting to the edge of the cone. Both require precise timing and a perfectly pitched "What about daddy?"

I honestly can't remember what it was like to eat ice cream as a kid, but I know that it's been decades since it tasted like this. Somehow, when I eat ice cream with other adults after a trip to the ice cream store with my children, it tastes tepid.

Witness, too, a trip to the playground and its long-forgotten swings, slides, and assorted climbing structures. When my older daughter first reached playground age, I was a little timid as I returned to the playground for the first time since my childhood. Now that's all in the past, as I find myself demonstrating how to pump a swing really high until one of my daughters finally kicks me off so she can have a turn. Actually, I like the slides best, especially the ones that spiral down. My daughters, aside from having reintroduced me to the fun of sliding ponds, also serve as my ticket to this activity, as any adult without a kid in his lap who took ride after ride down a slide among a crowd of children would, at best, be viewed with deep suspicion.

It makes me sad that for almost twenty years—from my early teens until my early thirties—I couldn't enjoy the playground. Fortunately, my youngest daughter is only three, so I have a few more years before I have to relinquish it and grow up again . . . until about twenty more years when my grandchildren give me one last fling at it all.

Witness, finally, the effect of a child's birthday party. Birthdays are events that most of us past our youth prefer to ignore, or—at best—are barely able to tolerate. With kids it's the opposite. My daughters begin looking forward to their next birthday the day after the last one. At any rate, the intensity of their feelings pulls the entire family into the maelstrom. This is especially true in my house, where the two chaotic days are less than two weeks apart.

In truth, my wife does most of the work. But there are still plenty of things for me to do, most of which I was blissfully unaware of for years. And not only do I do them, but I find myself caring as much as my daughters about such items as getting the right cartoon or magic show, or making sure that all the place cards are set out properly at the carefully set table. Sometimes I begin to feel like a kid even before the party starts. While selecting the ice cream for Eleza's seventh birthday party this year, I stood in front of the supermarket ice-cream case for about fifteen minutes in agonizing indecision and reappraisal, exactly what always happens and what I find so irritating when either of my daughters gets a chance to choose the ice cream we ought to bring home. In a slightly more serious vein, I worried no less than Eleza did when a couple of guests had to cancel, our shared wish being that enough children—and the all-important best friends—would show up and make the party a success (they did).

I have a photograph that sums it all up. It shows an ecstatic seven year old watching a magic show with her friends; it is ample proof that the day was worth the trouble. But there is more to the picture than that. For in the background, grinning from ear to ear, obviously delighted with the magic show and enjoying this party more than any other in about thirty years, are mom and dad, looking almost like a couple of kids.

I'd be the first to admit that raising children is not easy. It takes much of my time and energy and most of my patience. But in return, aside from happiness, pride, and love, my daughters have given me some simple pleasures—appreciating a butterfly, watching with fascination a perfectly ordinary bird in flight, playing Wiffle ball, riding a bike, building a sand castle at the beach, and so many more—whose existence I had forgotten or had come to ignore. They've given me, in short, a second taste of what it is like to be young. If you ask me, that remarkable gift, which could come from nowhere else, is worth far more than it cost.

> A college teacher, and author of *The Soviet Colossus: A History of the U.S.S.R.*, Michael Kort and his wife have two daughters, Eleza and Tamara. "Fatherhood keeps me too busy to worry about what I'm doing with my life, and that's a real relief."

The Joys of Fatherhood

David Riley

From the moment he was born, I've been smitten by Jake, more, I think, than even my wife dared hope. I never knew how much you could get by giving. Jake takes a lot of my time, but he gives back a dimension to my life that I cherish. And I've come to think that the world might be a very different place if its workaholics had more of this dimension in their lives.

I've always known that it's nice to be needed, but there's something so refreshingly simple and fundamental about the way Jake needs me: without words, without convoluted feelings to be sorted out, without mixed messages. He often needs simply to be held—nothing more—just loving, physical contact, accompanied by a soothing voice perhaps.

At certain predictable times, such as when he wakes up, Jake needs attention, no matter what our mood. Sometimes it's an interruption, and I don't like being interrupted. But I've come to look at it another way, too. If my work is going badly and I'm depressed about it, Jake still needs breakfast in the morning, and I know I can still make it for him and meet his need, which suggests that after breakfast I can still do my work, too, and meet some of my needs. There's comfort in the continuity of the routine; nurturing Jake has become a way of nurturing myself.

Jake makes my intellect take time off, which allows my senses and feelings to be more active. Raising a child requires plenty of intellect, certainly, but not in the same way writing does, at least not at his age. There's a refreshing difference between meticulously struggling to find the right phrase and instinctively knowing the right time to plant kisses on a soft cheek.

I get an atavistic joy out of listening to Jake's sounds. It's like watching a wildflower unfold. In the absence of words, he bursts out screams of excitement. He gestures with his voice, gurgling forth fresh, delightfully garbled notes that must sound like words to him. He is like an unfinished sculpture creating himself.

Nights are another new experience. How often do we enjoy the simplicity of total darkness? I'm much too busy (or self-important) to do so on my own accord. Only mystics soothe their souls with the experience of nothingness. And fathers and mothers walking infants at night. Normally if I can't sleep, I read. Now, even when I can sleep, I sometimes treat myself to the mystic's pleasures, or watch moonlight glisten off the stone wall outside our living room, punctuated by Jake's rhythmic breath warming the hollow of my shoulder.

Why do people glow so at the sight of babies? A month after Jake was born, we spent a weekend in New York at Christmastime. He won over the city for us. You might have thought we were carrying the deity for all the goodwill we encountered on the streets of this city where murderers and rapists prowl.

I used to resent the extra attention babies get. It seemed unfair to the rest of us. I understand it better now. There's a special charm in the way small children go about discovering the world. The slightest thing, like a piece of dust on a rug, brings squeals of delight. What an elixir for sadness! Infants delight adults by bringing them out of their frame of reference, out from under the weight of the world that hangs over them. It's hard to stay grumpy in the face of such innocent joy.

Humor often grows out of incongruity, and the sight of Jake parodying us, like a miniature adult, doubles the laughter in my life. I think of him walking around tapping a soup ladle on the floor like a cane, or looking in the mirror on the closet door, then peering behind it to see if he's there.

I don't mean to suggest, of course, that everything's easy. Jake's lack of language may be charming, but it's also frustrating and sometimes exhausting. So are the endless diaper changes and washings, the boundless energy, the constant picking up after him, the lack of sleep, the early morning risings, the arranging of baby-sitters and coordinating various siblings' needs, the car pooling, and so on.

But there's a freshness about the way this little boy meets every morning that lifts up our lives. It's like the freshness of the early morning sun sparkling off the dew on the grass. It's the same sun and the same grass every morning, but still it makes your heart stop and take notice.

I've learned that having a child doesn't have to turn you inward away from concern for the world. On the contrary. One evening my wife Martha and I watched the film, *War without Winners;* in it people were interviewed on the streets of New York and Moscow, speaking from their hearts, all saying the same thing: nuclear war would be unspeakably horrible, and it must never happen. The film also included interviews with government officials spouting nationalistic bravado, and interviews with retired officials saying that such talk is crazy. As I watched and held Jake—hovering in the hollow of my shoulder, wispy hair bobbing, dark eyes peering out, a soft ear against my cheek—I couldn't stop crying.

I was crying because Jake is so innocent and sweet and vulnerable, and we have brought him into a world being paved over with arms. Jake's being—

his size, his soul, his natural openness to the world—cuts through all the rationales that keep us building more arms for more people to use for killing even more people. Watching that movie with Jake, we knew that we would have to make room in our lives to work for disarmament in order for our lives to make sense.

Children remind us of our common humanity. Sometimes when I hold Jake at night, one small arm resting against my chest, the other on my shoulder, I think of the picture I saw in a magazine of a Russian father holding his young son in a car on the Trans-Siberian Railway. I see the twinkle in that boy's eye, much like Jake's when he gets the idea that we'll chase him. I think of that little Russian boy staggering across the floor, as Jake does, arms careening in all directions until he collapses in a pool of belly laughs when his parents capture him.

I don't read as many books as I used to because of the time I spend with Jake. I don't know as much about the sociology of that Russian father's life as I might if I had more time to read. But through Jake I make other connections—to myself and the world around me. When I'm sad, Jake's eyes still shine. He greets me as if I were shining. He greets the world as if it were shining, and before long it shines again for me, too. In an era that reveres intellectual and physical power, I learn from this little being, just up to my knees, whose power lies not in his body or his mind but in his soul. Through him I learn about my connection to that Russian father. It helps to believe— I guess I have to believe—that through such connections the world will some- how make its way toward peace.

David Riley is director of the National Campaign to Save the ABM Treaty. He lives in Washington, D.C., with his wife, Martha, and his three children, Seth, Heather, and Jake. He finds it vital as a father to "love and enjoy my children; put energy into being their father, including making time for them; let them know that it's okay to make mistakes, realizing that the main impact I have on them is by example."

Fatherhood Postponed

Carey Winfrey

My first wife and I were out of sync when it came to children. When I wanted them, she didn't, and vice versa. Perhaps that should have told us something, though even now I'm not sure quite what. In any case, the marriage was over before I knew it—literally—and once we were separated, people kept saying wasn't it fortunate there hadn't been any children. I couldn't argue with that.

For a while, after my divorce, I didn't give the idea of kids a lot of thought, though somewhere at the back of my mind lay the assumption that I would someday have them. If pressed, I would have said that being a father was not something I wanted to miss out on but that I was in no rush. There were still things I wanted to do before I got tied down.

By the time I got married again, at the age of 40, three and a half years ago, I was more than ready to be a daddy. It was as if some slow-release time capsule had suddenly gone off in my psyche, unleashing a pool of paternal yearnings. And when Jane and I had twin sons, most of our close friends our age were having babies, too. As much as I hate to think of myself as a part of any trend, it seems undeniable that Jane and I have become soldiers in a growing army of late-blooming urban parents.

The thing I was always warned against about waiting a long time to have children was that I wouldn't be able to throw a ball with them. Well, I'm here to say that I don't think it's going to be a problem. Either I'll throw balls with the best of them and that'll be that, or I won't and it won't matter a damn. Two-plus years into this fatherhood business, I know at least that what kids require of a father is a lot of attention, a lot of love and, I suspect, if mine ever reach the age of understanding, a lot of that, too. They can find other people to throw balls at them.

I like being a father. I *love* being a father. And I think I'm a better one for having waited. Though no number of years can ever adequately prepare one for the enormous delights and anxieties of fatherhood—worry and fear for his child's well-being will never be far from any father's consciousness—I also believe that coming late to it has some real pluses. One of them is the rejuvenating way kids force you to experience the world anew, a world filled with Dr. Seuss and showing off and funny animals and marching bands. Maybe some younger fathers get just as big a kick as I do vicariously viewing the world this way, but I wouldn't be surprised if it takes a bit of mileage on the old odometer to appreciate what Wordsworth was getting at with his line about the child's being the father of the man.

I know I resent the dramatic way my kids have circumscribed my life less than I would have a decade or more ago. I can hardly say I did it all, but I did enough—read enough books, saw enough movies, went to enough parties—not to mind much the degree to which those activities have been curtailed. I'm often grateful to my children for providing the excuse, as well as the reason, to stay home. I don't want to make too much of this because certainly there are times my wife and I would (and do) pay any price to escape "the boys" for a little while (and then, inevitably, we spend most of our precious time alone talking about them). But nine nights out of 10—O.K., four out of five—our sons (and whatever happens to be on the tube in the hour left to us after getting them to bed) provide sufficient diversion.

Of course, truth also compels me to confess that, lacking the energy I once had, my tyros can grind me exceedingly fine, particularly when they have a full day to do so. Many Saturday and Sunday nights find me close to tears from exhaustion. (Around *our* house, it's T.G.I.M.—"Thank God It's Monday.") But when morning comes around, assuming the boys have not awakened too many times in the wee small hours to wail for "appa juice," or "Mommy," or both, I'm again ready to give them as much of me as they want.

Then there's the money part. Admittedly, twins cost more than single babies (about double, roughly), but even one child these days creates financial burdens better born by mature than by starting salaries. Though the financial plateau I've reached after 20 years of for-the-most-part gainful employment remains modest by almost any objective standard, it is nonetheless proportionally higher than it was a decade or so ago. It is not hyperbole but fact that the woman who takes care of our children while Jane and I cavort at work makes as much money as I did not many years ago, even when the dollars are adjusted for inflation. But even if she didn't, children would have taken a much greater share of my expendable income just a few short years ago. More important, I almost certainly begrudge them the financial drain less today than I would have in all my yesterdays.

Recently, for example, my wife and I took out an amount of life insurance that makes each of us far more valuable as a dear departed than in the here and now. In my salad years, that money might have gone effortlessly into travel or clothes or cameras. I signed the insurance checks, if not joyously, with a satisfied sense that few expenditures could ever feel as warranted. It's hard to think of a better use for money than my sons' welfare.

Once the insurance was taken care of, Jane and I made out new wills. Since embarking on my fifth decade, I've given what she considers an indecent amount of thought on my own mortality; still, nothing so focuses the mind on the subject as the making out of a will. Sitting in the lawyer's office, listening to the stream of whereases and parties-of-the-first-parts, it occurred to me with the force of revelation that the expectation of being survived by one's children is yet another unanticipated pleasure of parenthood postponed. The thought of my sons carrying on after I'm gone is probably about as close to a belief in an afterlife as an aging pagan like myself is likely to get. But curiously, it's close enough for comfort.

Carey Winfrey is editorial director of CBS Magazines.

Peace of Mind

Richard Moore

This morning, about an hour ago, my young son discovered what it's like to drink the icy mist of a cold mountain stream. Dylan enjoyed it. His eyes opened wide and bright, as they do when he makes a discovery, and his mouth broke into a broad, if cockeyed, smile. Because my wife, Liz, and I have tried our best to pack his vacation with new adventures, the 4-month-old has worn that smile a lot this week. He has touched his first leaves and rocks, gazed at cows and horses, and heard the ice crunch beneath our feet. Friends and errands have been ignored, perhaps, but the Blue Ridge Mountains are so special that we have taken the time to indulge the boy in their steep and stunning treasures.

O.K. O.K. I suppose the child is a bit young to appreciate Appalachian pleasures fully. I admit, too, that the family's vacation is as much for me as it is for him. For many years, these mountains have served as a refuge into which I occasionally withdraw to take some measure of my past and make some sense of my direction. Becoming Dylan's father has sent me scampering once again for the rugged sanctuary.

Many men have such a refuge, a stretch of land they can turn to while sorting out the conflicts, doubts and challenges the world thrusts upon them. It might be a vacant beach or a backwoods cabin—private places. What we look for in these hideaways is peace of mind—an understanding of the person we have become and hope for the man we want to be. Especially in times of transition, our secluded shelters help preserve a precarious balance between the past and future.

It was in search of my past—in truth, yet another attempt to determine if peace of mind is just a childish fantasy—that I whisked Dylan and Liz to the smoky majesty of the Blue Ridge. Most men seeking solace head for familiar environments where they can rummage the pastures of past happiness. For me, happiness is nothing if not the contentment I knew as a child in the western North Carolina mountains. Their ground-down peaks stood only four hours from my family's low-country home, and in those years we made a habit of seasonal visits. Each trip was a glorious carpet ride to a mystical land far away. I remember lying outside our cabin on autumn nights and watching shooting stars scorch the sky. I remember shambling bears and wandering rocks and fat icicles congealing on treacherous ledges. I recall man-made mounds of dirt and stone slapped together by dynamite blasts and how my brother, Bill, and I would mine those mini-mountains for fool's gold. And I can still see the fog at Grandfather Mountain. It would blanket the road, the car and the picnic grounds, and I would punch and kick my way through it, across the Mile High Swinging Bridge, and sit on a shelf of round, blunt rocks. I could see nothing below me but a deep, radiant whiteness and feel nothing but the wind's tight hug. I sat secure, shining, in a magic kingdom all my own.

More than anything, the mountains bonded the generations of my family. My grandfather and I were never close until he accompanied us to the Blue Ridge in 1963. I didn't know then that Granddad was dying from heart disease. He would give out early every day and take a rest that Bill and I in our exuberant youth couldn't understand. During one hike up Mount Mitchell, Granddad leaned against a boulder, heaving, while we ran farther along the trail. When I asked him why he stayed behind, he answered: "The mountains are old and so they sit still. I am old and so I'm going to sit still, too. Don't worry. We are happy."

Granddad died the next year, and soon thereafter my peace of mind passed away, too. Oh, not just because he died, but because the world in the 1960's changed and began to blur and spin so fast that a 10-year-old boy lost his way. Adolescence, too, erected its mass of contradictory and muddled feelings. Even the mountains forfeited a lot of their enchantment. Vacations weren't carefree anymore.

Still, I hoped that someday, by luck or by work, I would uncover, beside some stream or in some valley, the tranquillity of my childhood.

Now my search has ended. Bringing Dylan here has done it. Carrying the baby in the Snugli, sitting with him in the sun, showing Dylan the bounce in a blade of grass, letting him feel its rubbery texture against his face—all these have brought back the warm tingles of a time long ago. And though mountain nights before the fire have always been toasty, even in bad years, this week I no longer needed Irish whisky to make them glow. I settled next to Dylan instead. I enjoyed the embers in the boy's eyes and the fire in the lad's smiles. Peace of mind, I can tell you, is much more than just a childish fantasy.

Two decades ago, my grandfather leaned against a Mount Mitchell boulder, aware of his impending death, and I know now one reason why he was at peace. It was the beauty of a man's childhood reborn in the squeals of children romping on a billion-year-old mountain. As I carried Dylan this morning along a cow-lined road, around its apple trees and grazing fields, through its clump of dark-green forest—stopping there for five minutes or so to see the trees pattern themselves against the sky and to watch Dylan bend his head back and shriek at the dragons poised above him—then finally over two hills into an open valley view of the Blue Ridge, I realized that my stony companions had welcomed my childhood back through my son. Once again the bears shambled, the rocks wandered, the fat icicles congealed on treacherous ledges. And the winds blew as fresh as ever. Dylan and I enjoyed a hearty laugh with them, and then, chilled to the bone, I brought him back to the cabin and fixed us all boiling hot chocolate.

Richard Moore is a freelance writer living in Brooklyn.